Prai[s]

"Lose yourself in this stunning true story following one young woman's transformative journey from the pulsing streets of New York City, to the tropical jungles in paradise, to the jaw-dropping cult world tucked away on an elite Dallas compound. With every astonishing twist and turn, Courtney Ramms's life falls deeper into the rabbit hole. This warrior woman must lose everything in order to find herself and save her unborn child. I could not put ***Eris Rising*** *down. This is a book you will insist your friends read next just so you can continue to talk about it long after you finish the final page."*

—Holly Kammier
Best-Selling author of *Kingston Court*

*"**Eris Rising** is a scary-good book. Scary because it tells a story of a beautiful life gone sideways—so far sideways that the author is dangerously close to going over the edge. Against compelling odds, Courtney manages to right herself. Therein lies profound life lessons.* ***Eris Rising*** *. . . get a copy, settle in, take your time, read it slowly, patiently, and learn."*

—Brad Alan Lewis
Olympic Gold Medalist and author of *Assault on Lake Casitas*

*"**Eris Rising** by Courtney Ramm should be required reading for every woman between 18–55. Ramm reveals a personal story that could happen to any one of us. While packed with nonstop gripping, dramatic moments,* ***Eris Rising*** *is simultaneously ripe with humor. By the end of her fateful journey, Ramm transforms into a grade-A heroine you'll cheer for and admire!"*

—Natalia Rose
New York Times Bestselling author

"Courtney's strength, determination, family bonds, and open heart formed the foundation for the warrior aspect of her soul to emerge. ***Eris Rising's*** *message is inspirational to all struggling to make sense of their personal journey."*

—Linda Freud
Co-author of *The Healing Gift*

"Courtney brings us on a deeply intimate and transformative journey of healing, forgiveness, and reclaiming our personal power. ***Eris Rising*** *reminds us of the sacred gift—our warrior within."*

—Sonia Choquette-Tully
Co-author of *You are Amazing* and daughter of
globally celebrated spiritual leader Sonia Choquette

*"**Eris Rising** is a compelling story of resilience. Courtney reaches out to anyone who, while searching for life-partnership, is taken in by alluring charm and in doing so, pardons the tell-tale signs of narcissism or sociopathy. This is a story of hope for anyone entangled in an intimate relationship with a destructive partner and, in writing this, Courtney offers connection to those feeling alone or stuck in their journey. **Eris Rising** is a call to everyone to be present with what is real versus what is wishful, to realize our true supports, and to honor one's inner voice."*

—Marie C. Carstens
Board Certified Dance/Movement Therapist

*"**Eris Rising** is a triumph that will inspire all those who need the encouragement to find their inner power when they need it the most. Kudos to Courtney! She proves that love, truth, and courage can conquer anything!"*

—Victoria Bearden
Astrologer and Intuitive Counselor

"Courtney writes with clarity of purpose, keeping track of the thread that pulled her into the strong warrior she is today."

—Thea Keats Beaulieu
Director, Biosonic Enterprises LTD
Author of the *Color Love Journal,*
and *Dancing with the Elements*

"In this captivating, searing, page turner of a memoir, Courtney Ramm describes the potential for deception that many young women may face, resulting in a devastating loss of personal power, along with the courageous steps that must somehow be taken in order to regain it. Courtney recounts the events of her life-changing saga with a precision that matches the depth of her mission. She finds within herself the planetary archetype of Eris, Feminine Warrior for Soul Purpose, as she learns to speak her truth."

—Henry Seltzer
author of *The Tenth Planet: Revelations from the Astrological Eris*

"Courtney inspires the reader with her honest self-reflection, reminding each of us that our next level of expansion is always within reach."

—Mark "Dr. DREAM" Peebler
Facilitator / Catalyst / Dreamer

Dear Petra,

I'm so glad we've had a chance to get to know each other, & that our little ones are friends ◡̈

I hope you enjoy this story ♡♡♡

ALOHA,

Courtney

A Memoir of Finding the Warrior Within

by

COURTNEY RAMM

FROM THE TINY ACORN . . .
GROWS THE MIGHTY OAK

Eris Rising

Printed in the United States of America. For information, address Acorn Publishing, LLC, 3943 Irvine Blvd. Ste. 218, Irvine, CA 92602

www.acornpublishingllc.com

Cover design by Damonza

Interior design and formatting by Debra Cranfield Kennedy

ISBN-13: 978-1-952112-12-6 (hardcover)
ISBN-13: 978-1-952112-11-9 (paperback)
Library of Congress Control Number: 2020914045

For my mom, Adrienne,
for helping me back up after every fall

Dance, when you're broken open.

Dance, if you've torn the bandage off.

Dance in the middle of fighting.

Dance in your blood.

Dance when you're perfectly free.

—Rumi

Contents

Author's Note

This book is a memoir. It reflects my truthful recollection of actual experiences and events in my life. In the interest of privacy, most names and identifying characteristics of individuals and organizations involved in this story have been changed, as have some locations. In addition, some conversations have been recreated to the best of my memory. This book is not intended to be an exposé or otherwise harm any of the real-life characters or organizations involved in this story. Because karma will take care of that, as it always does.

Prologue

I sat cross-legged on my twin-sized bed across from CNN journalist Lisa Ling, who posed a question I'd never been asked before, at least not this bluntly.

"Are you a genius?"

In the past two decades of interviews and television appearances about my unusual and controversial conception, I had received your garden-variety questions about my life, beliefs, and upbringing. All pretty much the same.

A typical question: "How did you do in school?"

My response: "I did very well. I always loved school."

I didn't elaborate. My answers were simple and to the point. Perhaps I was trying to get the interview over with as quickly as possible since talking about myself and the "genius sperm" that made me was rather uncomfortable.

Another common question: "What are your goals and dreams?"

With youthful hope and confidence, I'd say, "Keep dancing and choreographing professionally and one day to have my own well-known modern dance company."

"Growing up, did you ever feel any pressure to succeed?"

This question always landed in the interviews, and my answer was always the same.

"Never from the outside and definitely not from my parents. I always felt a strong inner drive to succeed and strive harder, particularly in dance but also in everything I do."

Although I consider myself just about as normal as every other person, I was indeed created in a unique way—out of sheer necessity.

After seven years of trying to start a family, my dad's infertility led my parents through a series of synchronistic events to find the Repository for Germinal Choice, otherwise known as the "Genius Sperm Bank." Though it existed only for a short time, this elite sperm bank collected the "highest quality sperm" from Nobel Prize winners and other high achievers in hopes of creating exceptionally bright, talented human beings. A total of 229 children were born from this experiment, the majority of whom have kept their lives private.

Not the Ramms.

My sister, Leandra, came first—outgoing, precocious, and adorable. Four years and two miscarriages later, on a hot mid-August day at Mount Sinai Hospital on the Upper East Side of Manhattan, I was born, thanks to Donor Fuchsia. (The Repository kept all sperm donors confidential and color-coded to keep track. My mom's two miscarriages were with Donor Coral, but Donor Fuchsia did the trick!)

There I was, twenty-five years after the experiment of my conception, in my parents' New York City apartment, sitting on a beautiful, antique bed passed down from my late grandmother, talking to CNN reporter Lisa Ling. Her question hung in the air, awaiting my response.

I giggled nervously. Was I a genius? I didn't know. I certainly didn't feel any more genius than anyone else based on genes alone. What about my younger brother, Logan? He also came from the sperm bank but turned out to be autistic. Would that make him less of a genius than me, since he has what's perceived as a disability?

Despite being thrown off kilter by her question, I managed to respond.

"I really believe that there is genius in every person."

By the time the show aired, I'd had a few more months to ponder what it meant to be a genius. Was the meaning confined to the most common definition, "a person who is exceptionally intelligent or creative, either generally or in some particular respect"? Or was it broader in scope so that every human being is a genius in his or her own right with gifts and talents waiting to be unearthed and cultivated from deep within?

The ancient origin of the word lends a different view. The Romans believed that all people had a guiding spirit that attended to them throughout their lives. Because this spirit was born with the person, it was called a "genius," from the Latin verb *gignere*, meaning "to give birth or bring forth." A person's genius dictated their unique personality and disposition, and if someone had an outstanding talent or ability, the genius by their side was believed to be responsible for it.

With the Roman definition of genius in mind, I can only ascertain that about two years after that interview with Lisa Ling, my own personal attendant genius (my little genie, if you will) left my side. Amid a budding dance career, I found myself in a whirlwind romantic relationship, one that resembled a perfect Hawaiian sunset at the beginning, and somehow, only sixteen months later, resembled the aftermath of a Midwestern tornado—a stark, scary scene of desolate destruction. I had longed for a "perfect" husband. The person who appeared turned out to be too good to be true, a façade, but I couldn't seem to let go. Yet as I devoted myself to my new partner, our relationship became unbalanced. Here was someone I trusted with my life who couldn't care less about mine. In the end, my former partner endangered my and my children's very existence.

The relationship was as intense as it was short-lived, leaving no facet of my previous reality in sight. I would have been happier to forget those sixteen months, to just move on with my life and restart my career as a dancer and choreographer, except it wasn't that easy. Not only did a tremendous amount of healing need to take place, but now there were children involved. I was forced to crawl out from beneath the rubble and piece together what was left of my life. Perhaps it was in that rubble that my attendant spirit reappeared and helped me set foot on a long, arduous, yet ultimately transformative road to reclaim my life and spirit. This book is an account of my journey and a testament that you too can reclaim your life after unthinkable upheaval.

The decision to recount my story was not an intellectual one. In fact, I didn't want to write this book—or, at the very least, my ego certainly didn't want to write it. I would rather have hidden everything I went through so that my name and image would remain untainted, leaving an unexplained two-year gap in my life story, which was the time it took to recover from the intensity of what I endured.

Despite my concerns, the words of this book continually washed over me in quiet moments, which, as a single mother of two babies, were few and far between. I felt as if something unexplainable was calling me to write, and this unexplainable force would find me whenever there was open space in my mind—on a long walk with the babies asleep in the stroller, in a hot bath late at night, or when I found myself awake at 3:30 a.m. for no apparent reason. In these quiet times, the words flowed into my imagination, and I knew, with growing certainty, that my story had to be shared. This book is not a mere journaling of my experiences but rather a journey of breaking a deep karmic pattern, which we all carry within us. When we go through the darkness and come out the other side, it's our duty to guide those still struggling toward the light.

When I was a little girl, I used to wish that life could be handed to me on a silver platter. My eight-year-old self envisioned everything I wanted—a handsome and charming husband, a dance career, a house on the beach in Hawaii—all of which would appear effortlessly, and I'd get to simply enjoy living out the life of my dreams for the rest of my days.

That little girl has grown up to see plenty of dreams manifest, but even more challenges. Despite valiant, type-A efforts, life has not been handed to me on a silver platter. And for that, I am grateful. I have learned again and again that the deepest, most profound growth comes out of the most intense struggles, just as the legendary phoenix combusts in its own flames in order to emerge renewed and even more beautiful than before.

In sharing my deeply personal story, my voice is no longer suppressed. I draw upon the collective female strength of those who have gone before me—strong, powerful women who were not afraid to step outside whatever contained them and let their voices be heard. I feel strongly that now is not the time to remain silent out of fear of authority or backlash but rather to have the courage to speak our truth. It is through our shared, celebrated victories that true freedom reigns.

The title of this book was inspired by Eris, a recently discovered planet in our solar system that has come onto the astrological scene as an archetypal force to be reckoned with. Eris represents the feminine warrior spirit, rising to reclaim her place in a world long fractured by patriarchal power. Eris, in all her mighty glory, comes to set things straight, to balance the scales.

While I was once highly skeptical of astrological woo-woo, I can't help but deny my connection to Eris and to the wisdom and feminine power she represents. But it's not just me. Look around at the feminine warrior spirit bubbling up in our society and you'll see her influence everywhere, perhaps even in your own life. Eris calls us to embrace our power and muster the courage to see the truth, to face oppression, and to fiercely protect what is sacred.

Now is the time for Eris to rise.

One Hawaii

Long before a fantasy love affair devolved into my worst nightmare, I was living out my life's greatest dream in the most beautiful place on the planet.

One spring several years ago, after years of dreaming, scheming, and planning, I left New York City—the place where I was born and raised—and moved to Oahu, Hawaii. Years before I made the leap, my soul began nudging me to make the move. I'd never been to Hawaii, nor knew a single person who lived there, but I imagined myself living a carefree yet productive and purposeful life in the tropical paradise promised by a compilation of Hawaiian Airlines posters on bus stop kiosks around the city. I was determined to make that new life a reality one day.

After one particularly brutal and endless winter, I'd finally had enough of the city. I was in my early twenties and living a dancer's dream. After graduating with top honors from a respected out-of-state university, I was a professional modern dancer performing with multiple dance companies. I also taught barre classes in Soho and Pilates on the ritzy Upper East Side. I rented my childhood bedroom from my parents and paid a fraction of what I would have paid living elsewhere in the city. My mom—a professional modern dancer, pianist, and composer—connected me with resources like studio space to choreograph new dance works, my true passion.

No one could understand why I would leave all I had going for me in New York to start over in Hawaii, which wasn't known for its arts and culture scene. But I had to answer what felt like a soul calling. I gave notice to my jobs and began preparing for my big move.

I found a place to land through craigslist—I planned to rent a room from a single, fifty-something woman who, like me, was vegetarian and into yoga. She owned a three-bedroom house in a neighborhood called Kailua, which didn't mean much since I didn't know the island, but a Google search revealed postcard-worthy photos of the nearby beach. I couldn't wait to finally escape the ubiquitous concrete, subways, and frigid winters.

I'd moved from one island to another, but they couldn't have been more different—one a concrete jungle and the other a tropical wilderness. Though New York City was home base, Hawaii felt like my true home. When I drove over the Pali Highway to get to work each day, I was always taken aback by the dramatic dark-green mountains that towered above, straight out of Jurassic Park. Commuting—especially once I learned to drive—became a real treat and a pleasure.

Once I arrived, I took some time to settle in and get used to a new way of life—extremely expensive groceries, lower pay for the same type of work, and appointments that ran on Hawaii time, meaning, no rush at all. Once I let go of such complaints and accepted the way things worked, I absolutely loved creating my new life in paradise.

As the saying goes, you can take the girl out of New York, but you can't take New York out of the girl. Many of my new friends couldn't believe the crazy schedules I set for myself. I had at least four different part-time jobs all over the island, and two years after I moved, I launched my own nonprofit dance company, RammDance, which comprised of a performing group and dance school in the trendy beach town of Kailua. My part-time jobs, which included teaching yoga, Pilates, and dance at health clubs or to private clients, dancing for two professional companies, and caregiving for a man with Parkinson's, among other things, served to support my main goal and dream—the newly founded RammDance.

For the first time, I felt fully on track—doing the right thing in the right place. Despite how busy I was, I felt a profound sense of peace. I could finally exhale, settle down, and build my life in the most beautiful spot on the planet. Unlike my career-centric New York life, Hawaii allowed for a whole new social world to open up to me. After only a few months, I jokingly told my mom, "Everything here's a potluck," and it was true—Hawaii life is centered around community. Locals would never consider showing up at a party empty-handed, and the greener, healthier, more local, more homemade, more organic, or kale-infused your dish was, the better. I couldn't have felt more in my element.

Without any conscious effort, I formed a group of close-knit friends shortly after I arrived. Perhaps because my energy was different in Hawaii, I attracted and developed several friendships that felt as close as family. I met several friends through a monthly spiritual meetup at a communal home called the Sanctuary and through Buddhist meetings and activities. I was raised Buddhist and had been practicing for my entire life with tangible benefits. Life had already thrown me a few curveballs, especially related to my health, and my Buddhist practice had given me faith to persevere and ultimately overcome severe digestive issues and possibly the worst case of adult cystic acne known to humankind, an unexpected souvenir from living in India. By the time I moved to this island, I had fully regained my health and felt ready to embark on this new journey with a renewed spirit.

Despite being driven and accomplished in other areas of my life, I was a late bloomer in love and relationships. I wasn't uninterested in men or socially awkward by any means. But finding a boyfriend and maintaining a relationship hadn't been a top priority when I was younger—I had too many other things to do. Men often pursued me, but once the relationship evolved from dating to something more serious, I found any reason I could to turn the guy away so I could focus on what was more important.

When I was a teenager, I witnessed my peers' priorities go flying out the window the moment they had a boyfriend. They became obsessed with their romantic relationships. I didn't have that kind of time to throw away—I had big dreams for what I wanted to accomplish in this lifetime and a long list of things to do to get me there. Starting at age eight, I trained at the prestigious School of American Ballet, and by age nine, I'd set my sights on becoming a professional ballerina. For the next decade, before branching out to other forms of dance, I was obsessed with ballet. Even in high school, I completed my studies in a correspondence program so I could train all day. Other girls often skipped class to meet up with their boyfriends, asking me to make up a story to explain their absence to our teachers. If I wanted to be a professional ballerina, I couldn't let boys distract me.

By the time I was twenty-five, however, I felt ready to get married and start a family. I just had to find the perfect guy. I'd only been in one long-term relationship since arriving on the island, but ultimately that union was not meant to last. So much else, however, had come together in the two years since I'd arrived on the island. I had a solid community of close friends, a business aligned with my soul's calling, and a life that seemed to flow in perfect order. In many ways, my life felt surreal. The only part of my dream that hadn't yet materialized was meeting the ideal partner. Where was he already? Why was it taking so long to meet him? Patience has never been one of my innate qualities.

All that changed one breezy evening in February two years after my move to Hawaii. I had just completed a full day's work teaching at my newly founded dance school followed by leading a stand-up paddle board yoga class floating atop the glistening Pacific Ocean at a beautiful beachside resort. The expansive views surrounding me in all directions enlivened my cells. Although I hadn't stopped moving all day, I felt energized and excited. I was doing exactly what I wanted to be doing, so the physical exertion filled me up rather than depleted me.

That evening, I planned to go to the Sanctuary to attend the monthly meetup, a gathering of new-age people, most of them in their twenties, who came together to eat, meditate, dance, and drum. The events often featured themes and a guest speaker who shared about their particular passions.

I showed up at the peak of the potluck and piled my plate with delicious vegan food, including three different varieties of organic kale salad. I loved being back with my tribe and reconnecting with friends I hadn't seen since the previous month's event. I sat down across from my dear friend Savannah, a warm, bubbly redhead I had met when I first moved to the island. Savannah lived in the community house where the monthly events took place.

"Hey, Courtney," she said. "This is my new roommate, Marcus."

Savannah gestured to a young man with chocolate-brown hair sitting next to her. His smile dazzled me, and pure charm emanated from his sparkling green eyes. As Marcus and I said hello, he held eye contact for an unusually long time. Through his intense, eye-locking gaze, I sensed he was flirting with me and reading deep into my soul. I was both highly flattered and put off by his bizarre stare. I had never met anyone with that type of energy before, and I didn't know what to make of it.

I was so captivated by his intense gaze that I hardly heard Savannah when she introduced her other new roommate, Annie, who was also sitting with us at the table. By the time I regained my sense of self, I assumed Marcus and Annie were a couple, evidenced by how he behaved toward her. Embarrassed, I turned back to my massive kale salad.

A few minutes later, both Savannah and Annie left the table, leaving me alone with Marcus. I wanted clarity right away. "So, Annie is your girlfriend?" I asked with a nonchalant tone.

"Annie?" he said with a laugh. "Definitely not—she's just a friend. I'm single."

He's single.

I felt both flattered and confused by this guy who seemed to read me like a book, despite only meeting me five minutes earlier. Could he sense I was looking for a new relationship? Or was he just another weird hippie, the typical guy who frequented these kinds of events in Hawaii? Either way, our interaction grew so awkward, I looked for a way out. I spotted a good friend across the room, took my plate, and got up from the table without giving Marcus another thought.

Over the next month, I stayed busy working on my dance company—growing enrollment, starting new classes, and forming a group of professional performers. I also created a nonprofit organization, wrote the bylaws, and researched grants. I spread the word about RammDance in every way I could think of—flyers at Whole Foods, Groupon promotions, and talking it up to everyone I met. I was on a roll!

On a warm March evening, I drove to the next gathering at the Sanctuary with fliers in tow, ready to give a presentation about my dance company as one of the evening's featured speakers. I led the group in a flowing movement exercise and then spoke about my current class offerings.

After the event ended, I was browsing a collection of donated items up for grabs when that familiar sparkly green-eyed guy came over to me. I had not only forgotten his name but had forgotten about him completely since the previous event.

He was so excited to see me that he seemed practically giddy with delight. He could barely get his words out fast enough. "My daughter's been asking nonstop for ballet lessons—it's all she can talk about! She needs to come to your class. She's seven years old, and she loves ballet! When can she start?"

The daughter thing threw me off a bit. He appeared so innocent and childlike I couldn't imagine him as a father. But I remained cool and composed and simply handed him my business card.

"Feel free to look up our classes online," I said. "I look forward to meeting your daughter in class—she could come as soon as next Saturday."

"We'll be there!" He skipped off in delight.

I picked up a few cute tops from the free stuff and then headed home.

The next day, I was walking into Whole Foods when my phone rang. I didn't recognize the number and usually let unknown calls go to voicemail, but since it was a Hawaii area code, I figured it was a mom calling about my new children's dance classes. When I answered, I was surprised to hear a male voice on the other end. He sounded familiar but I couldn't put my finger on who it was.

"Courtney?

"Yes, sorry, who is this?"

"It's Marcus."

I racked my brain. Did I know any Marcuses?

Thankfully he interrupted the awkward silence. "Marcus from last night. You gave me your business card."

"Oh! Yes, of course, Marcus!"

"I found your website," he said, excited and almost exasperated, "and I stayed up until four in the morning watching every one of your dance videos I could find online."

Although I had just launched my new dance company website, I hadn't posted any videos yet. He claimed to have seen every dance I had choreographed, naming and describing different pieces that I had, in fact, created. I realized that my old website was still live, although I planned to take it offline soon, and it hosted numerous videos and YouTube links.

My intuition spoke loud and clear. *Holy moly, this guy is nuts!* The last thing I wanted was a creepy, sparkly-eyed stalker watching videos of me online until nearly daybreak. I ended the call as soon as I could, and he promised to bring his daughter to my ballet class the next morning.

Oh, that's right. He has a young daughter. He must be a good guy if he takes care of her.

The single dad thing got to me. He portrayed himself as such a good guy, a dad trying to make his little girl's dreams come true by signing her up for ballet lessons. I didn't know what to make of his bizarre phone call and confession, so I took it as flattery. Though he knew nothing about dance, I appreciated having someone call me up to rave about my choreography. He had an air of mystery about him—I couldn't quite figure him out—and he exuded charisma and charm. Plus, he lived in the Sanctuary, a highly selective community house, with several friends I'd known for years. Surely he must be trustworthy.

The next morning, Marcus didn't show up to class with his daughter. I found myself surprisingly disappointed. I had attempted to look nice and actually bothered to apply mascara, despite not having worn makeup in years. The thought of seeing him again had made me giddy—I had butterflies in my stomach as I drove over the Pali into Kailua from my new Honolulu apartment. But, at the same time, he creeped me out—I intuited something was off about him.

Marcus's pattern of not showing up continued for another three weeks. Through voicemails, text messages, or Facebook messages, he relayed his apologies and gave all kinds of excuses for missing my performances, workshops, and other dance-related events that he had committed to attending. He also kept promising to bring his daughter to ballet class on Saturdays but never showed.

At each class or event, I would get my hopes up, as I had a major crush on him, despite barely knowing the guy. Every time he flaked, I felt a pang of sadness and disappointment. Yet, despite each missed meetup, I continued to like him.

One hot afternoon, I found myself stuck in unexpected traffic on the Pali highway into Kailua, one of the most scenic highways in the world. The road crests the peak of a mountain overlooking the Pacific Ocean with sweeping views of mountains below. Traffic on the Pali highway at that time of day was usually nonexistent, so I hadn't planned for any extra travel time and was now running late. The cars came to a complete standstill. I had perhaps the best view of anyone in any traffic jam anywhere, and I felt grateful for the inspiring and unbelievably beautiful scenery before me.

While I was deep in a daydream, my phone rang and shook me out of my altered state. It was Marcus. I contemplated whether or not to answer. I didn't want to hear any more lame excuses for why he missed my performance a few days ago. But I went against my gut and answered anyway.

As usual, he sounded completely high—his voice soft, spaced out, almost feminine. His words came out painfully slow, as if he was hand-picking them one at a time. He started off with another excuse for missing my big show—he claimed to be recovering from an illness—and promised again to bring his daughter to class on Saturday.

The combination of the sun glaring through the driver's seat window, the standstill traffic when I was already late to work, and his slow, stoned voice on top of everything pushed me past the point of patience. Something in me bubbled up, and my truth came out before I could stop it or sensor it.

"Look, you don't have to keep saying things that you're not going to follow through on. As much as I'd love to meet your daughter, it's okay if you don't bring her. Just please stop confirming that you're coming. It's been over a month of you not following through, and after about ten times, that doesn't work for me. It's not the kind of energy I want in my life."

Still speaking slowly, he switched to therapist mode and began counseling me on my strong feelings. "It . . . sounds . . . like . . . you're . . . upset."

"Yes, I am."

"I also hear frustration in your voice."

"Yes, I'm frustrated because you continue to go back on your word. And I'm stuck in crazy traffic, and I'm late for work. Maybe it's not the best time to talk."

"Or maybe it's the perfect time to talk," he said.

"How so?"

"Your feelings are what's causing me to miss your classes and events."

Come again?

"I'm a person of my word," he continued, "so I know that it's your feelings and emotions that are attracting the exact situations in your life you now find yourself in."

"Is there a reason you're talking so slow? It's driving me insane!"

The conversation went on for another several minutes, and he managed to convince me with his word salad that I was, in fact, to blame for his flakiness, and he had absolutely nothing to do with it whatsoever.

The next Saturday, he finally brought his seven-year-old daughter, Maya, to my ballet class, and instead of just dropping her off, he sat on the bench smiling throughout the entire class. He looked like something straight out of a magazine ad—the perfect combination of sexy and adorable. As much as his flakiness had bothered me over the past weeks, his overwhelming charm outweighed everything else. His presence, watching his little girl take her first ballet class, was the very definition of charming.

Two Two of Raphael

After Marcus started bringing his daughter to ballet, we had a way to see each other regularly, which I loved. What followed was a series of outings, adventures, and rendezvous that left me in a love-struck high. I was quickly becoming hooked.

One such outing was to the sacred Makua Valley on the far west side of the island, which is only open to the public a few times a year. I emailed to get our names on the list and then asked Marcus if he'd like to go. Thankfully, he said yes. We had to be at the entrance to the valley at 8:30 in the morning on a Sunday, which would mean I'd have to get a sub to teach my yoga class at the health club, but spending the day with Marcus was absolutely worth it.

Marcus arrived early to scoop me up in his big white pickup truck. I felt like I was the luckiest girl in the world, sitting next to him, singing out Hawaiian reggae songs, and sipping the organic green juice he'd brought for me. The day was pure magic, walking hand in hand through sacred Hawaiian land and then driving even farther west to Ka'ena Point, where we dipped in tide pools and skipped in the sand like there were truly no worries in the world.

On another afternoon, Marcus and I took a hike together deep into a valley outside of Honolulu. Our hike took us so far off the beaten path that I had no cell phone reception, and we didn't spot a single person for the next four hours. We had left the world to rejoin nature, which gave us plenty of time without any interruptions.

During the hike, I asked Marcus about his past, his daughter, and the rest of his life. I wanted to figure him out because, even after spending a good amount of time with him over the previous few weeks, I sensed something unusual about him that I couldn't identify. I wanted to figure him out and find out whether he was truly as he seemed or too good to be true. He answered all of my questions and was so open, blunt, and matter-of-fact that I ended up shocked and terrified. But he confessed the details of his past as if they were commonplace.

For example, he had spent a full ten years in a maximum-security prison. Though I sensed such information might be best left alone, my curiosity got the better of me.

"What for?"

"Oh, you know. I just got into trouble when I was younger."

Ten years is a really long time to spend in jail for just some "trouble." I kept probing until he admitted his crime.

"I stabbed someone," he said, "but it was only to protect myself and the others around me."

Terror invaded every cell of my body. We were far from civilization, and I was alone with someone capable of pushing me off the ledge and down the face of a cliff. He could be the end of me. I glanced at my phone to see "No Service." Scared but still curious, I continued to probe for more information.

"I was doing what was best and necessary in the moment for the good of all," he said in a priestly tone.

He never told me what happened to the person he stabbed. Perhaps I was naive and too trusting, but I figured since Marcus lived in the kale-loving Sanctuary with many of my friends—all of whom were spiritual and practiced conscious, healthy living—he must be a good guy, or at least a guy on the mend from a turbulent past. He deserved a second chance in life, didn't he? I decided to not hold his prison record against him nor let it deter me from pursuing a relationship with him.

But his decade in prison was just the start of his story.

When I asked who Maya's mother was, he replied, "She has lots of mothers. Several of them are here in Honolulu."

How was it possible to have lots of mothers?

"Several of my exes have bonded with Maya, but one in particular, Tina, is considered her mommy, but she's not her birth mom."

"Who's her birth mom?"

"That's a long story."

Marcus went on to explain that Maya's actual mother lived in Missouri, his home state, but she had no contact with their daughter whatsoever. According to him, he met some cute young girl behind the register at McDonald's just after he'd been released from prison, and the two of them hooked up right there in the parking lot. She ended up pregnant, but unbeknownst to him, she was heavily addicted to drugs.

"But how are you able to have Maya with you in Hawaii full time?" I asked.

Marcus went on to recount a detailed story about her acquisition, one that he repeated several times during the months that followed.

One night at a bar, he met Tina, another cute blonde, and they hit it off. Tina seemed to have her life together and offered him some lightness after life in prison. At the time, besides the fact that a drug addict was pregnant with his baby, he was also estranged from his son from yet another woman.

The drug addict baby mama invited Marcus to the birth of his little girl at a local Missouri hospital. He brought along his new girlfriend, Tina, since the two were now a tight-knit pair. Baby Maya was delivered via C-section, and she came out beautiful and perfect except for the fact that she was addicted to meth. The mother later left the hospital with Maya without telling Marcus where she was going. Every so often, she called Marcus and invited him to visit their daughter, but only on her terms, meaning that he would have to sleep with her in exchange for seeing the baby. Marcus agreed, and Tina understood that this was the price her boyfriend paid to see his daughter. After months of visiting various drug houses riddled with trash, excrement, and dirty needles, Marcus knew Maya needed to be rescued. The only problem was that the baby mama was constantly moving houses and nearly impossible to pin down.

After searching house after house, Marcus finally found out where she was living, deep in the back roads of Missouri. He and Tina drove over and hid behind some bushes. Late that night, the baby mama and her boyfriend pulled into the driveway with Maya in a car seat in the back of their vehicle. As Marcus recounted the story, he jumped out from the bushes and quickly knocked out both the baby mama and her boyfriend. While he was taking care of those two, Tina grabbed the car seat with baby Maya, and within minutes, the three were back in his car and driving off into the dark night.

Tina helped Marcus file for full custody of Maya, which he won by using the evidence he'd obtained of her mother's drug addiction. Then the three of them took off to Hawaii for a new start, leaving behind his young son to be raised by the maternal grandparents. Baby Maya lived with Tina and Marcus for years until they broke up, but Tina still considered herself Maya's mommy, and she ranked the highest of all Maya's other mommies. Despite having no legal rights to the child whatsoever, Maya lived with her half the time, and Tina paid for most of her expenses, including clothes, activities, food, and endless gifts.

The story featured way more drama than any woman wants to hear from someone she's starting to fall in love with, especially on an isolated hike deep in the valley with no phone reception to call 9-1-1 and not another soul in sight. His story sounded insane, and I had no way of verifying if anything he'd said was true. And that wasn't even the end of it. I heard loads of insane stories that afternoon. Any person in their right mind would have run the other way—assuming they were still in one piece after the hike—but infatuation does something funny to the brain. The myriad red flags waving frantically in my face turned into little annoyances too easily brushed aside. Marcus had such an intense air of enlightenment that clearly his past experiences must have been what shaped him into such an amazing person. Clearly.

More red flags continued to pop up like popcorn, but I was already charmed, quickly falling in love, and nothing could stop me.

At the end of April, about a month after the hike, I faced one of the most painful dilemmas of our relationship. I hadn't foreseen my heart getting broken quite this soon. We had been seeing each other on a fairly regular basis, and I'd just assumed, without a second thought, that I was the only woman he was involved with.

I had rented space at the Sanctuary for a dance and yoga event—followed by a potluck, of course—that I was hosting on Friday night. I had invited Marcus to attend, but he never committed. He simply said he'd stop by if he was free. His aloofness and lack of interest bothered me given how supportive he was of my dance company. I was hosting this event right in his home—how hard could it be to step out of his bedroom and participate?

Fifteen minutes before start time, I was prepping the sound system when Marcus walked right past me, dressed in crisp jeans and an ironed button-down shirt. This wasn't his usual attire—he looked clean and put together. Since we had recently spent a beautiful day in Makua Valley together, I waited for him to come over and give me a hug and kiss hello. Instead, he ignored me. He walked up to Savannah, my friend and his roommate, and gave her a huge hug and a peck on the lips. Instantly hurt and confused, I waited to see if he would acknowledge my presence—I was standing right in front of him.

But he didn't.

After giving me a passing glance, he continued getting ready to leave. I walked over to him, mortified and ashamed that he was treating me like a speck of dirt. Even as I stood right in front of him, he still ignored me—no hello, no hug, no greeting of any kind.

I finally spoke up in the nicest tone I could muster. "Are you coming to my event tonight?"

His reply was a nonchalant. "No, I have a dinner meeting."

"Must be an important meeting. I've never seen you so dressed up!"

"Yes," he replied. He gave me a smile and a wink and then hesitated for a second. "Taxes. Dinner and taxes."

What was he talking about? Who gets all dressed up on a Friday night to discuss taxes? The answer would be revealed about three months later. In the meantime, I was left to wonder.

Despite the emotional turmoil caused by our encounter, I tried my best to host a memorable and enjoyable dance event. After the evening ended, I sat at the kitchen table with Savannah and another roommate of hers. Instead of confronting Savannah, I stuffed my feelings and tried to keep it together.

"How's life?" I asked casually.

She replied in a breezy, sing-song way. "Life! It's amazing!"

"Oh, great!" I said, trying to sound enthused and supportive.

"Everything with Marcus is just going so great," she continued. "I could never imagine it would be this good. The whole thing just feels so right, and it's exactly what I need right now. He's so wonderful!"

I couldn't believe my ears. I thought maybe I misunderstood something.

"Which Marcus?" I asked, just in case there was someone else she could be referring to.

"Marcus, my roommate!"

What was going on? I had spent at least three days and nights with Marcus in the past week, and he'd never mentioned Savannah. She had been a good friend for years, and she clearly had no clue that we were both in love with the same man. Though the moment was ripe for a heart-to-heart about the truth, I was too embarrassed about being in love with someone who was also seeing my good friend.

Savannah continued to rave about her relationship while my insides writhed—I had been on the receiving end of Marcus's devoted passion inside his room at their community home just the night before—until she finally stopped to ask about me. "How about you? How's everything?"

How could I respond to this question without shattering her entire reality? I wanted to keep the peace and keep our friendship intact, so I answered vaguely while stuttering every few words. "I'm . . . going through a difficult time right now."

"Oh? What happened?"

"I was in love with someone, and we had incredible chemistry and spent a lot of time together, but I ended up getting really hurt."

"Who is he?"

She had given me another chance to speak my truth. Instead, I spared her the pain of bursting her little love bubble. "Oh, you don't know him."

"What's his name?"

I racked my brain to think of a name of someone I didn't know. "His name is Kevin."

"Oh, yeah, I don't know him."

Before she could ask me more about "Kevin" and figure out we were both in love with the same man, I said I had to go and quickly packed up my things.

Seated in my car, I began sobbing uncontrollably. I felt hurt, shamed, and angry at Marcus for leading me on and making me feel so incredibly special, only to find out he was also in some kind of relationship with my good friend, who had also been seemingly fooled to believe that she was the only one in the picture.

I drove half a block down the dark street but had to pull over. I was crying so much that I couldn't see well enough to drive. Despite the late hour—it was after 10 p.m. in Hawaii, which meant it was 3 a.m. in New York—I called my mom. Normally, I wouldn't have bothered her, but this was an emergency, and she would answer my call any time of day or night.

"Mom, don't worry, everything's okay. Please don't freak out. I'm just really upset."

Tears gushed like streams down my face. My mom did her best to help me lighten up. "Oh, honey! He's just a new-age hippie living in a new-age house with new-age roommates. He's into free love—but you're not! There's nothing to be upset about. Just know that he's not for you, detach, and move on."

Easier said than done, Mom, but thanks. However unrealistic, my mom's advice calmed me down enough to drive home, but I didn't take her words completely to heart.

I mustered the courage to confront Marcus about his relationship with Savannah the next time we hung out, which was the next night. We met up at 9 p.m. to get some tea and then headed to Kailua beach where we sat under a waning full moon. It was a beautiful night, warm and breezy, with countless stars overhead and the Mokulua Islands just visible in the moonlight. He acted as if everything was fine between us, despite having ignored me in front of Savannah the night prior.

I was mad. I spoke my truth, I didn't hold back, and I let him know that what he did was wrong. Savannah had been a close friend since I moved to the island years ago. I had barely known him three months. How dare he break up a friendship by being with both of us at the same time and hiding it from us! The more worked up I got, the more he seemed to lighten up, as if he enjoyed hearing me get so mad.

After my long rant, he denied having any relationship with her. "Oh, Savannah," he said in a tone of fatherly disappointment. "I thought I had her all straightened out. She's clearly confused again."

"What do you mean, confused?"

"She thinks we're a couple or something, when I continuously tell her I'm not interested in her at all. She's just so clingy."

"So, you're not in any kind of relationship with her?"

"Not at all. She's just a friend, a roommate."

I was wary of believing him, but Marcus convinced me that Savannah was the one at fault, not him. He continued to talk so negatively about her that I stopped liking her at all. According to him, Savannah had wanted to be with him so badly that she imagined they were in a relationship that didn't even exist.

We stood up to leave the beach, alone beneath a massive full moon. Out of the blue, Marcus asked, "Are you going to have my babies?"

Before I had a chance to register the inappropriateness of his question, I blurted out, "Yes."

His eyes sparkled. "We'll have two. A girl and then a boy."

I don't know where his question came from, whether an inner knowing of what was to come or his way of luring me with the dream of motherhood—most likely the latter. And where did my response come from? A deep knowing of our destiny or a lack of self-confidence that left me flattered by an offer of such magnitude?

Though Marcus had convinced me that Savannah was delusional about their supposed relationship, I later found out that was a complete lie, and one that destroyed a beautiful friendship. Over the next few months, multiple other lovers popped up. Savannah was just as confused as I was about his behavior.

One evening on the lanai of the Sanctuary, she spoke a truth I couldn't receive: "You're looking for a husband, Courtney, but he's never going to change."

Every time Marcus and I were together, however, he acted as if I were the only woman on the planet.

"He's that way with everyone," said Savannah.

Between Marcus's continued relationships with Savannah and other lovers, while also denying all such relationships, and the way he led me on and swept me off my feet again and again, I found myself on an exciting and exhilarating rollercoaster that was difficult, if not impossible, to exit. One day my heart was bursting, and the next it was broken.

He often created opportunities for all of his various women to meet up. On several occasions, he made us dinner at the Sanctuary, or we went out to eat together, or we ended up at the same spiritual gatherings. None of us were interested in a polyamorous relationship—none of us except Marcus, of course. He seemed to get a kick out of seeing our reactions to each other, all of us suspecting we were after the same man.

But at the end of every awkward and uncomfortable evening, he always went home with me. I was the *chosen one*, the special one, the one the other women started to hate and envy, which destroyed numerous long-standing friendships. The other women slowly faded out of the picture.

One sunny morning after a sleepover at my apartment, Marcus and I were making a mango smoothie when he told me he was thinking of moving to the Big Island in a couple of weeks. Oahu and the Big Island are separated by four islands and two hundred miles. He had met a woman who offered him an opportunity to work on rebuilding an old, rundown property in exchange for living on the property rent-free. The woman wouldn't return for at least a year, he said, so aside from minimal work, he could spend the rest of the time sitting on the beach and smoking pot.

Baffled at how he could possibly create value in the world by sitting on a beach stoned all day, I gave him a pep talk, telling him how much he had to offer the world.

"Besides, what would you do about Maya?" I asked.

"Oh, she can live with Tina—she'll take her full-time."

I was shocked by his nonchalance about leaving his seven-year-old daughter with an ex-girlfriend so he could withdraw from society.

As our conversation continued, he sounded increasingly certain about going. I helped him review the pros and cons, deeply hurt that he wasn't considering me in the equation. Our relationship, which had taken over my entire life, seemed to hold no weight in his life whatsoever. That was it for me—I decided to let him go. If he was ready to pick up and move to another island without even mentioning what that would mean for us, I was done.

I looked him right in the eye and said, "I fully support you in moving to the Big Island. I want you to be happy, and if that's what you want, I'm behind you one hundred percent. Why not go?"

He was so shocked that I wasn't begging him to stay with me that I had rendered him completely speechless. I felt a huge power come over me, and what proceeded next from my mouth seemed to be channeled from a higher source.

"In fact, it would be my inconspicuous benefit if you left. I may be sad for a while, but if you moved away, I truly feel it would be for my benefit in the long run. So, if you feel called to leave, I say go!"

The words I had spoken were not my own—I was just as surprised to hear them as he was.

"What do you mean, inconspicuous benefit?" he asked.

"In the Buddhism I practice," I explained, "there are two kinds of benefits—inconspicuous benefits and conspicuous benefits. Conspicuous benefits are immediately noticeable and often tangible, while inconspicuous benefits are less easily observed but often end up being even greater than conspicuous benefits. They're a result of a long, steady Buddhist practice that I've had my entire life growing up in a Buddhist family."

"And my leaving the island would be your inconspicuous benefit?" he asked, puzzled.

"Yes," I said.

And we left it at that.

In the midst of the drama Marcus created between his many lovers, girlfriends, and exes, I doubted the depth of our connection. I was likely just wasting my time with a man who would never fully commit, especially if he moved to the Big Island. But letting him go was not a decision I could make from my head. I needed to get out of my own way and ask the Universe for a sign.

One day, I had a two-hour break in between classes I was teaching, so I brought along one of my favorite tarot decks, the *Archangel Power Tarot*

Cards by Doreen Virtue. I drove to the nearby Magic Island, a beautiful peninsula in Honolulu with panoramic views of the Pacific Ocean, to watch the sunset. I felt open and ready to receive a powerful message about my relationship—it could go either way, and I wanted a clear sign of what to do.

For an entire hour, I walked around the park with the tarot cards in my hands, shuffling them over and over while meditating on my question: "Are we meant to be together?"

My heart was yearning to know. I sat down on the water's edge, closed my eyes, and prayed to receive one single card with clear guidance.

As I opened my eyes, a flock of beautiful birds swooped right past me, and a sense of sacredness hung in their wake. As the glowing orange orb dipped into the Pacific Ocean, I chanted a Buddhist mantra and continued to shuffle until I felt I had the perfect card in hand.

Whatever this card is, even if it's difficult to accept, I am strong enough to handle it!

I flipped over the card I had chosen out of the seventy-eight-card deck, and my heart instantly filled with warmth, peace, and overwhelming joy. The card was the Two of Raphael, the soulmate card. On one side was a picture of a man and woman standing on a beach with a radiant sunset behind them, facing each other, with their right palms pressing together, creating a prayer mudra. Underneath the image, it read, "Two hearts dedicated to creating something wonderful. Kindred spirits. Don't give up on those you love."

The longer description about the card seemed to speak directly to my question: *Two hearts can create something wonderful! A friendship can grow deeper, or a romance can flourish and bloom. Regardless of the nature of the relationship, time deepens the bond, and a long-term connection based on respect and understanding develops. This is the card of kindred spirits. Forgiveness heals wounded feelings. Relationships can be reconciled. Now is not the time to give up on those you love. Disagreements between people or groups will come to positive resolutions.*

I had full-body chills. *Yes, this is my answer. I asked for clear guidance and you can't get any clearer than this!* Picking this card was no mistake—I had spent an hour meditating beforehand. In that moment, I knew Marcus and I were destined to be together, and I knew I had to keep believing in our greatness as a partnership until he came around and saw it for himself.

Three Song to the Moon

My love for choreographing started at an early age, thanks to an old Russian teacher who gave the young students at the School of American Ballet a special and exciting assignment.

"Go home and pick some *vootiful* music, something you love," said Madame Olga in her thick Russian accent. "You back to class next week, and you show us. Da?"

We all nodded in agreement—our mouths never opened in ballet class—and something stirred in me. *I get to choose whatever music I want and create a dance to it? I get to make something amazing, something new and exciting, out of nothing?*

I picked a piano piece called "December" from Tchaikovsky's *The Seasons*, not to be confused with *Four Seasons* by Vivaldi. The more I listened and discovered the emotion underneath the melodic notes and rhythmic embellishments, the more I completely fell in love with the piece. I may have been only eight years old, but I already knew that every dance started with the music.

"See the music, hear the dance," said George Balanchine, the great American choreographer and founder of New York City Ballet. As I completed my assignment, in the very ballet school that the late Balanchine had founded decades ago, I was indeed following his guidance.

After that first assignment from Madame Olga, I was hooked. Sleep-overs with my friends were spent creating new dances and taking turns playing "director" while we honed our brand-new choreography skills.

Fast-forward twenty years and I was choreographing for my new dance company in Hawaii. The only problem was—with so few professional dancers on the island—finding male dancers was a challenge, as the good ones usually moved to bigger cities such as New York or San Francisco.

With my dance company scheduled to give two performances coming up in July, I needed to act fast. The brand-new piece I was choreographing was already underway and featured four female dancers, including me. Having even just one token guy would add more depth and dimension to the story.

One sunny Saturday morning, after teaching his daughter's ballet class, I asked Marcus, whose gig on the Big Island had fallen through after all, "Hey, do you happen to know any guys on the island who can dance?"

All of the other children and their parents had left, and Maya was across the room entertaining herself with colorful rubber dots, a prop for an earlier class of toddlers.

Stepping in closer, and towering over me at an impressive six foot three, Marcus now stood barely an inch away, his bright green eyes sparkling even more than usual. Sunlight from the large, open windows cast golden beams over his muscular arms and torso. The chemistry between us escalated, and although we were only having a conversation, much more seemed at play.

"Yes, me!" he answered.

I figured he was joking—he wasn't a professional dancer. So, I joked back, "Great! When can you start rehearsing?"

"Tomorrow!"

"Wait, you're serious?"

"Of course, I'm serious. I can dance!"

He proceeded to leap and waltz around the studio. As I watched him make an utter fool of himself, I considered his offer. He had just completed a yoga teacher training, and he was uncannily strong. I figured if he had basic body awareness from doing yoga, and he would be able to lift me, I could probably make it work. Plus, I had no other options and needed to find someone immediately. It was a huge risk to accept his offer, but he was so confident in himself and his ability to learn.

Training someone to perform who had no dance training whatsoever was a huge undertaking, one I never would have accepted if I hadn't already had such a massive crush on him. Working with a professional dancer would have required only a few rehearsals to learn basic partnering choreography, whereas working with Marcus required countless hours trying to catch him up on ten-plus years of training so that he'd remember basic things like to point his toes and not grunt when he picked me up. Basic dance concepts had to be broken down and taught before I could even get to the choreography. And then, making his dancing appear smooth and graceful was a whole new, almost impossible, project.

I had a limited number of hours to use the dance studio I rented in Kailua, and we needed somewhere that would allow us to rehearse as much as our schedule permitted. I had access to the high-end health club where I taught, which had four large mirrored rooms that were mostly free during the day, as classes were held either in the morning or evening. If I could get Marcus a membership, we could rehearse as much as we needed. As a yoga and Pilates teacher at the club, I was entitled to a spouse membership, yet Marcus and I weren't married or anything even close. But we were lovers—didn't that count? I went into my boss's office to inquire.

"As long as you and your boyfriend live together, you can sign him up," she said.

Boyfriend? Marcus had never claimed to be my boyfriend. But in this instance, maybe he would play along. I approached him with my genius idea, to which he immediately and happily agreed.

"I'll play being your boyfriend anytime."

The next day, as we rode up in the elevator to the health club, I whispered, "Remember, you're my boyfriend."

"I got this," he said with a smile.

The second the elevator doors opened, he grabbed my hand, intertwined his fingers into mine, and led me out of the elevator with the biggest love-struck smile I'd ever seen, which made me start laughing hysterically.

Oh, my God, he is so good at this. We marched into my boss's office, and she didn't question us—the quintessential couple—for even a moment before signing the papers.

An intensive rehearsal period commenced. It helped greatly that Marcus was unemployed and living off state disability for PTSD from prison, which gave him complete freedom to train all day long. With his new membership to the club, we could meet there every single day for the next twelve days until the show. He pawned his daughter off to various ex-girlfriends, other lovers, or female friends. Instead of seeing this neglect of his daughter as a possible red flag, I was just happy that we got so much alone time.

For my new piece, I chose "Song to the Moon," an aria, a lyrical piece for solo voice, that is part of an opera called Rusalka by Czech composer Antonín Dvořák. Ever since I first heard the aria on Hawaii's classical radio station, I had become obsessed with it, playing it over and over throughout the day. As the song was in Czech, I didn't know at first what the words meant, but I could feel the emotion, the yearning, the intense drama, and I saw a dance unfolding in front of my eyes.

As I later learned, the story of Rusalka is quite tragic, a heartbreaking tale of love and sacrifice, based on the same story that inspired my all-time favorite childhood movie, *The Little Mermaid*, but without the fairy-tale ending. The beautiful aria is sung in the first act when Rusalka, a water nymph, has fallen deeply in love with a prince who regularly visits the lake where she lives. Because the nymphs are invisible to humans, no matter how hard she tries to embrace him, he remains unaware of her existence. Against her father's warnings, Rusalka decides she wants to become human. As the full moon rises, Rusalka prays to the rising moon, asking the moon to reveal her love to the prince.

At one point, she sings, "Moon! Don't go. Allow me just a moment more to dream this sweet dream of love. Please, just a moment more before I awake or bless my beloved that we remember on the other side."

I didn't go into the rehearsal studio with Marcus intending to choreograph a love story, but somehow, that's what unfolded, both in the dance itself and in our lives, which were becoming more intertwined every day.

In the studio, although I was the director and he was the student, he constantly talked back to me, which I found hilarious. He truly seemed to think he knew more about dance than I did, though I'd been dancing my entire life.

"You need to point your toes," I said.

"They are pointed."

"No, your toes are flexed. That's not pointed."

If I hadn't been in love with him already, I would have been extremely annoyed. Though his defensiveness irritated me a bit, I thought it was cute and funny that he acted like the authority when he had no dance training of any kind.

Our favorite studio at the club had no windows toward the hallway, which we preferred for the sake of our privacy. These dance rehearsals created a haze of confusion as to what was real between Marcus and me and what wasn't. Dancing together just blurred the lines. He seemed to be seducing me, but wasn't he just acting the part? We entered this place where we had to pretend that we were a couple, and then we secluded ourselves in a cave-like room to create a love story. It felt so real. What was the dance and what wasn't the dance?

During this intense twelve-day rehearsal period, our relationship intensified, and I fell completely, head-over-heels in love. Often, our three-hour afternoon rehearsals turned into evenings under the stars in the hot tub, followed by late night dinners at whatever cafe was still open, and intimate nights. A high like no other. The maximum parking time at the health club was five hours, and on many occasions, we had to move our cars to a new spot because five hours flew by in what seemed like five minutes. We had rich, deep conversations, and I got to know him, or in retrospect, the version he crafted himself to be precisely for me.

Outside of the dance rehearsals, we spent every possible moment together. While working five different jobs, I somehow squeezed in time for hikes, camping, road trips, juice cleanses, dinner dates, and museum outings. We started staying over at each other's houses all the time, which was awkward given his communal living situation. We also met up regularly to work on our business plan for a joint juice shop and dance studio, and we drove around the island for hours, looking for retail space. This business idea was a shared dream that inspired us both to move forward in our lives.

The red flags all faded away, the prison sentence was long forgotten, and my other friends—some of whom expressed concern about this hippie slacker—fell to the wayside. I lost all sense of myself, living in my own personal paradise in the exquisite paradise of Hawaii. I felt like I had met my other half. He was mellow and easygoing, while I always ran after some kind of excitement. He was an Aquarius, whereas I was a Leo—he was go-with-the-flow, while I was not. And I felt like he knew and understood me better than anyone.

Too good to be true.

During a rehearsal at the Kailua studio, I told my cast of dancers, "This dance is like a prayer. Each of you is in your own world, performing your own ritual under the full moon. You are asking, praying, dancing under its luminescence."

Creating and rehearsing the "moon piece," as we called it, reflected my own deep internal prayer for Marcus to fall in love with me and commit to me. By the time we performed the piece under an actual full moon at a beautiful outdoor stage on the west side of Oahu, my prayer had been answered.

During one of our final rehearsals, while we were walking on a slow eight-count introduction in the music, he looked into my eyes and whispered, "I love you."

He'd never said that before. I was in shock. I pretended I didn't hear him and continued the dance. For months, I had been dying for him to say that—my dream of all dreams. At the same time, I still couldn't tell what was real and what was merely a role.

Either way, I could only imagine this was what someone high on Ecstasy must feel. Something clicked. I needed him and wanted him to be with me. We were meant to be together.

When the performances were over, I wasn't ready to give up my daily dose of dancing, and neither was Marcus. Our time in the dance studio had become the highlight of my day. Marcus made goals to be a better dancer—he set his sights on making dancing and choreographing his new career—and to devote himself to supporting my dreams. In those early days, he was completely selfless and the living image of the perfect partner. Since he wasn't doing much else, he made it his whole mission to support my dreams.

He eventually learned to dance well enough to perform. After the July performances wrapped up, we went to work creating a new dance piece, this time a duet called "Two of Raphael," named after the tarot card I pulled in May.

While I noticed his other paramours had been dropping off left and right, one day in early August, he shocked me with a new reveal. We had just finished a rehearsal when he turned to me, a casual look on his face.

"Do you mind if I invite my wife to see the upcoming performance?" he asked.

Wife?

I laughed, assuming he was joking. He laughed along with me, but then he said he also wanted to invite a few of his exes, including Tina. "If you don't mind."

I couldn't wrap my head around the idea that he was actually married to another woman. When I met him at the Sanctuary's monthly meetup, he had expressly said he was single. And after weeks of such an intense relationship, how could there possibly be anyone else in the picture? He hadn't explicitly stated his monogamous commitment, and he had mentioned back in April that he didn't believe in labels. But by now, we had grown so much closer.

"No, you're not married!"

"Yes, in fact, I am," he replied, clearly getting a kick out of how I had started bubbling up with emotion. I rarely lost my emotional balance before meeting him.

"Who are you married to?" I asked, a huge pit in my stomach.

"Oh, you don't know her," he replied, grinning. "Or actually, wait—you might know her. She goes to the monthly gatherings, so I'm sure you've seen her there."

I was dying to know her name and praying I wouldn't know her. What if it was Savannah? He held off on telling me, savoring my emotional disturbance as if licking frosting off a cupcake. After several minutes of my nagging, he finally replied, "Mariana. Her name is Mariana."

A huge sigh of relief. I had never met anyone named Mariana, although now I had to come to terms with why he had never told me he was married in the first place. He went on to explain that the marriage wasn't a big deal, just something to help a friend, and they weren't really together.

Deep breaths. I can handle this. They're not really together. But what does that mean? Do they still sleep together?

Of course, I had a hundred questions, though he seemed reluctant to say much.

"I'm helping a friend from Colombia who is having trouble with her visa," he explained. "You have absolutely nothing to be jealous about. We don't even live together."

And as it turned out, the day I met him at the monthly gathering, he'd only been married ten days. But he was still married—why had he said so adamantly that he was single?

"I don't know that I want her coming to our show," I said.

"I understand, but she loves dance, and she'd enjoy it."

"I'll think about it."

A few days later, he asked if I'd like to attend his wife's graduation from a personal development seminar. I couldn't believe he was asking me this. Did the wife know we were in a relationship? Were they going to act like they were in a relationship? I could never handle something like that!

Our rehearsal ended at 5 p.m., and Mariana's graduation started an hour later, which meant I'd have to go in sweaty dance clothes. My intuition spoke loud and clear. *Do not go. Just go home. Have the evening to yourself. Why put yourself in such an emotionally risky situation? Do you want your heart broken?*

But my ego spoke out. *I need to see my competition.* I was too curious, even though I knew I could get hurt by what I might witness.

We both took some time to shower and then we met up to drive to the event together in his truck. I fixed myself up as best I could, given that I didn't have a change of outfit. He looked gorgeous. He was wearing ironed clothes rather than the hippie pants and yoga top he usually wore.

While we drove, he gave me a warning. "Please be respectful."

"Of course, I'll be respectful!"

"What I mean is that when I signed her up for this course, I signed her up as my wife. So, for the evening, I need to be with her. But this could be a great course for you, too. You would really benefit from a personal-development seminar, so I hope you can enjoy the evening and get something out of it. I can even help you get signed up for the next one if you want."

"I don't think so, but thanks."

I considered just going home, except I didn't have my car and couldn't drive his manual-transmission truck. Of course, I also could have waited in the health food store across the street, but I stuck with my decision to go.

Before we stepped out of his truck, he reached into a small embroidered pouch and slipped on a beautiful Koa wedding band I had never seen before. My jaw dropped. As we walked toward the door, he was preoccupied with calling Mariana to see where she was. I suddenly didn't even recognize him—he had morphed into a completely different persona. *Who is this guy?* I suddenly realized this was the same cleaned-up Marcus who went out to dinner to "discuss taxes" months ago.

We walked up a long staircase, and he disappeared into in a sea of strangers. I stood alone and uncomfortable, wondering what on earth I was doing there. Everyone filed into a small ballroom set up with rows of chairs before a stage. I continued looking for him, unsure of what to do and feeling more awkward by the moment.

The next thing I knew, Marcus and Mariana were standing a few feet from me, holding hands and acting like the perfect, sexy couple. My stomach sank, and a lump bulged in my throat. Here was the man I thought was my best friend, lover, and companion, and suddenly I had no idea who he was. Plus, Mariana was gorgeous and ethnic, so I definitely wouldn't stand a chance next to her. They didn't see me staring at them. I didn't know if I should sit alone or next to them, so I found a seat in the back by myself, planning to walk out within a few minutes.

Then, I spotted them toward the front, on the other side of the room. Just as the event started, Marcus motioned for me to come sit in the empty seat on the other side of him. I walked over reluctantly, my feet heavier with each step. For the next hour and a half, I did my absolute best to "be respectful" and remain composed while he played out being the perfect husband to Mariana.

Once the graduation ended, he found me freaking out on an outside terrace.

"Meet me downstairs," he said.

Once we were together, he slipped off his wedding ring. We crossed the street to the health food store for dinner and then drove back to my apartment for a romantic night while his daughter stayed with one of her other "mommies." I never saw the wedding ring again.

Over the years, I had consulted a few trusted and highly regarded astrologers and intuitives, and they always steered me in the right direction, so I set up a couple of sessions once my relationship with Marcus was in full swing. I already knew what they'd say—that we were soulmates, meant to be together, and a beautiful couple—but I always liked to check out potential life partners, especially in the beginning when there was still room to wriggle out.

My first call was to one of the top psychics and channelers in the US, but our session didn't go as well as I expected.

In fact, she left me in tears because I didn't want to believe anything she said: "He is absolutely not genuine, not committed, and unable to be with one person, ever, in this lifetime."

She advised me to break off the relationship immediately: "Get the hell out, girl. He's a deceptive person, and this whole relationship is a big ball of karma. Your chemistry is strong because you recognize each other from past lives, and you've had several past lives in romantic relationships with each other."

At this point I was fighting back tears. I trusted this woman. I had worked with her for ten years—she had helped me overcome major life struggles and even severe mystery illnesses.

She gave me one more piece of strong advice: "Be very careful with your dance company. He wants to take it over and make it his. Keep it your thing. Do not merge with his ideas. Your dance company is *your* baby."

That struck me as funny because Marcus had been asserting strong opinions about my choreography and trying to change my dances. He even asserted he was the new artistic director of RammDance. He presented all sorts of grand ideas about how we could tour the world together with a multimillion-dollar production that would feature hundreds of naked aerial dancers hanging from the ceiling. I usually zoned out when he was talking because he droned on for so long and what he said didn't resonate.

"You lack vision," he said.

My response was to laugh at him. He knew very little about dance. He didn't care that he lacked the moves—he believed he held the overall vision. He had been doing the very thing the intuitive warned me about.

The reading with a top astrologer didn't go any better. With no other information besides his birth date and time, she gave an incredibly detailed description of him, echoing many of the same words I'd already heard. "Not genuine. Not to be trusted at all. Get out now."

Many of my friends also gave me their unsolicited advice. They didn't feel Marcus was a good person, and they begged me to break off the relationship for my own good. I listened to everyone's advice and meditated on it. My heart was pulling so strongly toward him, but my head knew that I was risking major heartbreak because he still was married to someone else.

At one point, I called my mom to ask what I should do, giving her as little detail as possible.

"If you think he's the right one," she said, "stick in there and play by his rules until he realizes how great you are."

I didn't listen to the intuitive or astrologer because I wanted to feel in control of my life and my choices, and I felt I had the power within me to turn the situation around. I felt that Marcus and I were destined to be together, and I needed to give him time to see that for himself. I loved being with him. I felt lit up, energized—the happiest, best version of myself imaginable. Every red flag ended up brushed aside by intense yearnings, no matter the consequences. Something deeper was at play—destiny, karma, soul patterns, or simply being head-over-heels in love—that kept me from heeding the clear warning signs.

Four Birthday Manifesto

The same summer that Marcus and I were starting our passionate, too-good-to-be-true love affair, my parents decided to sell the New York City apartment they'd owned for thirty years in preparation for a move to California.

My parents had purchased our home through the city's affordable housing lottery system on Roosevelt Island in a tree-lined, family friendly neighborhood when my younger brother, Logan, was born. The apartment was shaped like a subway car with a long hallway that ran from front to back with rooms off to the right and left—plenty of space for a family of five. Dad's health made it hard for him to endure the winters, and Mom was ready to retire from her career playing piano for dance, and they no longer needed so much space. Selling the apartment gave my parents the opportunity to overcome the financial struggles they had faced since I was a child. They had decided to move closer to my sister, Leandra, who was expecting her second baby at the time.

I took a trip back to New York City to help purge, pack, and organize the apartment in preparation for the sale. I figured two weeks would be enough time to sort through and pack up all of the belongings I'd collected throughout my life, as well as my parents' things.

Boy, was I wrong.

Those two weeks took everything out of me, emotionally, mentally, and physically. Two weeks of packing up my childhood bedroom—including drawings and schoolwork dating back to preschool—was an intense immersion in letting go.

The time away from Marcus only made us realize even more how completely in love we were. While my days in the city were full of packing and spending time with family and old friends, Marcus's life, according to him, was empty without me. Some of the videos he sent were outrageous—he filmed himself driving as the ocean zoomed by outside the car window while belting out Bruno Mars, "I think I wanna marry you." He told me he was out looking for the perfect retail space to house my dance company. Nothing could have made me feel more elated.

Day after day, I spent hours on end in my old bedroom, which I'd painted pink when I was thirteen, on the phone with Marcus while I sorted through piles of old clothes, dance leotards, notebooks, and books. Our phone conversations lasted sometimes four to five hours at a time.

By the time I was due to fly back home to Hawaii, there was still so much left to be done. Though I considered extending my trip, I couldn't take off any more time from work. I gave my parents instructions on what to do with the rest of my stuff and apologized profusely for not helping them as much as I'd planned.

I flew back to Hawaii the day after my twenty-eighth birthday. I purposely planned to fly home the day after my birthday so I could celebrate once in New York and again in Hawaii. I wondered what Marcus had in store for me. Soon, he'd be picking me up from the airport, along with the five large suitcases of stuff I'd saved from New York, and taking me on a surprise birthday adventure.

On the plane, I journaled in a large decorative sketchbook, thanking the Universe for Marcus. "Thank you for bringing me the world's best husband!" I wrote in my best cursive, filled with a deep sense of love and gratitude. Sure, he still had to get divorced before we could get married, but I didn't see that as a big deal. We were true soulmates, meant to be together, and the time apart seemed to clarify that for both of us.

That first, passionate kiss with Marcus, standing outside of baggage claim while people and cars moved quickly around us, was heaven. I was definitely back in paradise. I showed him the large pile of suitcases we needed to load into his pickup truck.

"What's all this?" he asked, alarmed.

"Everything from my whole life," I said, giggling. "I don't plan on ever leaving Hawaii, so I figured I'd bring everything here. Where else is it going to go?"

We loaded everything up and zipped away, ecstatic to be reunited.

"Do you think your parents can manage packing up the rest of their place without you?" Marcus asked, as we trudged through traffic.

"I'm not sure," I answered. "They seem pretty overwhelmed, and there's still so much to do."

"Why don't you make another trip before the apartment sells?"

I couldn't imagine doing that long flight again anytime soon. I was exhausted just thinking about it.

"What if I come with you?" Marcus asked, smiling.

My ears perked right up, and the creeping jet lag dissipated instantly. "Are you serious?"

Before he had a chance to answer, my mind was racing. *If he wants to meet my family, that's a major next step in our relationship. My prayer has already been answered! Wow, that was fast. We're getting married!*

"Of course, I'm serious!" he answered. "I'd be happy to come and help. When should we go? I'm ready anytime!"

I felt as if I had just won the lottery. If I hadn't been sitting down, I might have fainted with shock right then and there.

We crafted a plan to travel to New York City together in October, provided my parents still lived in the apartment. Though our focus would be packing, all I could think about was playing cute tour guide for Marcus's first-ever trip to Manhattan.

The rest of the evening was pure magic, our chemistry together out of this world. Marcus took me out to dinner at my favorite restaurant, and then we walked hand in hand along a deserted beach park under a huge, glowing full moon. We decided that the full moon was a special symbol in our relationship because the power of the moon dance had brought us together. We woke up the next morning in a blissful fog, entangled in each other's arms in my tiny twin-size bed.

Soon after waking, however, Marcus's countenance changed.

"I need to let you know that my wife's birthday is on Monday, and she expects me to be with her for a few days."

My birthday was just two days ago, and I had just returned after two weeks away. Why did her birthday take precedence over mine? I tried in vain to hide my anger.

"Why do you have to be with her on her birthday? You guys aren't even a couple!"

Marcus shook his head and walked into my bathroom to brush his teeth. I followed him and brushed my teeth alongside him. We continued talking and brushing at the same time.

"Can't you just be with me today to celebrate my birthday?" I asked, desperate to be with him a little while longer.

"Can't today. We're going to the North Shore. I'm picking her up at ten."

As I spit out the toothpaste, I felt a big lump in my throat. I tried to stifle the tears. *How had I gone from so elated last night to so miserable this morning?*

Before Marcus left, I asked if I'd see him on Sunday for my birthday party, which my friend Alana was hosting just up the mountain road from the Sanctuary where he lived.

"If I can, but don't count on it, okay?" He gave me a quick peck on the lips before turning around and leaving.

I stared at the closed door for a few seconds before quickly opening it back up. I ran toward him. "Text me! Have fun! Tell your wife I said happy birthday! I hope to see you Sunday!"

He smiled as he drove off, giving me a wave and then blowing kisses through the open window until he was out of sight.

Twenty hours passed without a word. He finally texted to request more frequent dance rehearsals, as he wanted to improve his dancing and work on a new piece we had talked about creating. I was equally elated and confused. Not knowing how I'd find time to privately train him but desperate to spend time with him, I agreed. We made a plan to start rehearsing three times per week, starting Monday at noon.

The next day, as I drove to Alana's house for my birthday gathering, I highly doubted Marcus would show up. Our relationship was still relatively under cover, and I was concerned that over the past decade that he'd lived in Hawaii he had slept with a good number of the female friends who'd be there to celebrate with me. In a way, his not being there would make the whole thing less stressful. Still, a part of me was dying for him to show up and be proud of being in a relationship with me. While I enjoyed the company of my friends, I still checked my phone every ten minutes to see if he had replied to any of my texts.

Twelve of my close friends gathered at Alana's beautiful bohemian jungle abode, just as the weather began to turn from a sparkly summer day into overcast, gray skies.

"We have our own climate up here in the jungle," Alana said, as the trees began dancing in the breeze. "It's probably sunny down the road right now. Up here, it just rains and rains."

As we enjoyed the potluck and engaged in lively conversation, I walked onto the lanai, surrounded by lush tropical foliage. I took a deep breath, allowing the incredible beauty and vibrant plants to fill me up. I said a prayer of gratitude for celebrating my birthday surrounded by beloved people in the most beautiful place on the planet.

By 10 p.m., only three guests remained, besides Alana and me—Mikey, Kim, and Liam. Rain fell steadily, and the surrounding jungle was even more vibrant and alive.

"What do you think about doing the bonfire now?" suggested Mikey.

"In the pouring rain? Is that even possible?" I asked.

"Come and see! I know you wanted to have one."

Mikey was also Alana's neighbor and lived on the same property. He was the outdoorsy, off-the-grid kind, and if anyone could start a bonfire in the pouring rain, it would be him. Alana chose to sit this part out. Using Mikey's strong flashlight as a guide, my fellow adventurers and I set off on a treacherous walk through shrubs and large rocks to the bonfire spot that he had prepared the day before. Though the rain had lightened, we were all soaked after the ten-minute walk. But Hawaii in August is still warm late at night, and it felt good to be outside in the freshly cleansed air.

Mikey worked hard to build up the fire as best he could in the drizzling rain. My friends' faces glowed in the faint light of the flames.

"I'd like to make some birthday intentions," I announced, with sweeping arm gestures. "First of all, I want to express my gratitude for this amazing life, for the absolutely incredible twenty-seventh year I've had, and for living in beautiful Hawaii, even if it rains on my birthday party."

I took a deep breath and closed my eyes, grounding into all that I saw manifesting in the twelve months ahead.

"This is the year," I said slowly and confidently, "that I'm getting married to the most amazing man on earth and having a baby."

Silence ensued, while my friends absorbed my perhaps unexpected intention.

"That's great! Who's the guy?" Kim asked.

"I'm not completely sure yet," I answered, giggling.

I thought and hoped it would be Marcus, but I felt uncomfortable saying so in front of my friends. All three of my friends affirmed my birthday wishes.

"I can totally see that for you, Court," said Liam.

"So can I," Mikey said.

"I want to meet this most amazing man on earth! Sounds like the perfect husband," Kim said.

And with that, as the last of the dwindling flames expired, our bonfire came to a close. Since Alana had already gone to bed, we went to Mikey's to warm up before saying our goodbyes. At the end of the night, I sat in my car waiting for cell phone reception in hopes that a message from Marcus would pop up. I found it strange that I hadn't heard from him, especially given that he lived so close by.

As I drove down the winding dirt road, I wondered if I should stop by the Sanctuary despite the late hour. At the main street into civilization, I was faced with a decision: left or right? Left would take me to the highway toward home. Right would take me to where Marcus lived, less than five hundred feet farther.

I debated what to do. My intuition said turn left and go home. *You're tired—just leave him be and take care of yourself.* Just as I neared the highway on-ramp, however, I changed my mind. Driving back toward his house, I wondered what the heck I was doing. Was I going to ring the doorbell at close to midnight when he lived with six other people? Was I going to send yet another text message and then sit outside the house waiting for him?

The lights were still on in the house. I decided to drive by slowly and peer into the kitchen window to get a glimpse. Once I knew that he was home and still awake, I could ring the doorbell and give him a big happy surprise. I imagined he'd be just as elated to see me as I would be to see him.

On first pass, I saw Savannah washing dishes in the kitchen. I stopped the car and waited to see if anyone else was still awake. Another woman came into sight but farther from the window. I couldn't quite tell who it was. I drove on. After a few blocks, I pulled into a random driveway to turn around and head back toward the highway. As I drove by the community house one last time, I turned my head to look. To my astonishment, there was Marcus—with another woman.

I slammed on the breaks, feeling extremely sick to my stomach. As I watched the scene unfold, every cell of my body was filled with rage, disgust, and jealously. Just two nights earlier, he was confessing his love to me. And now he had his arms wrapped around a short, dark-haired, ethnic-looking woman.

Marcus was carrying a large backpack, and his truck engine was running, as if the pair were about to take off somewhere together. Who was this woman? Where were they going? He was treating her with such tenderness, affection, and care that it seemed obvious he was completely in love with her.

After the embrace, he picked up her sandals from the many shoes sitting on the patio and delicately placed them on her feet while she held onto his shoulders for support. Suddenly aware of our close proximity, I turned off my headlights and then shut down the engine entirely, hoping to remain unnoticed. Marcus graciously opened his passenger door for this unidentified woman and then walked around to the driver's side.

And then he saw my car, with me sitting inside.

I thought he might just ignore me, but instead he walked right over and opened the door where I sat feeling shamed and heartbroken.

"Hey!" he said, with only an ounce of surprise.

"Hi," I answered. I was so embarrassed to be sitting in my car outside his house at midnight that I felt the need to explain myself. "I was just on my way home from my birthday party and wanted to see if you were home. Did you get my messages?"

"Nope," he replied, unapologetically.

"Really?" I didn't believe him one bit.

"No," he repeated. Then he changed the subject. "How was your party? Was it amazing?"

The party seemed like a lifetime ago.

"It was awesome, so much fun! But I wish you could've been there."

"I told you I didn't think I could make it. And now I'm heading out again, so I gotta go. But great to see you."

He started to head back to his truck where the dark-haired woman waited. My heart sank.

"Who's that girl you're with?"

Marcus answered by emphasizing each word loudly, deliberately, and slowly. "THAT'S. MY. WIFE." He slammed the door and walked away. Seconds later, the truck zoomed off.

I sat and cried for a good ten minutes before transitioning into deep anger. When I regained enough composure to drive, I began the journey home. More than anything, I was furious at myself for going against my intuition. *If I had just driven straight home, I would be an entirely different person right now.*

Then I remembered we had a dance rehearsal scheduled for the next afternoon. I wondered if he would call the whole thing off. I decided to change my typical *modus operandi* and not call or text him to see if he would reach out on his own. To my surprise and delight, my tactic worked.

A half hour before we had planned to meet, he sent me a text. "See you soon to dance?"

I replied yes and did my best to look extra nice before rushing out the door. Even in these early stages of our relationship, I was aware that I was playing by Marcus's rules, which had nothing to do with my happiness, security, or values. In fact, his rules were centered only around himself—making sure he could have any woman he desired with little regard for how they were affected. Fully mesmerized by him, however, I was willing to keep giving him more chances, fully investing myself, knowing that one day (hopefully soon), he'd come around and realize that we were destined to live a long, happy life together.

Part of me loved the challenge. Perhaps this was a product of all the years I spent at the School of American Ballet. Training in such a high-level atmosphere forged discipline, devotion, and determination amid an environment of competition and cattiness. I often felt that my ballet teachers ignored me, so I spent hours every afternoon trying to be increasingly closer to perfect in order to win their attention and approval. Something within me just never felt good enough. The casting for *The Nutcracker*, when I was nine, didn't help my self-defeating mind-set. I was one of five girls, the tallest in our class, who weren't cast that first year because we were too tall for the costume. I took that rejection personally, and even though us tall girls were given roles in New York City Ballet's *Firebird* that same year, and even though I danced in multiple performances of *The Nutcracker* in the ensuing years, that initial rejection carved a deep wound in my heart.

With Marcus, I was already confident that he loved me. The issue was getting him to drop all of the other women in his life who posed a threat to our being in an exclusive relationship. Something in me was not willing to give up the fight because the reward of our being together was too good to *not* fight for it. Deep down, I felt that he would change—in a matter of time, he would realize that we were soulmates.

I can see now that dropping all of my strong values and needs was absolutely the opposite way to enter into an intimate relationship, but I was so confused by Marcus's contradicting words and actions that I started to lose sight of what my own needs and values even were. I was convinced that with prayer, faith, and more investment into our relationship, he would come around and commit to me.

Five Cozy-rufu

That September, Marcus left Hawaii for a four-week visit to the mainland. Right before his departure, I found myself feeling incredibly sick—a massive, intense headache that brought on extreme nausea.

At his place, Marcus gave me one of his signature bear hugs. "Aww, Court-a-loo, you're just having withdrawal symptoms because I'm leaving for a month."

We were packing up his belongings so he could—get this—move in with me. He was paying too much rent at the Sanctuary for a room so small he and his daughter slept on yoga mats on the floor.

"No, I feel really sick," I said. "Maybe I need to lie down."

I stretched out on the floor, but my head only pounded even harder. I managed to get up and wander into the bathroom in case I threw up.

The next morning, after driving Marcus to the airport, I attempted to go to work—my morning job wouldn't require much of me physically. But my eyes were burning, and my whole body ached. I went home as soon as possible.

Marcus called me during one of his layovers, repeating the same thing he'd said the night before. "You miss me so much you're going through withdrawal! Poor baby. I'll be back, you know."

I was scared—I never got sick. That night, I started throwing up every hour all night long. Though I hadn't slept, not wanting to disappoint my students, I taught a mid-morning ballet class. Looking in the mirror on the wall, I noticed how pale and thin I looked.

A week after Marcus left for his trip to the Midwest, I noticed how much my appetite had increased. I called him while eating lentil chips out of a massive bag. Only half joking, I said, "Either there's a parasite inside of me eating all of this food, or there's a baby inside of me."

He didn't skip a beat. "It's a baby."

Could I really be pregnant? That would be crazy. Although not too crazy. In the past two months, we'd been intimate quite frequently. Although Marcus was only my second "boyfriend," and I'd spent the first twenty-four years of my life avoiding serious romantic relationships, something about him allowed me to change all of my rules, or maybe he just came in and changed them for me.

But I couldn't really be pregnant. With my former training and career as a professional ballet dancer, my hormones were perpetually out of balance—I didn't even get my period regularly until I was twenty-five. My period had been late, early, or just plain missing for years due to the way ballet threw my hormones out of whack. I always imagined that when my future husband and I decided to start a family, we would have to undergo fertility treatments and in vitro fertilization, perhaps even adoption. That is what doctors had told me for more than a decade, and I wholeheartedly believed them.

Another part of me enjoyed the risk, given how in love I was. The incredibly low chance of getting pregnant added a zest of thrill and excitement to our intimacy. Clearly, Marcus didn't mind taking that risk either, which made me feel even more special and loved.

He once said, "You're the only person I don't use condoms with. I even use them with my wife." In an odd and twisted way, I interpreted the statement as a compliment.

Dazed but somehow still functioning, I found myself in the pregnancy-test aisle of a local drug store. I spent forever looking over each box, trying to decide which would be the best and most reliable. I decided on one that seemed the easiest to read—rather than one line or two lines, it would spell out "pregnant" or "not pregnant."

The next morning, I told Marcus I had bought a pregnancy test.

"Great! Let's do it together when we're in New York."

There was no way I could wait three weeks. Plus, I wanted to know before we saw my parents. Though I told him I'd try to wait, I took the test the following morning. I turned the test into a beautiful ritual between me and my potential baby. I woke up at 4:30 a.m. out of pure excitement and anticipation and entered into deep meditation.

I asked my soul, "Am I pregnant?"

And I heard an immediate, clear, and resounding yes. With my eyes closed, I saw a vision of an adorable little girl doing somersaults in my belly. She had bright blue eyes, and her hair was golden blond and tied up in pigtails. She laughed and said, "Wee!" with utter delight as she flipped around and around. I was terrified at the prospect of becoming a mother without a committed husband. For as long as I could remember, my intention had always been to find an amazing husband and start a family—in that order.

At 5:15 a.m., I read the instruction pamphlet multiple times and took a few more deep breaths. I prayed that whatever the outcome, my life would be guided in the best direction.

And then I peed.

I had three minutes to wait. I closed my eyes and began chanting a Buddhist mantra. Twenty seconds later, I was already checking to see if the result had materialized.

There it was in plain English: "Pregnant."

I went into a state of shock.

More than anything else, I was truly astounded. *Could this really be true?* I started going into denial. Maybe the test was faulty, or I should have waited the full three minutes for an accurate result. I continued chanting until the timer on my phone went off, and then checked again.

"Pregnant."

Twilight Zone music played faintly in the back of my mind as I tried to make sense of the news. Life as I knew it was over. What would become of me? How would I go to work? How would I make money?

There was no way I could tell Marcus. First of all, he would be furious that I had taken the pregnancy test without him. And who knew how he would react to the results. Maybe he'd just say, "Good luck." Whatever his reaction might be, I couldn't deal with it. I attempted to have a normal morning, but I was in a complete daze as I prepared for the day. My mind went crazy with calculations and computations as I tried to figure out how a baby would fit into my life.

After an appointment later that day, against my own inclinations, I sent Marcus a text message. "I have some exciting news! When can you talk?"

He wrote back right away. "Now!"

My heart started racing. I sat in my car and took a deep, centering breath. *I can do this.* I couldn't keep the news from my beloved partner for even a single day. But once I had him on the phone, I found myself unable to speak the words. He grew impatient. He was at a sports event with his dad and had stepped out at a crucial point in the game. Unable to speak, I texted him a photo of the positive pregnancy test I had taken that morning and waited nervously for his reaction.

He wasn't just overjoyed but absolutely ecstatic! He sounded like he was jumping for joy across the phone line. He relieved all of my fears. Without my bringing it up, he promised to commit to me and to get divorced sooner than he originally planned.

"Given the circumstances, Mariana has to understand that I can't help her out with her green card any longer," he said. "I'll divorce her as soon as possible so we can get married."

I was overjoyed and felt like my dreams were finally coming true. After we hung up, he continued to text me selfies of his smiling face, showing just how happy he was about our news. I felt supported, loved, and so excited—and just a bit nervous—to become a parent with him.

Over the next few weeks, we talked daily, sometimes for hours on end. I shared what I was reading in parenting books. We seemed to be on the same page about everything, which comforted me.

But occasionally Marcus shared what he considered triumphs of not giving in to other women who were falling in love with him left and right. These stories were always odd for me to hear, and I wondered why he shared them. He seemed to think that he was making me feel better when quite the opposite was true. I was pregnant, deeply in love, and would never imagine in my wildest dreams even *considering* being with anyone else, so his triumphant tales of avoiding sleeping with other women made me feel uneasy, needy, and clingy, which I did my absolute best to hide since those feelings bothered him the most.

Late one night, for instance, he called me after a sound healing event in Dallas, Texas. He had driven down from his mom's house in Missouri to meet up with a friend who was the new minister at a pseudo-Christian church. Though I was happy to see his face pop up on my screen, I was surprised he was calling me so late.

When I answered, he was on a complete high from playing his gong at this bustling new-age spiritual meetup. But, according to him, his biggest moment was when a beautiful girl came up to talk to him. He felt instantly attracted to her and considered taking her up on her request to go out after the event. But a vision of me pregnant stopped him from leading her on any further.

Marcus was baffled and exclaimed that this had *never* happened to him before. He wasn't sure why, but it seemed the Universe was stopping him from being with other women so he could be with only me. He was so proud of this moment that he had to call me on the drive home to tell me about it.

Oy vey. His triumphant moment created only more angst and distrust. I could just imagine him at such an event, portraying himself as single and an Aquarian free spirit while I was back in Hawaii counting the days to our reunion in New York City. I quickly brushed my confusion aside and decided to wholeheartedly trust and believe in him. I reminded myself that we had an incredibly deep and profound relationship, and we talked at length every day. And we were having a baby! I forced myself to focus on the good and brush away any pesky doubt that crept up.

When I booked our tickets to New York City, I looked for the best deals possible, which resulted in the humorous decision to have Marcus arrive the day before I did, which meant he'd be staying with my parents for a night without me. I knew him well enough to trust that he could get along with absolutely anyone and instantly fit into any social situation. I knew he'd be fine meeting my parents and special-needs brother and staying with them for one night before I arrived.

My parents didn't know about my pregnancy or anything about our relationship. Marcus had never claimed to be my boyfriend, nor did he believe in such labels. He was married to another woman, yet he was about to move in with me along with his young daughter. My best shot at describing our relationship was to call him a dancer in my dance company, which didn't do justice to the extent of our passionate relationship.

He also didn't post any pictures or ever mention me on social media unless it was specifically related to my dance company. Since he was still married to Mariana, I respected his wishes to refrain from posting anything that depicted us as a couple. I figured that as soon as the divorce was final that would all change.

My plane landed just as daylight peeked through on a cold October morning. Thick clouds filled the sky and the chill of fall hung in the air. As I walked out of the airport to get in line for a cab, I felt that initial jolt to my nervous system as freezing cold air blew past my cheeks. Coming from the lush, green, tropical landscape of Hawaii to the gray, concrete urban jungle of New York City was always a shock to my system.

Once in the cab, I called my mom to check in, eager to hear how they were doing without me. She answered the phone in a wonderful mood and reassured me that they were having an incredible time. Marcus had given my parents and brother a full-on sound healing experience after he arrived, and thanks to the healing properties of his Tibetan gong, Logan had slept through the night for the first time in years. Now they were enjoying an egg breakfast that Marcus had graciously volunteered to cook and were engaged in sharing life stories with each other while they awaited my arrival.

I was relieved but not at all surprised to hear how well they were getting along. Marcus had a remarkable ability to connect with anyone and morph himself into exactly the type of person they wanted him to be. I recognized and capitalized on that quality of his right away. In my opinion, his relatability and magnetic social nature were some of his key talents.

My mom handed the phone to Marcus, and instantly I was giddy with delight. I turned into something resembling a lovestruck teenager who giggled uncontrollably after every couple of words. I could barely endure the thirty-minute cab ride. Once my cab finally crossed the bridge to Roosevelt Island, I called my parents to let them know I'd be arriving soon and to send Marcus to help me with my suitcase.

As the cab pulled up to my building, I saw Marcus running toward me, smiling from ear to ear. While my lifelong elderly neighbors walked by and our doorman of twenty years watched keenly, Marcus wrapped his arms around me and kissed me passionately. The cab driver realized we weren't going to stop anytime soon, so he got out of the car and took my suitcase out himself, leaving it on the sidewalk. He stood waiting for me to pay him. I broke away long enough to pay the driver and then went right back into another deep embrace.

We eventually made it back upstairs where I greeted my parents and brother in the midst of a high-flying state of oxytocin bliss. I asked Marcus if anyone had given him a tour, but he said no, he hadn't seen the whole apartment yet. When we got to the guest bedroom, which held a large wooden infrared sauna, I realized I could use a session after the overnight flight. Marcus was completely enthralled.

"How many people fit inside this thing?" he asked.

"Technically it's a two-person sauna, but it's a really tight squeeze."

I could already see the ideas forming in his head and wondered how we were going to swing going in there together with my family in the living room next door.

I announced to my mom, who was cleaning the kitchen, that I'd be taking a long sauna to recover from the flight. Marcus quietly followed me inside, and once the door closed, he gave me a seductive smile.

We left the sauna as quietly as we had entered and took a shower together while keeping our voices to a whisper. Afterward, I was ready for a nap and could feel the jet lag starting to creep in.

Twelve hours later, Marcus and I were wearing matching light-blue terry-cloth robes and drinking herbal tea as we sat on the floor, facing my parents, who sat on the couch directly in front of us.

The time had come.

My heart was beating faster and faster. I couldn't imagine how they'd react. I could only hope that my dad, whose health wasn't great to begin with, wouldn't die from shock.

Marcus sensed my nervousness and squeezed my hand. I whispered in his ear, "Make sure you talk about our relationship and our wedding first. Don't go straight to the news."

He smiled with sparkly eyes and whispered back, "Don't worry, honey. I love you. It's going to be fine."

My parents had no idea why we insisted having a meeting at 10 p.m., long past their bedtime, but they'd agreed to my request. I took a deep breath and cleared my throat.

"First of all," I began, "I wanted to let everyone know how happy I am that we're all together and that you've had a chance to meet and get to know Marcus over the past twenty-four hours. We have some things we want to share with you tonight."

I elbowed Marcus, and he jumped in. "Yes, I'm so happy we're here together, too. I love you guys so much already. And tonight, I wanted to talk about how in love I am with your amazing daughter. We've committed to spending our lives together."

Mom smiled, and Dad relaxed a bit. I could already read their minds. They thought we were to about to say we were getting engaged. *That would be so nice if we really were getting engaged and could set our wedding date right now.* I imagined myself in a gorgeous white lace dress with a huge, sexy baby bump on the beach in Hawaii with all of my friends and family cheering us on.

Marcus nudged me, and I was brought back to the present moment.

"Oh, yes!" I jumped right back in. "Marcus is truly the most amazing person I could ever imagine being with, and we're going to be together forever. But he has one little issue he has to take care of first, right Marcus?"

My parents' smiles started to fade.

"What kind of issue? Dad asked.

"It's a little complicated," I interrupted. "But it will all be sorted out soon. I'll let him explain."

Marcus launched into a long, complicated story about Mariana and her green card. His fifteen-minute explanation twisted and turned in all sorts of directions before leading us back to where he started—the land of utter confusion. He recounted so many different details about Mariana's past boyfriends and their betrayals, her love of Hawaii, and how he was the one person who had agreed to help her in her unfortunate situation. When he finally stopped talking, we were all so confused by his tale that no one said anything. I looked at my parents' faces, which were completely blank. Maybe they were still trying to figure out what he had just said. I know I was!

The silence was too much for me. "What I think Marcus was trying to say is that he's committed to me and just needs to work on getting divorced from Mariana so that we can get married as soon as possible. Right, Marcus?"

"Yes," he said, punctuating the moment with a peck on the lips.

Mom came down to where we were sitting so she could give us both a warm, loving hug. When she returned to the couch, Dad's eyes were starting to drift closed, and Mom looked pretty exhausted as well. I glanced at the clock. We'd talked for nearly forty-five minutes and still not told them I was pregnant.

"There's actually more we want to tell you," I said. My heart started to race again. My palms were so sweaty that I wiped them on my thick robe.

Marcus reached into his pocket. "Instead of tell you, I think showing you would be even better." He took out my six-week ultrasound photo, a tiny white bean on a black background, and handed it to my mom.

Mom let out a high-pitched gasp. "WHAT?"

Marcus grinned from ear to ear like a little boy. "Yep, Courtney's pregnant!"

Time froze. They froze. Mom gazed downward at the ultrasound photo, her jaw so wide in disbelief it looked like it had detached from the rest of her face. Dad stared at me with his mouth shaped like wide circle. They were in complete shock. I felt terrible. This was supposed to be a happy, celebratory moment. I worried that Mom might faint, or Dad might have another heart attack or stroke.

No one said anything. Marcus held my sweaty hand while tears formed in my eyes. As quickly as time had frozen, it all came back to life again. Mom's lower jaw rejoined the rest of her face, and Dad's expression shifted ever so slightly. *Phew.* At least everyone was still alive.

"Is this real?" asked Mom, pointing to the ultrasound photo, her eyes welling with tears. "Are you really pregnant?"

"Yes," I said. "And I'm having a baby girl!"

"You know already?" she asked.

"We don't know officially, but I'm one hundred percent certain I'm having a girl! Are you happy?"

"Are you kidding me? I'm ecstatic! Just shocked, but ecstatic!"

"What about you, Dad? Are you okay?"

"I'm more than okay," he said. "I'm overjoyed! And like your mother, I'm flabbergasted!"

I let out a huge sigh of relief. We had told them the news. I felt like a hundred-pound weight had been lifted off my chest. We continued to talk and celebrate for another hour, our previous tiredness transformed into excitement and an even deeper connection.

Several uncomfortable situations popped up while Marcus and I were in New York City. The first was how he laid claim to the library of books my father no longer wanted and spent most of his time packing those up for himself rather than helping my parents, which was the whole purpose of the trip. He also posted on social media about his amazing time in the city, while only including selfies and no mention of me or my family. Being pregnant amplified how much that hurt because I needed him to be there for me.

One night, while he was taking a shower, I cried to my mom like a little girl, curled up in a ball on the couch. I showed her the Facebook post and told her, in between sobs, how hurt and upset I was that according to the image he was putting out into the world, I didn't even exist. And yet, here I was, pregnant with his baby.

Another day, instead of being part of the dress rehearsal for a solo dance performance I was scheduled to perform, he took my bike and spent the day on a five-hour trip to New Jersey. None of my family could understand why he left at such a crucial time—he was largely involved with the technical aspects of the performance—and why would he go to New Jersey, of all places?

Despite the few negative moments, being in New York City with Marcus was like being on our own little honeymoon, and I especially appreciated not having to hide our relationship like we often did in Hawaii. The ratio of good to bad with him was about ten to one—the power of our connection, chemistry, and intimacy made me forget the hurtful, uncomfortable moments. I believed with my whole heart that he would change—he would grow up, get divorced, and become the loving, respectful, committed husband I envisioned. We were closer than ever by the end of those two weeks, as if we had merged into one solid unit.

The morning before we flew back to Hawaii, I was packing up a few final boxes when Marcus came in to tell me that Mom wanted to talk to us together. We walked into the living room where Mom was kneeling and chanting in front of her Buddhist altar. Her entire being glowed. She asked if we would chant with her for three minutes before she gave us a special gift.

Gift? That sparked my attention. After the final prayer, Mom opened a drawer in her custom-built wooden altar and took out a tiny box. I was intrigued—I'd never seen it before.

"This is from my grandmother," she said. And then Mom turned her attention to Marcus, holding out the box. "My grandmother passed down this ring to me, and now I'm passing it on to you, so you'll have a ring to give Courtney. I know you don't have much money so I thought this would help."

I watched with widening eyes as Marcus carefully opened the small box and then removed an even smaller pouch. He carefully took out a beautiful diamond ring and held it up as it glimmered in the daylight streaming through the windows. Time slowed as Marcus looked me in the eye for a long moment before slipping the ring onto my left finger.

A perfect fit, like Cinderella's glass slipper. I felt like the most special, chosen woman on earth. I was floating on air as I exclaimed my unending gratitude to Mom for giving us this beautiful engagement ring, a family heirloom that I had never even seen before. Marcus didn't say much, but he appeared to be genuinely happy, although not as much as I was. I barely noticed his subdued reaction because I was caught up in ecstasy seeing my childhood dream of marriage come true—he had the ring!

A minute later, Marcus took the gorgeous ring off my finger and put it back into the tiny pouch. I felt like a part of me was being ripped off. Wearing that diamond ring made me feel like an entirely different person, one who was confident, seen, and desired. Marcus promised to take good care of the ring until the time was right for him to propose, which he later confessed could only be after his divorce with Mariana was final. While I was overjoyed at Mom's incredible gift, I was deeply saddened that I had to wait to be engaged. I wanted it now, and I was tired of being number two on his list. Why couldn't Mariana just go back to Colombia where she belonged?

The ring became a prominent totem. Marcus alluded to it every so often when our relationship was going through particularly dismal times. He patronized me with comments like, "Remember the ring!" or "Do I need to get out the ring again?" Like a carrot on a string, that ring kept us going. But in the present moment, I was deeply in love, newly pregnant, and holding fervently to my fantasy of getting engaged by Christmas.

Dream on.

The morning of our departure was pitch black and below freezing. We decked ourselves in as many layers of clothing as we could fit. We pulled turtle-neck sweaters up over our chins and wrapped scarves around our heads like turbans. Right before we left my childhood apartment for the last time—it sold a month later—we looked at each other and started laughing hysterically.

I glanced in a full-length mirror and started laughing even harder. "I can't go out like this! I look ridiculous!"

Marcus came and put his arm around me. The two of us stood there laughing at what a sight we were—bundled-up bandits—before taking a selfie.

"At least you'll be cozy on the flight!" said Mom.

In a moment of genius, Marcus replied, "We're cozy-rufu partners!"

In Nichiren Buddhism, kosen-rufu means world peace, which starts with each individual. One of the daily prayers I had recited for as long as I could remember included one for kosen-rufu. A kosen-rufu partner is a nickname for a spouse or partner who enables your greater contribution to kosen-rufu. Through your partnership, the world at large is elevated.

"Cozy-rufu," or just "Cozy" for short, became our adorable made-up word that encompassed both world peace and cuddling. The nickname stuck—from that moment on, we called each other "Cozy," whether we were in public places or around other friends.

"Oh, Cozy!" I'd say.

"Yes, Cozy?" he'd reply.

After nearly twenty-four hours of traveling, we landed in Honolulu exhausted and jet-lagged. Since Marcus had given up his room in the Sanctuary six weeks earlier, we both headed back to my apartment. I was ecstatic that we'd finally be living in one place together. As we climbed into a taxi, I felt like we were truly partners. The whirlwind trip behind us, we had returned to beautiful, warm, Hawaii, and we had a whole, amazing life to build together. In just seven short months, our daughter would be born—it was time to plant deep roots and strengthen our relationship even more.

Six Forever and Ever

Three weeks after returning to Hawaii, my car broke down, and since I couldn't drive Marcus's manual pickup truck, we had to devise a plan for him to chauffeur me around.

One morning, Marcus decided to take the long way to my morning appointment, which meant driving along the coast on one of the most gorgeous routes on the entire island. As we took in the magnificent, dramatic dark-green cliffs and sparkly sky-blue shoreline, Marcus announced he had exciting news to share.

I bubbled up with excitement—he didn't make those kinds of statements often. I just knew he was going to tell me that Mariana had finally gotten her green card so he could divorce her. Maybe he was going to propose to me somewhere along this jaw-dropping drive. I imagined how he would pull over, and we would climb down the rocky cliffs toward the ocean, then he'd kneel down and—

"Cozy?" Marcus snapped me out of my intense daydream.

"Sorry, Cozy. I'm with you. I'm just so excited about this news. What is it?"

He joyfully exclaimed that his buddy Paul, who was the newly appointed senior minister at a church in Dallas, had called to offer him a position.

My heart plummeted. *He was offered a position at a church doing what? Who is this Paul guy? And why would he even consider moving while I was pregnant?*

Maybe Marcus just felt flattered about being offered a job since he had been jobless for quite a while. He was growing frustrated at my lack of enthusiasm, so he tried to explain. Paul had previously lived in Hawaii, and they had been buddies for many years. During Marcus's recent stay on the mainland, he had taken a road trip to Dallas to visit Paul. During his short overnight stay, Marcus had performed a successful sound-healing event at the Church—they fell in love with him and wanted more. So, Paul created a special position that would allow him to perform regular sound-healing events and help out with general tasks around the facility.

The proposed position would also allow Marcus time to complete his ministerial training, which he had begun several years prior but never finished. He had been expelled from the program for misconduct—yelling, fighting, and cursing with his then-girlfriend outside the preschool classrooms. (It was completely her fault, Marcus said.) Paul would ensure he could get back into the program under his mentorship.

We were a unit now. Where did I fit into his plan? I had just launched my nonprofit dance company less than a year earlier—I had students, company members, and an entire board of directors. The last thing I could ever consider was leaving Hawaii, my beloved home. I tried to think up something to ask that wouldn't upset him. The disconnected vibe between us was escalating, and I felt it my duty to keep it harmonious.

"How do *I* fit into your plan, Cozy?" I asked as sweetly as I could muster.

"You're invited, too! Paul is still working out the details, but hopefully we'll be able to live for free in the Blue House on the Church campus."

I was already living essentially rent-free. My landlord, Nancy, had leased me a large two-bedroom, two-bath detached apartment upstairs from her house. She suggested that I list the second bedroom on Airbnb and keep the proceeds, as long as I managed all the work it entailed. I was so successful that I'd made it to SuperHost status. Not only did the Airbnb cover my rent and then some, but I also had made friends from all over the world.

"What about Maya? She's settled here in school. Would she come, too?"

"Of course, she'll come with me. She's my daughter. I'm not leaving her here with Tina."

My mind raced to assess the situation. We couldn't possibly move to Dallas. I was having a baby in less than seven months; Maya went to school here; our lives were set up here. I'd already arranged for a close friend to serve as midwife for our home birth. Our daughter had to be born in Hawaii. Just the thought of her being born in Texas—of all places—made me cringe.

I looked out the wide-open window at the surreal beauty. I took a deep breath to slow my racing thoughts. Through eyes blurred by tears, I pondered the jagged mountain cliffs and the endless ocean glimmering in the radiant sun. A message came to me like a soft voice whispering into my cells: *You've worked so hard to get to this point, to live in Hawaii, and you have built a life you truly love. You can't just give this up.*

I reasoned with the voice. *Then what do I do? I'm nine weeks pregnant. I need to be with my partner.*

To my surprise, the voice answered right away. *You'll find a way. But you must stay strong.*

"When does Paul want you to start?" I asked as nonchalantly as possible.

"He has to present the idea of us moving as a family at their next board meeting, so it won't be immediately. But he'll let me know pretty soon."

"So, like, in a year? After the baby is born, right?"

"I would say probably sooner. Honestly, I think they could use me there now. But it all has to go through the board first."

I fell into heavy contemplative mode. The voice came back again, this time whispering more loudly. *Speak your truth!*

So I did.

"Marcus, this offer sounds like an incredible opportunity, and I'm genuinely happy for you. But I can't imagine living in Texas. I can't imagine leaving everything I've built here—my community of friends and all the clients. The only way I could possibly consider moving would be after the baby is born. I'm sure Paul would understand that the baby takes priority."

It felt so good to speak my truth. Until Marcus began replying.

First, he said nothing for a long time. When he finally spoke, he used the same stern voice he used to discipline his daughter. I felt like I had done something terribly wrong. Using that harsh tone and even harsher curse words, he negated every positive thing I had mentioned about living in Hawaii, devalued the level of success I had achieved, and accused me of having no respect for our relationship, for him, or for his career, while all he did all day long was drive around and support me and my artistic vision.

"You are a spoiled brat who only ever thinks about yourself," he said.

Tears streamed down my face. I felt like I had just been beaten up. He seemed so mad I feared he might stop the car and force me out right there in the middle of nowhere. I apologized to him profusely, fighting back more tears. I felt so incredibly misunderstood. I had absolutely no idea how the conversation had gone downhill so fast.

For three long minutes, neither of us spoke. Silently, I prayed for our relationship to magically heal itself. I needed harmony between us—I couldn't stand it any other way. We were almost at my teaching gig. I had to pull myself together enough to appear as though it was another normal day, despite having just lived through the first of countless such episodes to come.

Marcus broke the extended silence. "Hey, Cozy! You okay?" He reached out with his free hand to massage my neck and shoulders. His demeanor was so gentle, as if his outburst had never even happened.

Not quite sure how to respond, I answered with a fake smile. "I'll be fine." *I guess maybe my prayers worked.*

"Don't forget, Cozy, we're in this together—forever. Remember?" His tone had changed to childlike innocence.

"Yes, Cozy. Forever," I replied obediently.

"And ever and ever." He stroked my head, and a hit of oxytocin saturated my cells. I was hooked.

A month later, I had purchased our plane tickets to Dallas. We would be leaving in three weeks. I had tried to talk Marcus out of this move, but he wouldn't budge.

"I can't pass on such an incredible leap for my career," he said. "I sincerely hope you'll join me."

Being fourteen weeks pregnant and over-the-moon in love, I felt I had no choice, but I resented it. Maybe I could stay in Hawaii by myself and have the baby there. Or I could go live in Northern California near my siblings and parents. Mom could nanny, and I could get involved with the vibrant dance scene in San Francisco. I wrote out detailed life scenarios with pros and cons for each. I was surprised that both the Hawaii and California plans sounded like fun, awesome lives.

There was just one caveat—I would be a single mom.

I absolutely refused to be a single mom. If there was one thing that truly mattered to me, it was being in an inspiring and uplifting partnership with a loving husband and raising children together. Deep down, I didn't believe I was strong enough to have a natural birth and raise a child on my own.

In extreme emotional agony, I closed up my beautiful life in Hawaii—my business, jobs, apartment, community, friends, and support systems. I felt I owed it to myself to avoid becoming a single mother by being with my partner and supporting his dreams. That's what family does, right? And we'd be married soon enough. He already had the ring!

Most of my friends thought I was absolutely nuts. Over and over, I heard the same response: "I just can't see you in Texas."

"I can't see myself there either, but that's where I'm headed."

Our flights were scheduled to leave Honolulu on December 21. One month, however, hadn't been nearly enough time to properly close my dance school, disband my dance company, gracefully leave all of my jobs, and pack up an entire apartment. No matter how much Marcus tried to convince me that I could "leave in a week, what's the big deal?" I held my ground. I agreed to accompany Marcus and Maya to Dallas for three weeks, including the holidays. I'd fly back to Hawaii to close down my life and return to Dallas seven weeks later. That would give me time to prepare and produce a final dance performance in Hawaii on the first anniversary of my dance company's launch.

Every day before we left, Marcus let me know how disappointed he was that I wasn't moving to Dallas in one fell swoop with no looking back. No matter how many times I defended my decision and explained the significance of that extra time in Hawaii, he failed to understand. The heated conversations, which went on for hours at a time, wore me down. I was already making a sacrifice to be in Dallas for three full weeks. My sister's baby was due in early December, and instead of going to meet my brand-new niece and support my sister after giving birth, or visit my parents in their new home after my dad's recent emergency hospitalization, I'd be hanging out in Dallas with him, doing absolutely nothing.

He demonstrated zero understanding or appreciation for my decision to be with him over my immediate family at such an important time. He simply shook his head in disapproval.

"You need to get your priorities straight," he said. "We are our own family now, and family always comes first."

There was one major benefit to the whole situation—we'd be nearly four thousand miles away from his wife. I barely knew her, but she brought out the worst in me. Marcus didn't try to get me to like her but rather said terrible things about her, calling her "clingy," "needy," and "incapable of being in a healthy relationship."

We'd also be far away from any of his past lovers and girlfriends, which according to Marcus numbered more than two hundred. At times, he claimed to have been with around five hundred women before me, which I couldn't even fathom. *Yeehaw, we were leavin' his exes and goin' to Texas!* This was the one thing about the move that excited me. Rather than be stuck on an island surrounded by constant temptation, we'd be living on a church campus in a city neither of us had ever lived in before. There couldn't possibly be a safer place for us to be. I convinced myself that this move was the Universe's way of providing us an incubation period to focus on building our relationship away from possible distractions.

He couldn't even cheat on me if he wanted to.

I felt comforted by the vision of living a close-knit family life, in a huge blue house, where sweet old ladies kept close enough watch that he wouldn't dare even flirt with another woman.

We arrived in Dallas on a cold, damp December morning. I felt beyond exhausted after sixteen hours of traveling, and I vowed to never take an overnight flight again. Marcus, Maya, and I waited outside the airport for our ride to pick us up. None of us were wearing proper winter clothing, so we huddled together, shivering and giggling.

Standing outside the Dallas Love Field airport, I just knew I didn't fit in there. I wanted so badly to love it, so I pretended as best as I could from the get-go. I even held up my phone with freezing fingers to snap selfies of us with the big Welcome to Texas sign in the background. I couldn't believe this was our new home.

Paul sent a church staff member named Monica to pick us up, except he sent her to the wrong airport, so it took another forty-five minutes before she showed up. Monica was in her late forties and dressed up just to come and greet us. I felt embarrassed about my disheveled appearance—I was wearing pajama pants, and my first trimester hormones had caused unrelenting breakouts on my cheeks and jawline. By Dallas standards, I looked like your average homeless person.

Monica said it was her day off, but she wouldn't miss a chance to pick Marcus up from the airport! She'd been waiting for him to come back. The two of them began flirting playfully, but I was too tired to care. I had grown accustomed to him flirting with any and all women—and often men. Plus, I could see by her large diamond ring that she was married, so what did I have to worry about? I just wanted to get to our house and lie down. I felt ill from missing an entire night's sleep.

We piled into an old black Volvo SUV that Monica said had been the Church's "company car," but Paul had since lent it to her. She took the scenic route to the Church. I gazed out the window at magnificent mansions, each with their own style, architecture, and charm. As well-traveled as I was, I had never seen homes this big before, one after another. Focusing on the mansions distracted me from how unwell I felt.

Monica slowed way down as we approached a large church campus on the left. "Here we are!" she said.

A modern angular building made its way into view, surrounded by gardens, tree-lined pathways, and a small creek. Sleek, eye-catching, and huge, the building didn't look much a traditional church. Outside of the large building was an even larger parking lot, massive enough for several hundred cars.

As we drove farther back into the parking lot, I saw our house. Light-blue wood panels covered the exterior of the long, ranch-style home, which had a large front porch and three cute little steps leading up to a beautiful stained-glass door. Despite being a fraction of the size of the homes down the street, the Blue House looked pretty darn big. Our little family now had a real place to call home—not an apartment, not a rented room, but an actual house.

Monica parked close to the house and handed Marcus a key with a twinkle in her eye. After she noticed Maya and I staring at her, she looked away with a high-pitched nervous laugh.

She's seriously after my man while I'm pregnant and she's married? Was she truly after him? Who knows, but there was enough chemistry between them that even the eight-year-old picked up on it.

We walked inside the heavy, stained-glass door to find ourselves in the first of two large living rooms. I later learned that our house would also be used for various Church activities. On Sunday mornings, teenagers met in the first living room, replete with twenty extra-large beanbags, chalkboards, and a colorful rug.

Past the first living room was a spacious kitchen and dining area that opened up into the second living room, which was even bigger than the first and had an entire wall of floor-to-ceiling windows that opened onto the backyard. We could grow a vegetable garden, get a massive trampoline, or turn the yard into our own sacred meditation zone! (Eventually, we did all three.)

The possibilities at the Blue House seemed endless. Despite the expansive square footage, there were only two bedrooms. Maya's room came first down a long hallway, the biggest bedroom I'd ever seen for a child, even counting my days nannying in Park Avenue penthouses. She also had her own walk-in closet and an attached bathroom covered in delicate light-pink tile.

After three oversized hallway closets and a laundry room large enough to be a third bedroom, we came to the master bedroom, which had its own entryway into the backyard, two ridiculously large walk-in closets, and a grand bathroom suite in a beautiful blue tile. Even the oversized bathtub was a unique shade of blue. I felt a tickle run through my body. We were like a real married couple!

The house was everything I'd imagined from Marcus's descriptions and more. We were in Texas now, where everything is just bigger.

On the kitchen counter was a gift basket that Paul had put together for us, filled with random foods that none of us ate—generic brands of creme-filled cookies and cans of ravioli. Clearly Paul wasn't up to speed with our family's mostly vegan, organic dietary preferences, but it was the thought that counted. Amid the hodgepodge of groceries was a blue sheet of paper typed with large, all-capital letters: WELCOME TO YOUR NEW PARADISE.

We unpacked the food in the walk-in pantry (I wanted to throw it all away, but Marcus insisted on keeping it) and taped the sign to the refrigerator, where it remained for the entirety of our stay at the Blue House.

Three days before Christmas, while Marcus prepared for the busiest church season of the year, I poured myself into unpacking. Our house was only a minute's walk to the main building, so our work and personal lives merged fluidly. One moment we'd be waltzing around our living room putting ornaments on a tacky gold Christmas tree, and the next moment, we'd be standing at the main building's entrance, greeting people for the evening service.

Marcus made it clear that my job was to make as many connections as possible, schmooze as much as possible, and present myself as the beautiful, perfect, pregnant housewife and mother of Maya. I was honored that he had given me such a job! Always trying to please, I took it upon myself to do everything he asked and more.

The Dallas churchgoers—mostly older, retired folks—were very friendly people. And although I felt completely out of place—and living a lie anytime someone referred to my "husband" or "our" daughter—the people I met were genuinely good and kind and seemed to be strangely overjoyed that we had moved there.

As I held the door on Christmas Eve, wearing high heels and makeup, I wondered what they would think if they knew all of our secrets—that Marcus was not actually my husband but married to another woman in Hawaii, that Maya was not my biological daughter, that I was Jewish and Buddhist and had never been to a church service in my entire life, and that in addition to our unborn daughter and Maya, Marcus had a grown son, and possibly other children, all from other women.

Our first Christmas together, Marcus wanted to share how his ex-girlfriend had taught him to "do Christmas." I had no idea what that entailed until twelve large boxes arrived in the mail, all gifts for Maya that Marcus's ex had purchased online.

On Christmas morning, like a little kid, I was the first one awake. Santa Claus had indeed made his way into our living room. Under the tree and across half the massive living room were boxes and boxes of gifts, each wrapped to perfection—a red bow here, a long curly white ribbon there. I knew Maya was getting tons of presents, but I was shocked to see how many gifts there were for me. The gift tags read things like: "To my dear Cozy, have you been naughty or nice this year? Love, Your One and Cozily." I was so tickled and filled with a deep sense of appreciation for our home and family.

When Marcus woke up a bit later, he told me he had stayed up until four in the morning wrapping everything. He was invested in giving Maya and me an incredible Christmas. Seeing how tired he was, Maya and I crawled into the queen-size bed with him where we cuddled together for another half hour.

While I didn't give Marcus a multitude of gifts, the few I did give him were especially meaningful. One was a large framed black-and-white photograph of us, a selfie we had taken just two weeks prior in Hawaii right after we'd woken up one morning. Although it was a headshot, you could see that Marcus was shirtless, and I was wearing a white lacy top.

Something magical happened in this photo—you would never guess we'd just woken up. It looked more like a Calvin Klein ad on the back cover of a magazine, our faces close together with small smiles and deep, soulful gazes into the camera. And the antique wooden frame transformed the photo into a piece of art.

Marcus wasted no time in hanging the photo right over our fireplace. He turned on a dimmer switch that put a golden spotlight directly on the photo. Maya and I were incredibly impressed by his impromptu handiwork.

"It's like the paintings in museums, Daddy!" Maya exclaimed.

"Do you like it?" I asked Marcus for the tenth time.

"Like it? I love it! That's why I'm hanging it right here. When you go back to Hawaii, I'll just come out here every night, turn on the spotlight, and sit on this couch and stare at you."

Maya started giggling. I gushed in delight.

"This photo is going to save us when you're gone for so long," he added.

"Good," I answered, not exactly sure what he meant.

On New Year's Eve, Marcus's job was to supervise the building during a large Alcoholics Anonymous party. The local AA organization had rented the entire main building and were throwing what sounded like quite an event, including a theatrical comedy performance. The three of us dressed up and walked over to the church where Marcus quickly disappeared, attending to various technical tasks. Maya went to sit in her dad's office and watch a movie, and I was left to roam around feeling awkward, trying to fit in with a crowd to which I had absolutely no connections.

As I paced the long hallway trying to figure out how to get past the usher without a ticket, Minister Paul walked through the front door with a big, goofy smile on his face. I instantly felt happy and relieved to see someone I knew. A gorgeous, model-thin woman accompanied him.

"This is my girlfriend, Lacy," he said.

Lacy wore incredibly high heels, which rendered her a whopping six feet tall, and a strappy, revealing black dress with a long, Cruella de Vil–style white fur coat. She had long arched eyebrows and a bizarre, slightly uneven haircut. She looked not a day over twenty-five. She had also brought along her eight-year-old son, a bouncy, energetic boy named Maddox.

At first glance, and especially at a distance, she appeared strikingly gorgeous. Up close, she had slightly odd features like a unique top model. Lacy didn't live in Dallas but a few states over, where Paul had last worked as a minister. They were now in a long-distance relationship and visited each other every couple of weeks. Paul had never mentioned he had a girlfriend, though we'd spent quite a bit of time with him in the past ten days.

Paul let the organizers know that he was the "CEO of this place," and we all walked in without question. I didn't know churches had CEOs and thought that was an odd way to put it.

"I have to go to my office to print out notes for tomorrow's sermon," he said, "so I'll meet up with you later in the theater."

Lacy and I continued along the long corridor together. Even at five foot nine, I felt like a shrimp next to her. We were walking down the carpeted hallway when Marcus came skipping down a flight of stairs in front of us like a Christmas elf. He had eyes only for Lacy. *I knew I should've worn something sexier.*

Marcus walked right up to her, ignoring me all together, and looked her up and down as if he were admiring a rare work of art. A few seconds later, with a sparkle in his eyes and a small alluring smile, he stated softly—but loud enough for us all to hear—"Stunning."

I felt sick and utterly worthless—ugly, fat, short—not to mention completely embarrassed that he was acting so inappropriately. He was blatantly turned on by the minster's girlfriend.

I watched Lacy take in the compliment with only slight apprehension and smile back at him. Marcus introduced himself and the two of them were lost in la-la land for about three seconds, until I snapped them out of it by putting my hand on his shoulder. I turned into my alter ego, Clingy Needy Pregnant Partner. Lacy was shocked when I told her I was pregnant. She hadn't realized that Marcus and I were a couple—she thought I was just some girl from the Church.

The rest of the evening was long and painful. Marcus was clearly captivated by Lacy. Each of them parents of an eight-year-old, they discussed planning playdates in the coming weeks for Maya and Maddox. Marcus ignored me the rest of the evening. While on the surface I was all smiles, I was slowly realizing that I was in a relationship with a man who had absolutely zero self-control around other women, which terrified me to pieces. He knew how strongly I felt about monogamy, faithfulness, and honesty, but he didn't seem to care one bit.

While I didn't think he'd cheat on me, and while I trusted him with my life, I had to contend constantly with his desire to flirt with other women. I just couldn't understand or relate whatsoever. *Wasn't I enough? Couldn't he be proud to be with me?* Little did I understand at the time that a zebra, no matter how much they meditate or play a gong, cannot change their stripes.

Three weeks later, at 9:30 p.m. on a Saturday night, I was back in Hawaii and soaking in a warm Epsom salts bath, my baby bump poking above the water. I finally looked pregnant rather than simply bloated.

My eyes, on the other hand, were red and swollen. The second trimester of my pregnancy was an emotional time. I needed a stable partner, but Marcus had been ignoring my texts and calls all day long. Something was off. Was he cheating on me? I couldn't figure it out. Something must be wrong with me.

Or, maybe he wasn't cheating on me at all.

With an ounce of hope, I realized that I had no proof. Maybe he was just busy. Maybe all my intuitive feelings were just pregnancy hormones gone haywire. But it wasn't like him to completely ignore me for an entire day.

At 9:45 p.m., which was 1:45 a.m. in Dallas, I decided to surrender. After checking my phone obsessively all day, I decided to let go and turn it off. But as I reached for my phone, it started buzzing. Marcus's smiling photo popped up. *He's calling me now?* What could he possibly have to say for himself? Staring at his shirtless, sexy photo, I was equally furious and elated. I wasn't sure I even wanted to talk, so I just stared at the phone. At the last moment, I decided I would rather hear what he had to say than ignore his call.

"Hello?" I tried to act calm, cool, and collected.

"Hey," he whispered, like he was trying not to wake anyone up.

"Are you okay?" I asked. "I've been trying to reach you all day!"

"I told you I was working nonstop all weekend."

I knew he was lying.

"Did you get my texts?" I asked.

"Yes."

An awkward silence. We were both thinking of how to proceed. Perhaps he sensed that I knew something was up.

"I was working today, like I told you the last time we talked, remember?" His voice was annoyed, rude, and although still quiet, a bit angry.

My eyes welled up with tears again. "You were working all day? Like, until now?" I never should've answered the stupid phone.

"If you want to know," he said, "I was working from six-thirty this morning until three this afternoon, nonstop."

Silence.

"You've been free since three, but you couldn't call or text me back because . . . ?"

Marcus let out an angry sigh. He hated any sense of control I tried to have over his life, including asking too many questions.

"Lacy came over with Maddox. She had driven up to Dallas to see Paul, but he's out of town this weekend, so she came here instead."

I knew there was a woman at our house. I would have loved to have been wrong. I tried to return to my calm-cool-collected voice to encourage Marcus to share even more. "Did Maya and Maddox get to play while you guys hung out?"

"Yep, they had a great time. They get along so well."

"That's great."

Another awkward silence.

The conversation progressed slowly. Every time I tried to question him about his evening, he grew angrier. I tried to shift the conversation to our baby's first kicks. We switched to video chat so he could see them live, which helped lighten the mood. Our connection seemed to improve, and the energy between us was somewhat lighter, although something was still off.

During the course of our bathtub conversation, all I had to do was piece together the tidbits of information Marcus dropped to figure out what had gone on that evening and why he hadn't called. He said things like, "I have such a bad headache from all the wine we drank," and "Everyone loved the potato soup I cooked." Clearly, Lacy and her son had been at our house all afternoon and evening. In fact, they were probably still there right now, hence his whispering. While Marcus was declining my phone calls all day, he was enjoying quality time with his sexy, model lover (and boss's girlfriend) while their kids were playing together in Maya's room. If Paul was out of town, surely they had planned this.

"Why did Lacy drive all the way to Dallas if Paul was out of town?"

Marcus had no logical answer. He never admitted to sleeping with her, to kissing her, or to anything beyond cooking her dinner, drinking a couple of bottles of wine, and talking. But his lies were practically written across his face. Knowing him, how could he not have slept with her?

My boundaries were stretched to the max. I needed things to improve between us. By the end of our hour-long conversation, I found myself apologizing for calling so many times, texting him when I knew he was busy, and for even thinking he could have been cheating on me. I had been reduced to a lowly, submissive version of myself. I didn't know what to believe: that he was cheating on me with the minister's sexy girlfriend or that he simply had a new friend over for dinner while the kids played. I chose the latter in an attempt to protect myself and our unborn baby from the piercing pain of betrayal.

The next day, I made affirmation cards saying exactly what I wanted and desperately needed to believe: *I trust Marcus completely. I have total faith in our beautiful, healthy relationship. I am confident in my secure, loving relationship with Marcus.*

These cards soothed my aching soul like a delicate balm. I needed these affirmations to get through the times he didn't call back and my insecurities took over. Though my affirmations later proved false, I fully believe that they were necessary to keep my unborn baby healthy and alive. If I had known the reality of what he would later do, the grief may have been too much to bear.

Seven Countdown

It was just after seven and completely dark outside as I scurried somewhat frantically along a deserted cul-de-sac, trying to find the birth class I'd signed up for. I missed the first class of the series while I was in Dallas and hoped I'd be able to catch up in the next four classes. I knew I wanted a natural birth, but I had a lot to learn.

A bit out of breath, I slowed down as I arrived at a brightly lit storefront that, as far as I could see, must have been a rented space because it had no logo or identifying characteristics like a sign or banner. I found that a little odd, but as soon as I walked inside and saw a dozen pregnant women walking around, I felt right at home.

With a bit of online research, I had found a free local birth class called Trust Birth held on the windward side of Oahu and hosted by a group of women who were all doulas—an emotional support for women giving birth. While not medically trained, a doula acts as a birth companion and coach and provides continuous care during childbirth in the form of information, physical support, and emotional support. I couldn't believe the generosity of the women who put this together. They cooked an organic meal for thirty people, taught a jam-packed three-hour class, and didn't charge a penny. I felt like I had struck the jackpot, despite getting ice-cold fingers and toes from the Arctic temperature in the room.

Rather than advocating for either a hospital or home birth, the doulas presented accurate and detailed information about different birth practices and then left us to decide what was right for each of us. After that first Monday night, all I could think of was how Marcus needed to be there with me. I wondered how we'd ever get on the same page with our birth plans without his receiving this same information. In our daily calls, I did my best to share what I'd learned, but relaying an entire three-hour class wasn't feasible. I also felt slightly uncomfortable being the only one in the room without a significant other, but I knew that if Marcus were there, every other woman in the room would be jealous because of how playful, connected, and perfect we were together. I was definitely not a single mom going it alone.

I sat in the same chair at the same round table every week with two nice young couples whose babies were due much sooner than mine. Any chance I got, I gushed about Marcus. I missed him so much that he was constantly on my mind, and even more so at these birth classes since I was the only pregnant woman there without a partner.

Before the second to last class, I talked to Marcus while sitting outside the health food store. I gazed at the beautiful wetland marsh. My Hawaiian paradise was even more beautiful knowing my time there was coming to an end.

To my dismay, I could tell something was off between us again. Even through the phone, thousands of miles away, I picked up on the fact that he wasn't acting the same as usual. I had an instant gut feeling. *He's probably cheating on me with another woman in Dallas.* Mid-conversation, I pulled out my affirmation cards and started reading them silently. *I trust Marcus completely. I have total faith in our beautiful, healthy relationship. I am confident in my secure, loving relationship with Marcus.*

My intuition spoke loudly in response. *Yeah, right. In your dreams.*

I asked Marcus if he had seen Lacy again. My simple question infuriated him, and we found ourselves going down the rabbit hole, repeating much of the same conversation from the other night, except with more intensity. I could tell this was going to be a long, drawn-out episode, so I packed up my things, took a large sip of water, and started off on a walk while he went on for twenty minutes about my "paranoia and insecurities." I couldn't get a single word in.

Held captive on the other end of the line, I simply sobbed like a child. It never occurred me to hang up, defend myself, or speak back to him. That would be too risky. He might leave me forever—and then I'd end up a single mom. Plus, I started to wonder if he was right. Maybe I did need to get over my "deep issues." Either way, Marcus's accusations cut to the core, and being emotionally hooked to him only made it all the more painful.

I deeply craved a sense of stability, security, and love from him, but he said things like, "What? We don't have agreements about only being with each other."

Yes, we did, and we do!

When he finally paused to breathe, I spoke up. "Look, given what you just said—which is completely untrue because we do have agreements—is that your way of telling me you've been with other women since I left Dallas?"

I held my breath, praying I could somehow handle whatever answer he was about to tell me.

"No," he said quietly. "I haven't been with anyone."

I exhaled. His soft answer sounded honest and truthful. *Maybe I was just "paranoid and insecure" like he said.*

When we hung up two hours later, my head was spinning. I no longer felt like myself. These emotional rollercoasters during our weeks of separation were agonizing. My journal entries from this time are painful to read even today. In one entry, halfway into our time apart, I made a bulleted list titled, "Everything I can't stand about Marcus," with thirteen distinct items. Some were small paragraphs that said things such as, "He takes zero responsibility for our baby. He puts it all on me, yet he wanted a baby with me the second he saw me and didn't use a condom dozens of times prior to our getting pregnant!"

Others were one-liners:

"He owes me money—about a thousand dollars."

"He never says thank you."

And this one, which cracks me up a little bit: "I don't like him."

Looking back, I can't believe I stayed with him for even a minute longer. I didn't realize that if things were so bad while I was pregnant—my needs weren't being met and he wouldn't divorce his wife—then it was time to leave. Underneath the hurt, I was still in love and desperately trying to figure out how to get love flowing between us again. Perhaps I thought moving to Dallas would make all of our problems magically disappear. I was in for some big surprises.

Marcus's episodes, as I came to call them, left me in a bind. I didn't want to play by his rules, but I felt forced to. I tried to explain my needs to him in ways that wouldn't trigger his unrelenting rage, but such conversations always ended in disaster anyway. What if he was purposely trying to torture me so that I would change my mind about going to Dallas? But I was pregnant, and my mind was made up.

After that two-hour phone call, I felt like someone had put me through a meat shredder, leaving me in a pile of mere pieces of myself. I decided to seek some advice from Marie, the older, more experienced doula who ran the class and a sweet, kind lady. I walked into the ice-cold room, this time prepared with a shopping bag full of fuzzy socks, a fleece sweater, scarves, and a knitted hat that I'd bought at the Salvation Army.

I found Marie in the kitchen, preparing to bring out a big tray of rice and veggies. After helping her bring out the rest of the food, I asked if we could talk for a minute. We walked into the classroom where we'd have a little more privacy.

She looked at me with the kindest, most comforting eyes. "Honey, what is it?"

Just hearing those words and sensing her pure, kind heart, I burst into tears. It was strange to witness myself cry like this. Before Marcus, I had always been such a balanced, stable person. But now, I couldn't even get any words out. What was I going to say anyhow?

I'm hurt and upset because my partner refuses to divorce his wife and claims she came first. We're apart for two months while he's living thousands of miles away, and now I think he's cheating on me with the minister's girlfriend, but he won't admit it. I want to have a home birth here in Hawaii with my close friend as my midwife but now I can't, and I have no idea where I'm going to give birth in Texas. I'm going to arrive there more than six months pregnant, and I don't want to go, but I have to go.

When the tears subsided enough that I could talk, all I could muster was, "My partner and I aren't connecting anymore. It's been really difficult having him so far away during my pregnancy."

She gave me a huge hug and continued to hold me for what felt like an eternity. Although I didn't tell her the details, she seemed to understand somehow.

"It's normal to feel extra emotional during the second trimester," she said, "and I know how hard it is for you to be here alone. Why doesn't Marcus join through video chat?"

I had thought about that, but given the time difference, the class would start at midnight his time, and go until three in the morning. I told her I'd ask him anyway. He often stayed up into the night to talk to me.

A few minutes later, pregnant mamas with baby bumps of all sizes began filling up the room, and I wiped my teary eyes and runny nose one last time and took my seat. I zoned out while everyone around me chatted and ate dinner. What if I changed my mind about moving? Could I go through a birth alone? I wondered if maybe I should trust my gut that he wasn't being faithful. What if I moved there and the whole thing fell apart anyway?

The buzz of my phone shook me out of deep contemplation—a text from Marcus. I couldn't believe his impeccable timing. I desperately needed to hear from him. After the initial relief, my heart raced. *What was he going to say?* I opened the text, a paragraph of poetic "blah blah," as I called it—ramblings about spiritual topics that he usually brought up after smoking marijuana.

Somehow his nonsensical ramblings sounded incredibly poetic and often reminded me of warped love poems from the 1800s. This particular one was about how "all was working in divine ways to bring us closer together if we could continue to trust the process and sink into it." He punctuated the message with several emojis: a pink heart, yellow heart, angel smiley face, and last but not least, a diamond wedding ring.

I couldn't help but smile, despite the message not making any sense. The emojis said it all. He loved me. I wrote back with a simple emoji of three pink hearts and felt like I had received a new lease on life. My mood lifted, and my appetite returned. I heaped up a large plate of food and happily chatted with my classmates, doing my best to put the day's difficulties behind me.

The countdown was on—I had a little over four weeks until the big move.

Not only was I downsizing my belongings and giving away as much as I could, but I was also planning and rehearsing an anniversary performance for my dance company. I had invested thousands of hours (and dollars) into growing, nurturing, and sustaining my first baby. I had a board of directors who believed in and supported me, a troupe of wonderful dancers, and a group of adoring young students. The least I could do before leaving it all was to put on a beautiful performance to commemorate its one-year birthday.

Two other personal events I'd planned before leaving included a Blessingway ceremony—a sort of spiritual version of a baby shower—and a maternity photo shoot. I wanted my belly to be as big as possible for the photo shoot, so I wanted to wait as long as possible.

One early morning in the middle of meditation, an idea popped into my mind out of nowhere, leaving me feeling elated. I called Marcus on my morning drive to teach a yoga class.

He answered with a chirpy, friendly voice. "Hey, Cozy!"

"Cozy! I have a genius idea to tell you!" I was practically bouncing in my seat with excitement.

"What's that?"

"You know how my mom is coming to Hawaii to help me pack up and move during my last week? I was thinking maybe you could come too! That way you could be part of my dance company's final performance, attend the Blessingway ceremony, and be in my maternity photo shoot!"

I waited for an enthusiastic reply but faced instead an unanticipated silence. Maybe the call had dropped. "Cozy, are you still there?"

"I'm still here, Cozy," he answered. "That's an interesting idea, but I don't know if it's doable for me."

My heart sank. "Why isn't it doable?"

"Lots of reasons," he said. "For one, I can't afford a plane ticket to Hawaii to play around with you. Plus, I'm busy here. I can't just take a week off because you want to see me. And I could get a call about my marriage interview anytime now and have to be in Hawaii with only a few weeks' notice."

I had forgotten about the dreaded marriage interview, where he would sit with Mariana across from a United States Citizenship and Immigration Services officer, and they'd pretend they were a happy married couple—never mentioning me, my pregnancy, or my moving to Dallas with Marcus—and present all sorts of fake evidence to make their marriage seem real. This interview terrified me for many reasons—what if they found out he was lying? Marriage fraud is a felony offense.

"When do you think the interview will be?" I asked.

"There's no way of knowing. Everything's backed up at Immigration so it could be several months from now. Or it could be in two weeks."

My stomach turned into knots. All I wanted was for the interview to be over as soon as possible so that I could relax and know that my future husband wouldn't be sitting in jail for the next five years. That would certainly put a wrench in my plan.

Aside from the looming marriage interview, I reasoned that Marcus's main reason for not coming was financial. I couldn't blame him for that—he had only a small salary because living at the Blue House was considered part of his compensation. I continued to tell him how much his presence would mean to me. Without him, what were my mom and I going to do? Neither of us could lift a fifty-pound suitcase, and I would have ten of them. We needed him.

Marcus assured me with no measure of enthusiasm that he'd think about it.

My next call was to Mom to see if she'd be interested in financing Marcus's trip. "How could we possibly do this move without him?" I asked.

She offered to put eight hundred dollars toward his roundtrip flight from Dallas to Honolulu, and I would pay the difference. I couldn't wait to share the wonderful news with Marcus. In the text message conversation that ensued, he not only never said thank you, but he also remained hesitant to committing for the week. He didn't want to miss work, and he had to figure out who would watch his daughter.

As the day progressed, I found myself begging him to come. Stooping that low made me feel a bit worthless, but eventually, he started to budge. He said he would look into childcare for Maya and would get back to me the next day. We had to act fast—tickets were already close to eight hundred dollars, and there weren't many good flight options to begin with.

I woke up the next morning to wonderful news: Marcus had found someone to watch Maya for the week! I asked who, thinking it must be one of the sweet old ladies from the Church.

"Alice agreed to watch her," he said.

"Who's Alice?" I asked.

"You know Alice. Alice who's been helping me paint my office. Alice whose daughter comes and plays with Maya during the day. I know I've mentioned her to you before."

He probably had mentioned Alice once or twice, but only in relation to her daughter, who was Maya's new best friend. I thought she was just some random church person—I didn't realize he had such a close relationship with her to have her watch Maya for an entire week. Either way, I was thrilled he'd found someone to watch Maya so he could come and be with me in Hawaii.

By that evening, ticket prices had risen to nearly nine hundred dollars round-trip, so Marcus told me to go ahead and book it. He still had a few weeks to get his duties covered at the church. In the days to come, time seemed to slow down. I didn't know if I could last any longer without him. He was a drug to which I was heavily addicted, and I yearned for him.

So much had happened in our weeks apart—my body was completely different from the last time Marcus saw me. I now had an official baby bump. My skin had cleared, and I was starting to have the pregnancy glow I'd only read about. Baby was kicking her legs, poking her elbows, and somersaulting inside me. I was truly transforming into a mother.

On Friday, a week before Mom and Marcus both arrived in Hawaii, Marcus called to say the plan was off—Maya could no longer stay with Alice for the week he'd be gone.

"What do you mean, she can't stay with Alice? You're leaving in a week!"

Marcus replied with a notable charge in his voice. "I'll bring Maya with me to Hawaii if I have to, but there's no way she's staying with Alice."

"What happened?"

"Alice has now agreed to watch Maya only if she can stay at the Blue House," he said, his tone slightly mocking. "I told her, 'Courtney's moving here! I can't have another woman staying in our house!'"

What's the big deal about her staying at our house? There was clearly more to the situation than I realized.

"Why would she need to stay at our house for the week if she has her own house?" I asked.

Marcus said that Alice was going through a divorce, and at a recent playdate at her home, Maya witnessed a domestic dispute between her and her husband, who was so enraged he banged his hand against a dresser and broke his wrist. The rest of the playdate involved getting him to the emergency room where Marcus picked Maya up. After the incident, Marcus no longer felt comfortable letting Maya go to their house, especially for a whole week. Alice still wanted to help out, but only if she could stay at our house, along with the youngest of her four children, her nine-year-old daughter, Maya's new best friend.

I felt compassion for Alice. I didn't see the big deal in her staying at our house. She was going through a divorce, her husband sounded nuts and possibly dangerous, and according to Marcus, she had nowhere else to go. Why not give her and her youngest daughter a place to stay, away from her husband, which would then give us the benefit of free childcare for Maya?

When I mentioned this to Marcus, he was adamantly against it.

"I could never do that to you," he said. "Out of the question."

He spoke with such authority and gusto that I felt compelled to agree. I even felt oddly flattered that he wanted to keep our house so private and free from other women, despite Alice's desperate circumstances. *That says a lot about his character. He's really changed in the past few weeks. He doesn't even want other women in our home!*

"You're right," I said, agreeing just for the heck of it. "That would be strange to have Alice stay at our house the week before I arrive. Is there anyone else who can watch her?"

"No, I don't want anyone to watch her. She's going to come to Hawaii with me, or I won't come at all."

I'd been daydreaming about our magical week in Hawaii, full of romance and passion, which didn't include his eight-year-old daughter. I suddenly felt extremely frustrated and angry. My mom and I were now paying nine hundred dollars for him to come help with my move, not to spend the week taking care of his daughter.

"My mom isn't going to be able to pay for Maya's ticket, if that's what you were counting on, so it would be best if she could stay with a church member while you're here."

He answered without skipping a beat. "I was never expecting your mom to pay for her flight. I'll figure something out."

And with that, he hung up.

Eight Goodbye to Paradise

The day my mom and Marcus were due to arrive in Honolulu couldn't have been more perfect. I had been counting down the days especially to Marcus's arrival, which would put an end to the incessant yearning I'd been feeling for seven weeks.

To my dismay, however, he ended up bringing Maya along after all—and her last-minute plane ticket cost a whopping twelve hundred dollars. I couldn't imagine how he could have afforded such an expense. He hadn't even paid for his own ticket.

According to Marcus, Tina had paid for half of Maya's ticket, and a nice couple at the church had donated a hundred dollars toward her airfare because they were so proud of him for stepping up and "doing the right thing."

"I made the right decision," he said, "so that Alice wouldn't have to watch Maya at our house."

I didn't understand the issue with Alice, but I had too much else to worry about.

My mom arrived at two-thirty in the afternoon. I picked her up from the airport wearing a blue flowery dress with plenty of room for my baby bump. Our reunion was joyous, and I adorned her with a fresh lei to welcome her to Hawaii in the true spirit of *aloha*.

We had exactly seven days together, which I jam-packed from morning until night. We had only a brief respite at my apartment before heading to a dance rehearsal so my company could receive expert coaching from my mom, the artistic advisor of RammDance. My mom had a performing career in a specific style of early modern dance created in the early 1900s by Isadora

Duncan, the pioneer of modern dance in America. Although Duncan's style looks simple, the technique is difficult to master. My mom was (and still is) an amazing dancer. One thing that makes her so amazing, perhaps, is that she had no other conflicting dance training. One of her teachers was Anna Duncan, Isadora's adopted daughter, and Anna made her vow to never study any other form of dance, including ballet. My mom grew up only training in Duncan, which makes for a very pure quality.

Mom performed extensively in New York and Europe in her twenties and thirties before shifting her focus to having a family. She remains a sought-after teacher and coach. Though I had minimal interest in the Duncan style until I was twenty, I was fortunate to train under my mom, who passed down much of the repertoire to me.

I could tell Mom was tired from the long day of travel.

"Mom, if you want to stay home and rest, that's okay, too," I said. "We can rehearse without you if we need to."

"No, I'll be okay," she replied. "I'll make sure I get to bed early. I'm not on this time zone yet."

I smiled. "Of course, you should go to bed early! We'll come right home after rehearsal."

That would give me and Marcus the whole night to ourselves. I definitely needed some alone time with him after all these weeks apart.

Having Mom coach the seven dancers in my company was an incredible experience—each woman was not only a lovely dancer but a beautiful person. Beyond her creative contribution, Mom seemed to connect well with the dancers. I was so in love with the scenario—my own modern dance company rehearsing for an upcoming performance in Honolulu, Mom visiting from California to coach us, the dancers getting along and offering to help me in preparation for the show.

The whole drive home, all I could say, with my heart aching, was how much I didn't want to leave Hawaii. I loved what I had created. I had worked so hard to build something beautiful.

"If you can create this in Hawaii, you can create it in Dallas, too," said Mom.

"I couldn't care less about creating anything in Dallas," I responded. "I need to be near the ocean and in nature."

My suitcases were mostly packed, my apartment mostly cleared out. I was going—albeit reluctantly. I loved Hawaii, but I loved Marcus even more. That evening, I skipped to my car to pick him up from the airport. The twelve-minute drive felt like twelve hours. Not only were my hands and feet cold and clammy, but the baby kicked away in my tummy, apparently just as thrilled as I was to have him back after seven weeks apart. I couldn't wait to never, ever be separated this long again.

Marcus's ex-girlfriend Tina planned to meet us at the airport to pick up Maya and take care of her for the week, which was a relief. I wanted to bond with Maya before the baby was born, but now was not the time.

As I approached the airport, with his fresh lei at the ready, I called him to find out where he was. I practically shrieked with delight when he answered the phone.

"Cozy, is it you?" he answered, his voice playful.

"Cozy, you're here! Aloha, welcome to Hawaii!"

"Thank you, Cozy!" His enthusiasm matched mine.

"I'm here at the airport, so where are you?"

He asked me to hold on for a moment, and I heard voices and laughter in the background.

"I'm with Tina! She's getting my bags into her car."

"What?" I asked, confused. "I'm here at the airport to pick you up. I told you I'd be here, remember?"

"I don't remember that," he answered, "but we can meet you somewhere."

Given how complicated the Honolulu airport was, we decided to meet at the lei stands near the exit. I parked my car and waited. After several minutes, they hadn't arrived yet. I called Marcus back.

"Where are you guys?" I asked, slightly annoyed.

"We stopped to get something to eat—we were starving. We'll be just a few more minutes."

"Are you still at the airport?"

"No, we're at a drive-through. Be there soon."

I couldn't believe he was at a fast-food drive-through with his ex when I had driven to the airport to pick him up—and had a delicious vegan feast ready for him back at home. The longer I sat at the lei stands, the angrier I became. I climbed out of the car to do some yoga. I needed to move the anger and extreme frustration out of my body.

A petite, elderly Hawaiian lady at a nearby lei stand started up a conversation. "Waiting for your husband?" she asked with a smile, seeing my prominent baby bump and the lei I was holding.

I picked my words carefully. "I am waiting for someone. He's not my husband yet."

She nodded, smiling from ear to ear. Then she walked into her lei stand, opened up the refrigerator, and pulled out a single, delicate, pink plumeria flower with a long, thin toothpick stuck through the stem. She motioned for me to come closer and then secured the flower behind my ear.

"This is for you. This man you're waiting for, he is very lucky to have you."

Touched, I smiled and thanked her profusely.

Although she had no clue about my bizarre situation—having a baby with man who refused to divorce his wife and who was, at that moment, with his ex-girlfriend instead of me after we'd spent seven weeks apart—she seemed to sense what I was going through. Her simple adornment was a profound reminder of my worth, even if only for a moment.

A few minutes later, Tina's black MINI Cooper pulled up next to my car. The passenger car door opened, and Marcus stepped out. Incredibly handsome, he looked even better than I remembered, impossibly clean, fresh, and sexy after fifteen hours of flights. Everything about him was so put-together that he seemed unreal.

We ran toward each other squealing with delight and landed in an embrace. We both giggled for a moment—we'd never hugged with a balloon-sized baby bump between us. He pulled me into a long, passionate kiss that made the whole wait worth it. After our embrace, he knelt down and put his hands on my stomach and started talking and singing into my belly. By now I was laughing out loud—the warmth and vibrations of his mouth tickled, not to mention the whole sight was just plain ridiculous. I glanced toward the lei stands to see the old Hawaiian lady beaming at us and our passionate reunion.

A minute later, I slowly came back down to earth long enough to say hello to Tina and give her a quick hug. After she transferred Marcus's bags into my car, I had a few minutes to say hello to Maya, who was amazed at how much my belly had grown, and then we all said our goodbyes.

Back at the apartment, Mom had waited up, despite being exhausted from traveling. She and Marcus enjoyed a joyous reunion of their own. I still couldn't believe how much the two of them connected and got along—they too had a dream relationship as future son-in-law and mother-in-law, which was a joy to witness.

The following seven days were a complete whirlwind. I had spent the last several weeks methodically organizing, giving away, and packing up most of my stuff, so we didn't have to spend much time on actual packing until the last day or two, which freed us up to focus on more meaningful activities.

My final days in Hawaii were a grand culmination of all I'd created over the past three years. My dance company's anniversary performance packed the house and brought us all a sense of deep fulfillment. Both director and dancer, I performed in a silk tunic over my six-month baby bump, basking in delight over how the final performance came together—my mom performed, as well as my youngest students and company dancers, while Marcus ran music and sound, smiling at me in awe and amazement the entire time.

Two mornings later, Marcus and I raced over jagged rocks through pitch darkness, laughing like hyenas, toward the shore for our sunrise photo shoot. We posed together against dramatic, jagged cliffs as the sun rose over the expansive ocean. Getting up at four in the morning to put on makeup isn't something I'd want to repeat, but the results were epic, magazine-worthy shots.

There remained only one more event before the big move—my Blessingway ceremony, an ancient Navajo tradition and a spiritual rite of passage that prepares the mom-to-be for her journey into motherhood. Traditionally, the Blessingway is a women-only ceremony with a small group of close friends who gather to nourish, pamper, and support the mom-to-be. Though I had never attended a Blessingway, I just knew I had to have one in Hawaii with my close friends.

Marcus's presence added an extra sparkle to an already magical afternoon. Kealoha, my dear elder Hawaiian friend, led the ceremony at the Sanctuary, along with her partner, a medicine man well-versed in Native American traditions. I decided to break from tradition by including a few men—aside from Marcus and Kealoha's partner, I also invited my good friend Liam to play his set of large crystal bowls during a meditation.

We arrived at Kealoha's thirty minutes ahead of the guests. I wore a white strapless dress and a sheer turquoise cardigan on top, both loose and flowing. Marcus had matched his outfit to mine and wore a freshly ironed white linen button-up shirt, delicately embroidered with elephants along the bottom, and his typical loose Thai pants.

As we began, candles glowed around the room, and large Tibetan gongs and crystal bowls stood at each corner. Under a high cathedral-style ceiling and on top of thick wool carpet, a decorative red woven tapestry from Thailand lay in the middle of the living room floor as the backdrop for our altar. On top of the red tapestry, arranged in perfect symmetry were meaningful items Marcus and I had selected, including two sets of ultrasound photos, crystals, a photo of us from our trip to New York, a small stuffed lion named Sandy that I'd had since I was two, a special turquoise candle that we'd be using during the ceremony itself, and in the center, a woven basket filled with fresh fragrant rose pedals from the dance performance, a mélange of dark red, pink, and yellow. Our guests added their own contributions to the altar until it overflowed with beauty and emanated friendship, support, and love.

As Mom's original piano compositions played in the background, Kealoha motioned for me. She instructed me to stand with my arms outstretched while she wafted sage smoke over my body to clear the energy. She then brought me a white, rectangular box, which I opened to find the most delicate, gorgeous haku lei, or head wreath, I'd ever seen—full of creamy-white orchids, light-pink baby rose buds, baby's breath, and greenery.

"Kealoha! You didn't have to get me this!" I could barely accept something so beautiful.

"I know, but I wanted to," she said softly.

Kealoha tied the white ribbon to secure the haku lei on my head, and I felt like a Hawaiian queen. Surrounded by my *ohana* (family), blessing my baby girl in the presence of my beloved, I was radiant beyond belief.

We formed a circle as best we could given that there were twenty-seven people in the Sanctuary living room. Kealoha's partner thanked Mother Earth and Father Sky and called in the four directions and the power animals that resided in each. With Marcus on my right, Mom on my left, and surrounded by my soul sisters, I couldn't possibly have been more at peace. All the stress of the past seven weeks evaporated as if it had never existed. All I could feel was support and endless, overflowing love. Marcus's hand rested firmly on my thigh, giving me an extra sense of grounding, warmth, and comfort.

About thirty minutes into the ceremony, Kealoha reached for the unlit turquoise candle on the altar and removed its bamboo lid. "Now we're going to do a special ritual for Courtney."

Out of the several Blessingway rituals I had read about, this one called to me the most.

"We're going to pass the candle around the circle," explained Kealoha, "each offering a blessing to Courtney in any way you choose—a song, a story, or some words of wisdom. Your blessing will be stored in the candle. We'll blow it out after we're done, and it will remain unlit until Courtney goes into labor. Once in labor, she'll light the candle again and be reminded of the strength, wisdom, and support she received from all of you today."

As the candle moved around the circle, my highly creative and talented group of friends blessed me through song, story, words of encouragement, a violin solo, and even an interpretive modern dance. During those two hours, the ambience remained focused and serious. We had cultivated an atmosphere of strong intent, and each blessing was a unique gem, entering the glowing candle beam where it would remain on hold, ready and waiting to emerge again when our baby began her arrival into this world.

After the candle blessings, my hosts rearranged the altar so I could lie down in the middle of the tapestry. Liam played his crystal bowls near my head, bathing us all in deep, resonate sound. Baby started kicking in response to the bowls' gentle, healing sound waves, which made me giggle with gratitude for the moment.

Afterward, one at a time, each sister took a handful of fragrant rose pedals and prayerfully sprinkled the petals over my body, each a colorful visual of the blessings I was receiving, a symbol of grace, beauty, and receptivity. Other sisters massaged my feet and hands, and still others placed their hands on my belly, sending loving energy to the baby and me.

The ceremony concluded with an improvised duet between Marcus on his Native American flute and my friend Kim, a professional violinist. And then we feasted. The potluck gathered together from this many health-minded guests was impressive, a colorful array across every surface of the kitchen—chopped honeydew and cantaloupe, kale salads, homemade hummus with organic veggies, fresh mango salsa, gluten-free mochi, banana bread, and much more.

While conversation and laughter buzzed around the Sanctuary, Marcus and I sat on the center of the red tapestry, basking in the blessings still lingering in the air. We posed for smiling photos, kissing photos, arm-in-arm photos, and embracing photos, radiating the profound joy and connection we were feeling after such a mesmerizingly beautiful experience.

Though I remained immersed in the experience of the Blessingway, one of my friends, a professional photographer, snapped more than two hundred images of this divine gathering. The next day, she emailed me a link to the images, each glowing in a warm golden hue, a sight too beautiful to behold.

I wanted so much to share these photos—the inspiring vision of spiritual sisterhood and my vibrantly healthy pregnant body—with friends and family far and wide who weren't able to be there. Those who weren't part of my daily life in Hawaii didn't even know I was pregnant. But not even one picture of my first pregnancy could be posted on any social media platform. I had to keep to a particular agreement, one that threatened to rob me of the joy this day had bestowed.

Three months earlier, on a gray, cloudy morning in November, Marcus asked me to accompany him to see his wife, Mariana.

"Why would I want to do that?" I asked, trying to sniff out his reasons.

"I think you two should get on the same page," he answered, half laughing. "You know, about the divorce."

Mariana and I pretty much hated the mere idea of each other. I despised her for being married to Marcus, and she resented me for having a baby with him and risking her green card if their arrangement was ever found out.

Despite all of this, I agreed to go and talk to her anyway—a once-in-a-lifetime opportunity to speak my mind and express my needs. Marcus drove us in his white pickup, which bumped along a small paved mountain road made slick by the misty rain.

The higher we climbed, the more nervous I grew. I started to regret that I'd agreed to this visit. I was terrified of talking to Mariana face-to-face. What if she started yelling at me in Spanish and throwing things, like Marcus had described her doing when he tried to talk to her about divorce? Marcus, on the other hand, wasn't nervous at all. He might get to witness two Leos having a catfight—pure entertainment.

Marcus parked outside a run-down, makeshift house that looked like it had been pieced together from construction scraps. As we walked toward the clear glass front door, Mariana, perhaps hearing us giggle, appeared with a huge smile. She looked Marcus straight in the eye, while ignoring my presence altogether. I instantly resented her. Didn't she realize there was no hope for her?

During their extended embrace, I looked around. Her house felt like a cool cave with colorful tapestries over the windows and walls, as well as amateur paintings of sunsets and beaches. A mattress on the floor with a dozen patterned pillows served as a couch.

When the two of them finally detached from each other, Mariana approached me, her arms outstretched. I wondered in horror, *Is she going to hug me? Yes, there she goes.* Thankfully this hug lasted a mere millisecond, followed by a Colombian-style kiss on the cheek. I was amazed at her audacity, but Marcus just smiled.

"Courtney, dear Courtney!" Mariana said, in her thick Colombian accent, as if we were long-lost friends. "How are you feeling, honey?" She motioned to my belly, which was still fairly flat at only two months pregnant.

"I'm feeling fine," I answered, wondering why she was being so nice. At her graduation, she had given me only evil glares.

"What can I get for you both? Water? Tea? Marcus, you want coffee, honey?" she asked.

I looked at her in disbelief. "No thanks, I'm fine."

"I would love coffee," Marcus answered with his signature charm.

Mariana scurried into the kitchen. The next few minutes passed slowly and strangely. As the coffee brewed, Mariana treated me more nicely than I thought humanly possible, despite that we were practically sister wives. She went out of her way to offer me a chair, a pillow for the chair, a fan, open windows, and endless compliments in broken English.

"You look great. Wow. You have beautiful hair. I wish my hair looked like that. Hahaha! You are so in shape. I guess I need to work out more!"

I ignored her and cut to the point. "Marcus said you wanted to talk to me."

Mariana and I walked outside to a small balcony with an incredible view over Honolulu, although covered in a thick cloudy haze. Marcus stayed inside enjoying his coffee. There was a small green sofa outside, but I didn't want to sit that close to her, so I went back inside to grab the purple yoga ball I'd spotted in the living room. That way, we could sit across from each other and I could channel my nervous energy by bouncing on the ball.

"First of all, I want to tell you congratulations! You must be so excited to be having a baby!" She leaned over to rub my flat belly, which made me shudder. "There are some things I want to discuss with you so that we get on the same page, you know?"

"Yes," I answered.

Mariana began describing how much it meant to her to live in the United States, how she first came to the country with her Colombian boyfriend eight years earlier, and how she knew she had to stay in the US after they broke up a year later. She couldn't imagine leaving, and this marriage agreement with Marcus was her one and only option. I had heard this story before from Marcus.

"What I need from you," she continued, with her plastered-on smile, "is to agree to some things that will keep me and Marcus safe."

"Shouldn't Marcus come out here for this?" I asked, fearing I was about to be bullied into something.

"We already discussed everything, so now it's between us."

I kept bouncing up and down on the yoga ball, unconcerned that I might look a little ridiculous.

The stipulations were laid out: I wasn't allowed to post any photos or announcements of being pregnant on social media or anywhere else online.

Even emails like my dance company's weekly newsletters were questionable—if the immigration officers got suspicious, they could look into our private email accounts. Mariana needed her marriage to Marcus to appear real, despite that he was in a relationship with me, until her green card was finalized, which wouldn't happen until after their marriage interview.

"And when is the interview?" I asked, though I already knew the answer.

"I don't know. Hopefully soon."

My heart sank. "What happens if I don't agree? What if I just post photos anyway?"

Mariana's voice changed from overly sweet to deadpan serious. "Then you risk putting Marcus and me in jail, and you'll be left raising a baby on your own."

I stopped bouncing, and the tears started flowing. As if on cue, the light misty rain became a heavy downpour, turning both me and the city of Honolulu below into faded, dismal versions of ourselves.

Mariana stood up, patted me on the shoulder, and went back inside. Instead of following her, I repositioned myself under a large awning to stay dry. She returned a few minutes later with a box of tissues and with Marcus by her side.

"I know this is difficult for you," he said, "so let's make an agreement on our end as well."

My ears perked, thinking the stress on me and my unborn baby might inspire him to have their marriage annulled, the obvious solution.

"We'll be divorced in six months, just before the baby is born," he said. "You'll then be free to share whatever you want."

Six months seemed like a lifetime. What if the baby came early? Marcus and Mariana waited for my relieved, appreciative response, but instead all I had was concern and more questions.

"What if your interview isn't done by May?" I asked.

"We'll still get divorced," said Mariana.

"What if Immigration wants to further investigate your marriage and it drags on for months?"

"We'll still get divorced," she said.

I continued to ask about every worst-case scenario I could think of, and they assured me that they would be divorced by May. In Hawaii, a divorce from filing to finish only took thirty to ninety days, so I imagined it could be done. I begrudgingly agreed to their terms.

Fast forward to the Blessingway ceremony three months later. There had been no notice of a marriage interview nor any word on filing paperwork for their divorce. The only thing about Mariana that Marcus mentioned at all during this trip was how he needed to take some photos with her for documentation to make the trip seem like a visit to see her rather than me.

"You want me to take a photo of you two so you can pretend this trip is to visit her?" I asked, shocked.

"Only if you care about me," replied Marcus. "Remember, we're a team."

He had a way of stretching every boundary I attempted to set. Despite being six months pregnant with his baby, I snapped a shot of my fiancé with his "wife," while they pretended to be a couple.

Though I was dying to share my own photos and ecstatic news, I suppressed all expression of my joy. The Blessingway photos would remain hidden in a folder on my computer indefinitely.

Nine All In

"Cozy! Where are you, my Cozy?" asked Marcus with unmistakable sweetness and excitement in his voice on the other end of the line.

After our week in paradise, Marcus and his daughter had flown back to Dallas a day ahead of me. After seven weeks apart, those twenty-seven hours between his departure and my arrival in Dallas were agonizing—an unbearable craving penetrated every fiber of my being. The last thing I wanted was to be separated from him ever again.

"I'm almost there, Cozy!" I answered, as I made my way toward baggage claim at the Dallas Love Field airport. I held my cell phone in one hand and wheeled a small carry-on with the other, a massive, overstuffed pink plaid backpack on my shoulders. I had walked this same walk before the holidays, but this time was different—this was the real deal, ten large checked suitcases and all. There was no turning back now, Dallas—I'm all in.

My speed-walking turned into discombobulated jogging as I headed toward Love Landing—a small, comfortable lounge area for people reuniting after time apart. Like an addict knowing her fix is mere moments away, I felt elated with anticipation.

As I approached, I slowed down to catch my breath. I spotted my Cozy holding a beautiful bouquet of light pink roses. He looked absolutely gorgeous. We became the object of the everyone's attention as we ran toward each other, magnetizing into a passionate kiss while his hands ran all over my pregnant body. After thirty seconds or so, I pushed him away, laughing.

"We don't want security to come break us up," I said. (Little did I know that wouldn't have been the first time that sort of thing happened to him!)

As a true romantic well-versed in fairytales and happily-ever-afters, there were certain things I'd only dreamt about. One of those things was having my very own tall, dark, and handsome Prince Charming pick me up from the airport—luggage cart, flowers, organic coconut water, and all.

Marcus had arrived at the airport early, parked in the garage rather than just drive by to scoop me up, and had two luggage carts ready. Like a true Prince Charming, he held not only the bouquet of roses but also a small gift bag. He showered me with so much love, praise, and affection that within ten minutes, my jaw actually hurt from laughing and smiling so much.

After getting our full use out of the appropriately named Love Landing, we made our way to baggage claim, hand in hand, fingers interlaced, bouncing in unison with each step.

"There's another one!" I exclaimed each time one of my suitcases clunked onto the conveyer belt.

Marcus skipped over to the conveyor belt like a merry Peter Pan, grabbed the fifty-pound suitcase with one hand, and ran it back over to the cart. Despite my long layover in San Francisco, all ten suitcases made it to Dallas. Marcus was beaming. The only other time I'd witnessed him this happy was when I told him I was pregnant. It made me so happy to see him so happy.

When they saw the two carts piled with my bags, airport workers and travelers alike asked us the same question: "You two moving here?"

Marcus proudly replied with a thick Southern twang that I'd never heard before, "Yessir, my woman is here to stay! See all dem bags? She's here for good!"

"It's true!" I added. "There's no way I can turn back to Hawaii now—I have way too much stuff!"

Outside, bright sunlight beamed down on the chilly March day. The air was so different in Dallas than in Hawaii. I felt a newness in my cells. More than ever, Marcus and I felt like a solid, unified couple, destined to make it to old-people status, sitting in rocking chairs and still giggling and in love at ninety-five years old. That image had been encapsulated in my mind ever since Marcus shared a vision he'd had months ago of us as old people. After hearing him mention words like rocking chairs, front porch, and gray hair, I fully believed, without question, that we were in it for the long haul.

After loading my belongings into a pickup truck Marcus had borrowed from one of the members of the Church, he shuffled through a few bags at his feet and pulled out a selection of beverages: bottled alkaline water, organic coconut water, and freshly pressed green juice. He wasn't sure what I would want after the long hours of travel, so he decided to get me all three and let me decide.

He took out a paper grocery bag filled with all kinds of fruit, treats, and snacks. And finally, I opened the little gift bag he had given me earlier when we met on the Love Landing. I was silent with suspense as I unwrapped a tiny parcel to find two keys, one light blue and one pink, inscribed in curvy script: *Home.*

"These are your set," Marcus said, beaming proudly. "One for the front door and one for the back door leading out of our bedroom. Now there's no way you can get confused. You'll always know where home is."

"You didn't have to do all this for me!" I found it hard to accept all of this generosity and thoughtfulness.

"But I love you, and you made it here," he replied warmly.

Filled with endless gratitude for being welcomed like a queen, I leaned over to give him a hug and then a kiss. The kiss quickly took on a life of its own, and soon we were crawling into the blue velour backseat where Marcus gave me a full-fledged Texas welcome. Our new life together was off to a good start.

At the Blue House, Marcus opened the passenger door for me, gracefully offering me his hand as I stepped out of the truck.

"Let's leave the bags here for now," he said as he led me toward the large, stained-glass front door.

I wondered why the rush to get inside.

"Try out your key, Cozy." He exuded the innocent excitement of a little boy.

I took out the shiny, light-blue key and savored it for a moment before sliding it into the keyhole and turning the lock. "It works!"

Marcus began giving me a tour of our house, just as he had months earlier, only this time he had tucked away a special surprise in every corner. The living room had been transformed by an entirely new couch set, a new mahogany kitchen table and chairs, large potted plants and trees galore with painted affirmation stones artistically arranged in the pots, a set of miniature ceramic turtles on the fireplace mantel, and the big shocker—a piano! I had played piano since I was six years old. Now I could relearn all of my old pieces—a long-standing item on my to-do list—plus learn new pieces to play for our baby.

I let out a shriek. "How did you do all this? Where did you even find a piano?" I was amazed and befuddled at how much time and energy he had spent redoing the living room.

"I've been working on it since you left. But I wanted it all to be a surprise so that's why I never mentioned it to you. See this?" He pointed to the black-and-white framed photo of us above the fireplace that I had given him for Christmas. "That was my inspiration. The beauty of us together. Just imagine what we can create."

I sat on the comfy dark green couch, taking it all in. No one had ever spent months redoing a house and planning for my arrival. No one had ever bought me a *piano*.

"There's more to see—let's keep going!" he said, as he led me into the kitchen.

I felt like I was on a treasure hunt, and Marcus was clearly enjoying this little game as much as I was. I shrieked again as I saw our refrigerator door.

"Cozy, did you make these?" I peeled off a three-by-five-inch photo magnet—a gorgeous photo of us dancing together in the moon piece I'd choreographed.

"Yes, well, I designed them."

More photo magnets on the fridge brought back other wonderful memories: our trip to Manhattan, dancing together, road trips in Hawaii. In the middle of the magnets was a quote he had saved from a teabag that read, "Trust is the union between intelligence and integrity."

But there was more. Marcus had truly outdone himself—from the exquisite antique dresser and full-length mirror he set up in my massive walk-in closet, to the stunning potted white orchid on my desk, to the stainless steel enema bucket with accompanying hilarious memo, to the fluffy blue bath towels (one for each of us), to a canvas wall-hanging custom-printed with a photo collage of us, to gift after gift after gift—I was blown away.

These gifts weren't just gifts to me. I interpreted this abundance as a deep, powerful symbol of his undying and unwavering love. Gifts of any kind, whether a yellow dandelion picked from the grass or a diamond necklace, hold a special place in my heart. His gifts said to me, *I love you.*

I couldn't believe I had spent the past two months being so paranoid about Marcus having affairs when he clearly was just busy getting our new house set up. I suddenly understood why he didn't want Alice staying here while he was in Hawaii. Every little detail had been precisely and immaculately placed, which wouldn't have been possible if she had been there for a week.

Marcus had arranged for Maya to have a sleepover for the whole weekend, which I deeply appreciated. As much as I loved his adorable daughter, Marcus and I needed time by ourselves to strengthen and develop our relationship. After the tour, we brought in all of my suitcases and enjoyed a good meal, followed by a sweet cuddle in the backyard.

"Why don't we go somewhere off campus tonight?" he asked. "Or we could go to the spiritual movie night at the Church, but they're not expecting me—Alice is covering for me at my event, so it's our chance to get out."

"Movie night sounds great. I don't know if I'm up for going out tonight." I was thoroughly exhausted from the stress of the move.

"Are you sure? No one knows we're even here! We could leave the campus, and I won't have to work tonight."

"I think the movie night sounds great. I'm pooped."

After a bit more back-and-forth, Marcus finally gave in. I didn't understand why he didn't want to attend the event he had planned and marketed himself, which was part of his new ministry. I thought it sounded like the perfect opportunity to relax, meet some people, and see what his events were like.

We walked across our front lawn beneath a canopy of stars and a minute later entered the Church through the back door. In the darkened fellowship hall, which had been set up with a large screen and rows of chairs, the movie had already started. I hadn't met Alice yet, but she was upstairs in the sound booth.

I was amazed at how many people were present—about a hundred, all older, gray-haired folks. Marcus and I found two seats toward the front and watched the rest of the movie while giggling, talking, cuddling, and giving each other shoulder massages.

After the movie ended, several couples came up to introduce themselves to me. "You must be Marcus's wife."

I could barely stay awake. The hectic final days in Hawaii and the long day of travel had all caught up with me. I longed to go to our cozy new home and sleep in our cozy bed with my Cozy. I walked outside of the fellowship hall into a large, wide hallway complete with stone fountains and so many plants and flowers it resembled a green house. As the last of the moviegoers trickled out the front door, I went searching for Marcus, who had disappeared fifteen minutes earlier, to see if he was ready to go home.

In the hallway, a woman in her mid-forties with bright red hair was steam-cleaning the carpet with a massive, loud machine. A quarter to eleven at night seemed like an odd time for cleaning staff, but I was too tired to think much of it. When she saw me peering in random rooms, she turned off the machine.

"Can I help you with something?" Her voice was rude and direct.

"Yes, I'm looking for my—"

"Marcus?"

"Yes," I answered, giving her a quizzical look.

She propped up the steam cleaner and walked toward me with a strange expression, as if she was trying to smile but couldn't quite muster the kindness to do so.

She held her hand out. "You must be Courtney. I'm Alice. I've heard so much about you."

Alice? This is Alice?

I had pictured someone much plainer than this plump, scantily dressed woman in front of me. I shook her hand, embarrassed that I had mistaken her for a cleaning lady.

"Do you know where Marcus is?" I asked.

"Why do you need him right now? He's probably busy."

"I need to tell him I'm going back to the house," I answered, unsure why I had to explain myself to her.

"I'll tell him for you. He doesn't need to be distracted." Alice was getting worked up—her face started to turn a deeper shade of pink. "He doesn't have time to play house with you right now."

I stared at her, trying to figure out how to respond. Just then, Marcus dashed down the stairs from the offices and jumped right in. He gave Alice a massive hug, to which she responded by pulling him even closer toward her.

"Have you two had a chance to meet?" he asked with a huge grin. "Alice, this is Courtney. Courtney, this is Alice."

I nodded. "Are you ready to go back to the house? I'm about to fall asleep."

Marcus started to answer, but Alice interrupted him mid-sentence. "You can go back by yourself. He has work to do here."

I looked at Marcus. *What's with this crazy lady?*

"Alice is right," he said. "I have a lot to do tonight. Can you go back by yourself?"

"No, I don't think so. It's so dark out there, I don't want to walk back alone." Alice had triggered me—the way she spoke to me and the way she pulled Marcus into her when they hugged gave me a strange vibe. "Can't you at least walk me across the lawn and come back to finish up?"

Alice butted in again. "I can walk you back!"

"Great idea!" Marcus said.

"What?" I asked, exasperated.

"I feel perfectly safe walking back to the Blue House," said Alice. "I'll walk you home and then come back to finish cleaning. That way Marcus won't be constantly distracted and interrupted. He has important work to do here."

His "important work" was putting away the chairs. I put up a fuss for another few minutes, which turned into a slight argument with Alice about Marcus's priorities, but I finally gave in, too tired to keep going in circles.

The walk back to the Blue House with Alice was strange. I couldn't figure her out at all. She was the only other adult under the age of sixty-five that I'd met at the Church, and I just didn't see how she belonged there, or why she was steam-cleaning the carpet on a Friday night. At the door, I mustered a thank-you for walking me home, and we parted ways—Alice went back to the Church to join Marcus, and I walked into a big, empty house alone.

Three days after my grand welcome in Texas, I felt an insatiable urge to unpack, organize, and settle into our house as soon as possible. Nesting was in full swing. As much as I loved preparing our home for the baby, I found it unsettling to have my days so open that I didn't even know what day of the week it was. In Hawaii, I worked seven days a week. In Texas, I had no work, appointments, or commitments outside of the tight-knit trio of my new family: Marcus, Maya, and me.

Given the newness of my life in Texas, I was shocked on the third day when Marcus asked, "How would you feel about taking care of Maya for a week all by yourself?"

"What do you mean?" Maya wasn't even in school yet—Marcus wanted me to homeschool her, which I adamantly refused to do. I insisted that regular school was important and necessary for her.

"I need to be in Hawaii next Monday. Do you think you can watch her? Or should I ask Alice?"

"What?" I still didn't understand. "We were just in Hawaii in a few days ago! Why would you go back again?"

The date for his long-awaited marriage interview had finally been set, and it would take place in less than two weeks. I couldn't believe the timing. We were just in Hawaii a matter of days ago! If only I had known sooner, I would have stayed in Hawaii where I could subtly supervise the two of them until the interview was over. Now I'd be forced to trust him from thousands of miles away.

Marcus thought I'd be ecstatic over the news, but instead I started crying.

"Why do you have to go for a whole week?" I asked.

He attempted to slurp up the tears from my face, causing me to laugh and cry at the same time.

"Because we need to prepare! Do you want me to just show up in Hawaii and go straight to Immigration? Are you crazy?"

"What do you mean, prepare?"

Marcus spoke slowly and plainly as if talking to a preschooler. "Mariana and I need to know everything about each other. When we go into this interview, we need to appear married."

This made me cry even more, which made Marcus more upset.

"I can't believe you're crying over this," he said. "I thought we'd be celebrating together. I just don't understand you."

"You want me to celebrate that you're going to Hawaii where you'll pretend you're married to another woman while I'm all alone in Texas?"

Marcus's face went blank.

"What are you going to say to the Church about leaving again?"

He paused for a moment. "Good point. I'll call it a business trip!"

His lightness and laughter in the midst of my emotional breakdown tortured me. "Can't you just be here for me and try to see what I'm going through?"

His question mirrored mine. "How about you try being here for me for once? Do you want to be a team? Or do you want to always be against me?"

"I want to be a team," I answered, as my tears subsided.

"Then support me in this. It's almost over. Just a week of camping, the interview, and I'll be back here with you."

"Camping?" I practically shrieked.

"Yes, camping. What better way for me to get to know Mariana than to go camping with her on the beach with no distractions?"

During the week he was gone, my stress level was so off the charts I feared I might go into premature labor or have a miscarriage. Under such circumstances, I would usually talk to my close friends and receive much-needed compassion, connection, and insights, but most of them didn't know he was secretly married to Mariana. My mom, who knew about his sham marriage, had enough on her plate without hearing me complain constantly. As a result, I felt completely alone.

I went over to the Church daily for different classes and groups, but that was difficult too, since socializing meant I had to play along with the lie of "my husband's business trip" and appear as if all was well in my world. Feeling like a fake doesn't help forge connections with others. I couldn't escape the Church either—Marcus had taken our car so he could drop Maya off in Missouri with his mother before flying to Hawaii.

Only after Marcus finally returned could we slowly settle into our new life in Texas together.

My new reality soon hit me hard. My life had been completely upended—no jobs, no money to pay for expenses like gas and groceries

(Marcus didn't share his salary), no friends, and still no midwife or place to give birth. For weeks, I would think back with nostalgia to my old Hawaii schedule. *It's Friday afternoon—right now, I'd be teaching my Pilates class.* I missed my old life terribly but tried to keep myself busy with what still had to be done—finding a midwife, putting up family photos, attending mandatory Sunday church services, making dinner, and doing all of our laundry.

Though it had never before been important, laundry became a central part of my life, and I had to live up to a new and unexpected standard. A few days into our new life together, Marcus came into the bedroom with a serious look on his face.

"Come with me, Courtney. I want to show you something."

That he called me Courtney and not Cozy meant something was way off. I knew I was in trouble—he never called me Courtney. I panicked that I must have done something terribly wrong. Marcus led me down the hallway into the laundry room. He opened up the dryer to reveal our clothes in one big mash-up, the dryer so stuffed that underwear and socks fell onto the floor.

"Do you have any clue how to do laundry?" he asked, his tone mocking me. He grew angrier. "Please, explain this to me."

"You take the clothes, sort them by lights or darks, put them in the washer and then into the dryer." I wondered how our dynamic had shifted from loving partners to a father and his disobedient child.

He fumed over my straightforward answer. "And then?"

I sensed where this was going. "Then . . . you take them out and fold them?"

"And what do we have here?" His entire countenance became unrecognizable.

"I was tired last night, so I thought I'd sort and fold all this in the morning. Thanks for reminding me." I brought over a laundry basket and began pulling out the pile.

Marcus lost it. "You can't leave laundry in the dryer overnight! Don't you know anything about doing laundry?"

I paused for a moment before answering calmly. "Clearly, no, I don't. Why can't it sit overnight in the dryer?" I thought of the many times back in Hawaii when I left my laundry in the washing machine overnight. When we lived at my apartment, Marcus laughed with me over my laundry habits. But what was the big deal about letting dry clothes sit in the dryer?

"Look at this!" Marcus pulled out one of his signature dark gray T-shirts. "I can't wear this!"

"Looks fine to me," I said.

"Are you fucking blind? Can you not see it's wrinkled?"

Tears welled from my eyes. I offered to spend my day ironing his clothes, but Marcus told me instead to not touch his laundry again. I felt so defeated. I had been an A-plus student my entire life, never feeling satisfied until I reached a certain level of perfection, and now, I was told to stay away from my (fake) husband's laundry, because I wasn't good enough. I had failed at the most basic of domestic tasks.

My determined and persistent personality got the better of me three days later when I found there was more laundry to be done. Craving a sense of acceptance and appreciation, I asked Marcus for another chance.

"If I don't get it right this time, I'll forget it," I begged.

Marcus agreed. And my new life as an amateur housewife began to take shape.

During those first weeks in Dallas, I did my best to please him as much as humanly possible. After another yelling episode over the fact that I "had no fucking clue how to fold towels," I watched YouTube videos to become a towel-folding pro. Even his daughter was impressed!

Once Marcus had finally enrolled Maya in elementary school, part of my day included taking Maya to school in the mornings and picking her up in the afternoons, which gave me a sense of routine and grounding as I transitioned to being a Dallas housewife. Eager to stay in shape as my pregnancy advanced, I made it a priority to drive to her school forty-five minutes early for a fast-paced walk in the affluent neighborhood. Despite the beauty of the awe-inspiring mansions and their impeccably manicured front lawns, I couldn't shake an underlying sad and heartbroken longing for Hawaii. One afternoon, I called my mom.

"I feel like my heart is actually broken," I said. "That's how much I miss Hawaii."

Mom couldn't say much to cheer me up besides the old cliché, "Bloom where you're planted," and her Buddhist wisdom, "Look at all the wonderful things you have there. Focus on the good. Plus, you don't have time to be heartbroken—you have a lot to do!"

I tried to focus on the good, but I still felt heartsick for the ocean, the mountains, my community of friends, and my old life. But Mom was right that I didn't have much time to complain. Moving at twenty-eight weeks pregnant left a massive number of things to do in a short time—our baby could arrive in as soon as eight weeks.

Ten Night on the Lanai

As Marcus and I continued to settle into our daily life, he asked if I wanted to start teaching dance or yoga classes at the Church. Eager to stay busy, I said sure.

The Church already had a full schedule of classes and events that ran the gamut—spiritual formation, conscious communication, women's groups. I completed an online application, which felt odd given that I was a staff member's "wife" living at the Blue House. I then had to attend a meeting with the events team to propose my idea and have them formally approve it.

At the Tuesday meeting, a group of four women all about fifteen years older, including Alice, along with the senior minister, Paul, and Marcus, sat around and read through the proposals, often laughing and joking at some of the ideas in the pile. They decided on the spot to approve the proposal or not. After three hours of reviewing submissions, they still hadn't arrived at mine, but Paul later approved it himself and told Monica—the staff member who had picked us up from the airport—to add it to the Church website and Sunday bulletin.

I offered my yoga class two mornings a week, but despite advertising through fliers, Sunday service announcements, and online newsletters, the class never picked up. Two regulars never missed a class—both retired seniors and the kindest people, full of Southern charm. A handful of other retired people came on occasion, but the class usually topped out at five people. Given the fact that I was paid a percentage of what came in, I was essentially working for free.

Marcus came when he could or felt like it, though never without Alice, his self-proclaimed volunteer personal assistant. In the beginning, Alice brought along her friend Katie, the first normal young person I had met at the Church. I was excited to make friends with someone in my age range, and Katie and I bonded from the start.

A month into our friendship, however, Katie simply disappeared. One day we were friends, and the next, she stopped coming to yoga altogether. She frequently texted me, "I'll be there tomorrow," but after a few more months, she finally dropped off for good. Little did I know that Katie had a reason for staying away from me and from the Church, but in the moment, her departure hurt and confused me.

One morning after yoga class, I ran into Paul in the hallway. He pulled me into a hug so tight that I felt my round belly squishing against his tall, strong body.

"I'm so glad to run into you," he said, "because I want to talk to you about something."

"What's that?" I asked.

Paul led me into his massive office, complete with floor-to-ceiling windows that overlooked the campus's streams and colorful spring pansies. There were two oversized blue antique chairs angled toward each other. He motioned for me to sit down.

"Monica is no longer working here," he said casually, "so I wanted to see if you were interested in her position."

"What? What do you mean she's not working here? Is she still going to come to the Church services?"

I was completely shocked—I had just seen her the day before, and she didn't mention leaving. Her whole family was heavily involved with the Church and had been for years. Paul didn't share any details about her departure after a decade as the marketing director but rather focused on how her leaving would benefit me.

"You can have her office, computer, the whole setup," he said.

I was instantly intrigued. Her office was even bigger than Paul's and right next door to Marcus's office. But I hesitated given that I had no real marketing background. Monica made all the Church fliers and bulletins and coordinated building rentals for weddings and other events. I didn't know how to do any of that. Plus, my due date was only three weeks away.

At the same time, I was actively seeking a sense of purpose to my life in Dallas, so I agreed to take on Monica's former duties and in return inhabit her massive office, complete with multiple balconies and antique furnishings, and receive a small salary of a few hundred dollars per month. With my baby's pending arrival, my life in Dallas had solidified. Although my days weren't full of things I was passionate about like in Hawaii, staying busy helped me adjust to this new Texas life.

The Church formed the core of our home and work life, and in general, we only left the campus for necessities, such as grocery shopping or the occasional Sunday night out to dinner, which Maya and I loved. When I suggested we take outings to places like the Dallas Arboretum and Botanical Garden—we purchased a family membership when I first arrived, which we rarely used—Marcus complained.

"Why do we have to leave if we have everything we need right here?" he asked.

I learned, unhappily so, to live a very different kind of life—one that didn't involve driving to five different jobs like I had in Hawaii but was instead more contained and incredibly isolated. The Church community, filled with mostly retirees, was my only place to form friendships. As time passed and my due date neared, I began to make more connections with other women at the Church.

One Thursday night in June, Marcus agreed to let our friend Samantha host a girls' night at the Blue House. Beautifully decorated, spacious, and airy, our house was slowly gaining traction as a place to hold events and gatherings. In the past few months, we had hosted a men's group, a Hay House author, and a gong workshop—all in our living room.

The girls' night drew a handful of women mostly fifteen to twenty years older, all friends of Samantha's and none of whom were members of the Church. Samantha had gathered us all together to watch a DVD about relationship dynamics between men and women, as she was shifting careers and entering into relationship coaching. I was eager to watch this DVD and learn what I could do to fix my relationship with Marcus, which was great most of the time, but the rest of the time, I encountered more and more of his episodes of verbal lashing and his constant flirtations with other women.

After the viewing, we discussed at length what we'd just learned and how we could apply it to our own lives. I said not a single word during the whole discussion, which was quite uncharacteristic of me, as I was trying to process why the simple truths about men, women, and relationship dynamics didn't seem to apply to our relationship. For example: Say your needs clearly to a man, and he will do everything in his power to get them met. What a joke! That gave me a better chance of getting slapped than getting my needs met.

As would any conversation between women trying to improve their stale marriages, the topic soon shifted to sex and intimacy. Again, I sat in complete silence, this time listening to the other women complain about their husbands' lack of desire. I nodded along with them, hoping they wouldn't call me out to chime in. I couldn't relate at all—Marcus constantly seduced me, left and right, at any time and place imaginable. That was the one part of our relationship that worked. He loved the thrill of bringing me to all sorts of places in the Church and around the Church, and I never put up a fight since I believed sex was his way of showing me that he really did love me. The more pregnant I got, the more intense our chemistry was.

"Being pregnant makes you extra sexy!" he said. His flattery and the abundance of intimacy made me feel more connected to him, emotionally attached, and totally, completely in love. Our sexual life was the glue that bonded us together and made me feel as though I were swimming in a love bubble, high on hormones of bliss.

As good as it was between us, our intimacy didn't start out that way but in fact quite the opposite.

Just one year earlier, the dynamic between us was extremely different. During the early stages of our relationship, when Marcus and I were still just friends, I had a huge crush on him. Since he had kissed me a few times, I assumed the infatuation was mutual.

One warm spring night, I was trying to fall asleep on the back lanai of the Sanctuary. I had attended a spiritual business networking event at the house that had lasted past ten, so I asked Kealoha for permission to stay over, which would save me more than an hour of driving in traffic the next morning to teach a yoga class just a few blocks away.

A little voice, perhaps my subconscious, said, *If you stay over, maybe you'll get to see Marcus!* Even just a short conversation with him would make staying there worth it.

"Of course, you can stay over!" she said. "We've got guests staying in all the other spaces, but there's a couch on the back lanai, and it's quite comfortable."

Despite my exhaustion, I was still awake an hour later, with sounds of a rushing stream and crickets echoing loudly throughout the lanai. I draped a large, heavy blanket over my entire body and tucked it around my head. Despite barely being able to breathe, I needed the blanket to protect myself from the multitude of bugs. Sleeping outdoors on an open balcony was perhaps not the best idea after all, I realized, after seeing giant flying cockroaches zipping by just a few feet above.

I thought of a perfectly logical solution—go inside and sleep in Marcus's room. The living room couches were already taken by other moochers, so his room felt like my best bet. I hadn't seen him come in that night, so I couldn't be sure that he was home, but I assumed he probably was.

I tiptoed into the dark, silent hallway with my blanket in tow and knocked on his door. I wasn't after anything except some safe, bug-free floor space to sleep on and maybe some cuddles on the makeshift bed next to him. I was wiped out from a long day and had to teach early in the morning—I had no other desires whatsoever.

I stood in the hallway, feeling completely ridiculous, and quietly knocked on his door.

No answer.

He was probably already asleep, since it was almost midnight. I waited a minute and knocked again, a little louder.

"Who's there?" He sounded annoyed.

"It's Courtney. I can't fall asleep on the lanai. Could I come sleep in there?"

He didn't answer. Feeling annoyed that I couldn't just talk to him face to face, I had the audacity to turn the doorknob to let myself in, thinking that if he saw how miserably tired I looked, with a blanket draped over me from head to toe, he'd have some compassion and let me in. Yet the moment I began to open his door, in one sharp movement, he quickly slammed it shut and turned the lock whose loud click reverberated through the silent hallway.

Flat-out rejected, I was mortified. I thought I'd never be able to face him again. I slowly walked back out on the lanai and pulled the covers over my head. After replaying the events over and over in my mind with increasing amounts of shame, I fell asleep at close to 1 a.m., desperate for morning to come so I could get the heck out of there.

I woke up out of my brief sleep to see a dark figure crouched directly on top of me. Terrified to my core, I shrieked, but the figure put a hand over my mouth to muffle the sound.

"Shh! You'll wake up Savannah!" said a familiar voice with a chuckle.

I couldn't make out his face in the pitch darkness, but I knew that voice well enough to conclude it was Marcus. Relieved it wasn't some random rapist lurking in this sketchy neighborhood, for a brief moment I felt okay about the unusual situation I now found myself in.

Too naive for my own good, I thought that maybe Marcus felt bad about not letting me in his room earlier and had come out to apologize. Maybe he'd invite me back into his room and—

My thoughts were interrupted by a crinkling sound that I later realized was a condom wrapper. Without thinking, I attempted to scream yet again. This time, instead of his hand, Marcus shoved his tongue into my mouth, kissing me ferociously but with no love or kindness whatsoever. His kiss felt more like an aggressive attack. I entered into the ultimate state of confusion, partly because I had just been woken up in the middle of the night and partly because I actually had a crush on this guy who now appeared to be raping me.

Over the last several months, I had been desperate for our relationship to go to the next level, and now it was happening, but this was not okay. My thoughts continued to race. *What do I do? Should I try to push him off? He's way stronger than me.*

Marcus was quick, to the point, and devoid of any connection. Ten minutes later, at most, I was left feeling used, shamed, and disgusting. I had spent my whole life protecting my sacred body, opening up to only one other boyfriend before Marcus after waiting months to make sure that relationship was committed and stable first. I lay there in shock and complete disbelief that Marcus could do such a thing and then just leave.

"Please, can't you sleep out here the rest of the night?" I asked as he got dressed.

He simply smiled and said, "I bid you adieu," before leaving me alone, completely unable to fall asleep, yet again.

The next morning was almost as unsettling as the ten-minute rendezvous on the lanai. My heart sank deep in my chest as Savannah, Marcus, and I found ourselves in the kitchen at the same time. He didn't say hi or good morning to me, but instead looked at me with twinkling eyes that seemed to say, "Yes, Gorgeous, I remember what happened last night, but I'm going to pretend it never happened, while making your morning miserable."

Still in deep confusion about the previous night and whether or not he even liked me, I tried to get his attention while he made himself breakfast, but he was too busy giving Savannah as much attention as possible—kissing her and tickling her. When she left for work several minutes later, they said, "I love you!" and kissed each other before she left.

My self-worth, already low to begin with, was now plummeting into the depths of the earth by the second. Although Savannah and I had to leave early for work, Marcus didn't have to be anywhere and could have easily stayed in his room until we both left. I wondered if he'd staged the whole thing on purpose, creating a scene where the three of us would have an awkward interaction, and I would be completely silenced, unable to tell Savannah what happened.

I didn't tell anyone about what happened on the lanai. My immense shame and sheer confusion over having a guy I was in love with completely violate me was too complicated to put into words. But I was desperate to feel better about myself and about what had happened that night.

I thought about a book called *The Way of the Superior Man* by David Deida, a down-to-earth guidebook for living a life of masculine integrity. *Maybe Marcus just didn't know any better. Maybe if I give him this book, he'll understand more about how spirituality and sexuality are linked, and there's still hope for us to have a healthy relationship.*

In other words, *Maybe I can change him.*

I gave him a copy a few weeks later when I was at the Sanctuary for an event. He laughed and threw it onto a bookshelf, and then he brought me into the garage where he seduced me, but this time he was a completely different person—our encounter was ripe with connection, chemistry, and romance.

"Yeah, I don't need a book," he said, smiling.

As much as had happened in our relationship since that night on the lanai—becoming a couple, getting pregnant, creating a family, moving to Texas—I never quite felt healed from being assaulted by him, though I thought about it often. As our daughter's birth drew nearer, I felt it was something that needed to be aired out so we could have the beautiful, connected, natural birth we were planning.

In our usual hangout, the spacious blue bathroom, I mustered the courage to bring up what had happened a year prior. I made sure that Marcus was in a great mood before broaching the subject, since I didn't want to upset him or cause him to be defensive.

"There's something I want to talk to you about, and I think it needs to be expressed before the birth," I said, speaking as kindly as I could.

"What's that?" Marcus asked, his arms wrapped around me.

I reminded him about that night on the lanai. I made sure to sprinkle my sentences with phrases like, "This is just my experience of what happened. I'm sure you didn't mean to hurt me," along with plenty of apologies for having to bring this up now. Marcus didn't get angry at all, which was a huge relief. In fact, he didn't even seem surprised or have any emotional reaction whatsoever.

Instead, he simply stated, "I just gave you what you asked for."

This baffled me. *Did I ever ask you to assault me?* I shook my head in confusion. "What are you talking about?"

Marcus remained cool. "You wouldn't leave me alone that night—I felt you psychically calling for me all night long. I was pretty annoyed. I was just trying to get some sleep. But eventually I figured I'd give you what you wanted."

I pulled myself away from him, shaking my head in frustration. "So, it's my fault? Is that what you're saying? You came out to the lanai and forced yourself on me because I was *calling* for you?"

"Fault is a strong word. I never said you did anything wrong. But yes, I was simply giving you what you asked for, and I can't take any responsibility for that."

Eleven The Third Wheel

Every weekday morning between nine and ten, Marcus and I came together for what we called "baby time." We set aside this hour to meditate side by side for fifteen minutes, followed by doing one thing from my to-do list to prepare for the birth. The typed to-do list for the baby ran two full pages long and included your standard baby prep things, like cervical massage, natural childbirth practice, and putting together the crib, bassinet, and stroller, among other preparatory tasks for our baby girl's grand arrival.

One hour a day never felt like enough time to make real progress on the list, and I grew increasingly anxious that we wouldn't be ready before I went into labor, but an hour was all Marcus could devote, given his busy schedule building his ministry and doing janitorial work for the Church. We made it a point to keep the time sacred, and when the clock struck nine, we dropped whatever we were doing to sit in silent meditation next to each other in an attempt to get clear and connected before moving on to the list.

One morning, a few minutes before nine, Marcus started getting dressed to leave the house.

"Where are you going? We have baby time in two minutes!" I exclaimed.

I was paranoid about starting precisely on time because two days prior, when I showed up five minutes late, Marcus let me have it.

As he slipped on his shoes, he said, "I'm going to let someone in at the Church. Just start without me."

He walked out a minute before nine. I was in shock at his total disregard for our sacred agreement. During the last weeks of my pregnancy, I was needier than ever, and his walking out before our guaranteed hour left me feeling incredibly unimportant. *Everyone else matters to him except me.*

He returned twenty minutes later, running through the back door into our bedroom, sweating slightly. In the moment, I didn't think much of it. One of his main jobs at the Church was setting up and breaking down large tables and chairs, which was hard physical work. But his pattern of leaving right before or even during baby time began to repeat frequently as my due date approached.

"Don't you understand you're taking away from our sacred time together to prepare for our baby?" I asked him one day after he came home at 9:25 a.m., leaving us barely enough time for one task.

"You need to remember that it's my work that gives us this house," he declared, "this house that our baby will live in and grow up in! My work is the reason we're here."

"What kind of work do you need to do before the building even opens?"

"That's the thing—I need to open the church."

"Who needs to get in before ten?" I already had an idea.

"Alice," he said, confirming my suspicions.

"If all you need to do is unlock the door, why are you gone for thirty minutes? Shouldn't that take more like thirty seconds?"

"You know how Alice is," he said. "She has a hard time staying focused, so I have to stay and make sure she's on task before I leave."

I scanned him from head to toe, trying to sense whether what he was saying had any truth in it. A part of me didn't believe a word, incredibly suspicious of what he was doing with her alone at the Church.

"Come on, Cozy. Don't be jealous of *Alice*!"

Jealous was not quite the right word. I definitely didn't envy Alice or want to be anything like her—she was too messed up. Perhaps infuriated was a more accurate word for my feelings toward her. Since I had arrived three months earlier, Alice had been seeping into our lives at a most rapid and uncomfortable pace. As Marcus's self-proclaimed volunteer personal assistant, she stood at his beck and call, ready and eager to help him with anything and everything, any time of day or night.

She was an unusual character. For starters, she was unashamedly, unabashedly in love with Marcus. As I learned more about her dysfunctional life, I realized that her obsession with him appeared to be her life's sole purpose and lifeline. Worst of all was the fact that she didn't bother trying to hide her lust for my fake husband—I could see it written all over her face whenever she was around him. She displayed it daily when she delivered large Starbucks lattes to his desk every morning, never asking for a dime, after walking right by me without the slightest embarrassment.

Though she was going through a divorce and had four children at home, her time and attention went not to her own family but instead to Marcus, Maya, and, because of our constant proximity, me. Our entire family, including our unborn daughter, became her light at the end of a dark tunnel, and she clung to us desperately, completely disregarding the inappropriateness of falling in love with an unavailable man expecting a baby. Moderately overweight and severely underloved, Alice was a jiggling, giggling recipient of all the attention and flattery she so desperately craved from Marcus, who doled it out to her in ample doses while she soaked it up like a sponge.

Marcus's flirtatious affection toward Alice often took place right in front of my eyes. Sitting on the comfortable gray couch in Marcus's office, which Alice had upholstered herself, I watched scenes unfold between the two of them that created the same nauseating, gut-wrenching feelings I felt when I saw him interact with Savannah at the Sanctuary.

Day in and day out, Alice spent as many hours as possible away from her chaotic home and in the peaceful confines of the Church campus—from early morning to late at night. She called the Church her happy place, yet her presence made the Church anything but a happy place for me.

I developed a new ritual where soon after waking up I'd run to the window and look for her dark red van, praying it wasn't there. She always parked in the same spot—the one closest to our house and thus one of the farthest spots from the Church. If her van wasn't there, I breathed a sigh of relief, as the day was off to a good start. But if her van was there at seven in the morning, while she waited for Marcus to open up the building, then I'd be overcome by a cacophony of thoughts that ranged from paranoia to anger to depression over this new, unwanted mosquito buzzing all around us to no one's delight but her own.

I repeated the ritual every night before I went to bed. At night, it was a rare miracle if the van was gone when classes ended at eight. Her usual departure—and I know this because I checked every fifteen minutes—was closer to eleven, but sometimes she stayed until the early morning hours when Marcus had a big ministerial project or event to prepare for.

Lying in bed alone and very pregnant, while Marcus and Alice were the only two people inside the Church, was the most painful thing I'd experienced thus far in our relationship. My nightly journal entries from those first months in Dallas are all centered around the "Alice issues," which robbed me of so much daily peace during my third trimester that I was already toying with the idea of leaving Dallas and Marcus.

One day, while Marcus was in an especially great mood after smoking a joint, I broached the subject. "Why do you flirt with Alice so much? Don't you know you're completely leading her on?"

"Come on, I'm helping her! You can see how much she needs this."

"I think you need to put up some boundaries with her."

"I think you need to mind your own business. Alice is doing so much better now that I'm giving her the attention she needs. What harm can a little flirting do?"

I was trying to describe the emotional distress his flirting caused me and our unborn baby when he interrupted by tickling me all over, which caused me to fall to the ground and break down into hysterical laughter while trying to push his strong arms away. The tickles got so intense I was gasping for air, but he wouldn't stop.

"Please, Cozy," he said smiling, while I writhed around trying to escape, "don't be so selfish. Not everything has to be about you."

I finally pushed him off and ran into the living room, but he followed close behind, the two of us resembling a pair of hyenas. I eventually caught my breath enough to speak.

"What are you talking about?"

"Flirting is the best medicine for her right now. Her self-esteem needs it," he said before initiating another tickle fight.

Though I was practically going insane, I tried to have an open mind and be nice to Alice rather than confront her face to face as I desired to do. Although I had my constant suspicions and felt too paranoid to leave them alone for more than a minute—lest his *medicinal flirting* get out of hand—I never truly thought I had anything to worry about. Alice wasn't attractive by any conventional standards, despite cosmetic surgery, and her choice of clothing—bright colors with minimal coverage of her plus-sized body—didn't help either. There was no way Marcus could ever be attracted to her. I considered her swooning over him annoying, frustrating, and insanely disrespectful but not a real threat to our relationship.

As time went on, Alice began to join us for lunches and family dinners, and she hung out at our house so much that we had to kick her out on nights when we wanted time to ourselves.

"Can I just stay over tonight on the couch?" she frequently asked.

"No!" Marcus and I would shout in unison, before physically escorting her to the door.

Just as I was trying to stabilize and build our relationship before our baby girl arrived, Alice became an unwanted third wheel. The first time I walked into the kitchen to find that Marcus had cooked enough food for her to have lunch with us, I lost my appetite completely, fuming with such emotional fury I could've packed my bags and left for Hawaii right then and there.

"Did you invite Alice for lunch, honey?" I asked with the sweetest voice I could muster.

"No, but she's here anyway, so I guess we have to feed her."

I rolled my eyes, but I knew that by giving her lunch, Marcus was securing more free work. The more he gave her to do, the happier she seemed. Truth be told, she never stopped talking, and she was incredibly distracted and unfocused, but after being redirected a number of times, she was moderately helpful running errands, watching Maya for hours and sometimes days at a time, and helping Marcus move tables and chairs for events at the Church. Though we were, in a sense, using her, a strange dynamic between Alice and Marcus persisted so that no matter how much she did for us, she always came back wanting to do more, as if they had an unspoken agreement that she owed him something.

Besides my frustration over her joining our family uninvited, I also experienced sheer confusion. When she came up in conversation with Marcus, which was frequently, he acted as if he detested her, making comments too awful and degrading to repeat. When she wasn't around, he referred to her more like low-class hired help rather than a friend and human being doing us a multitude of favors. His horrible remarks both shocked and comforted me at the same time. *At least I know he's not in love with her*. But the dichotomy between how he spoke *about* Alice and how he spoke *to* Alice was something I couldn't figure out.

In a strange way, I benefited from having Alice around as well. Of course, I would have done anything to get her out of our lives, but since she was hanging around with nowhere else to go, I figured I'd jump onboard and have her start doing things for me, too.

Alice helped me complete my house beautification project by printing out several large prints of Marcus and me from our Hawaii maternity photo shoot, which I had framed and hung all over the house. She offered me a sisterly sort of friendship and support when I had no other friends in Dallas (not that I wanted it), and she made promises to make me things and gift me things (many of which I never received but appreciated anyway). She had been a professional photographer before being sidelined by depression, so she gave us another maternity photo shoot in the Texas countryside. She also watched Maya so that Marcus and I could go on date nights and have plenty of time to ourselves without her. She did all of this and more without asking or expecting anything in return. As time passed, I realized we could ask her to do pretty much anything at all, and she would do it.

One scorching spring day, I decided to muster the courage to have an honest conversation with Alice and set some boundaries since Marcus wasn't going to do it. She answered on the first ring.

"Hi, Courtney!" she said, in her usual quick, frenetic tone.

"Hey! I want to talk to you about something. Could we meet up today?"

"I would love to meet up, but right now, I'm at the Church helping Marcus create an email list from his event sign-in sheets. This is probably going to take me a while."

In the background, I heard papers shuffling and then Marcus's voice giving her instructions.

"When do you think you'll be free? It's kind of important." I suddenly felt that the long-standing problem of her infatuation with my almost husband and baby daddy had to be addressed now.

Marcus and Alice conversed for a moment before she responded. "He says I can take a break at three this afternoon."

"Can't we meet any sooner?" It was only ten-thirty in the morning—did it really take that many hours to enter email addresses into a computer?

After more hushed conversation, Alice said, "How about quarter to three?"

"I leave to pick up Maya at two. Her school gets out at three. Can you meet me at her school? She loves to play in the yard so that will give us some time to talk."

Alice agreed, and I began to prep myself for the big meeting, where I'd finally assert myself and tell her to back off my man. I was equally excited and extremely nervous. After this day, everything would change, and my life would become stable again.

That afternoon, Alice strutted across the playground in three-inch heels, a short jean skirt, and a bright orange tube top that accented her long, orange hair and made her black eyebrows seem even more out of place. I sat on a bench waiting for her, hands resting on my beachball belly, in a sort of meditation. I tried to send my soon-to-be-born baby loving vibes often and felt bad about the amount of stress she'd probably experienced over the last nine months. *Not to worry, everything is going to be okay, and you're going to be born into a very loving family.*

Alice gave me a big hug and then put her hands on my belly, talking in a gentle, soft voice and then swirling her hands all around like some kind of made-up energy work. Baby kicked and poked an elbow in response, to which Alice was mightily amused.

"Where's Maya?" she asked.

I pointed to the top of the jungle gym, and Alice waved hello. As soon as Maya got a glimpse of Alice, she ran right over to us and practically jumped into Alice's arms. The two of them had developed a deep bond since we moved to Texas. In one sense, I appreciated their close relationship because it gave me and my Cozy more alone time. We sent Maya to Alice's for sleepovers nearly every weekend. But it was also strange to see that Maya was becoming more attached to Alice than me, her new stepmother.

During a recent off-campus outing, Alice tagged along with our family uninvited, which annoyed both Marcus and me. Our odd ensemble prompted a complete stranger to ask, "Are you guys poly?" I had to think for a moment—poly meant polyamorous. I was in such shock that someone thought Marcus, Alice, and I were in a polyamorous relationship that my whole body froze, unable to mutter an answer, while Marcus and Alice doubled over in laughter at the stranger's outrageous assumption.

Once Maya resumed playing in the schoolyard, the conversation that brought Alice and me together on this hot afternoon finally began, but my confidence had disappeared, along with the words I'd articulated in my mind over and over. In the safe space of an elementary schoolyard, away from the Church, I had the perfect opportunity to express my feelings, woman to woman, but I lost my nerve. This made for an awkward start, especially since Alice wondered why I'd asked her to meet in the first place.

In the heat of the moment, I decided to take a detective-style approach and gather some background information to help me understand why she thought it was okay to act the way she did around Marcus. She was more than happy to talk and talk and talk about her childhood, her upbringing, her recent debilitating depression, her complicated relationship with her husband, and even the first moment she saw—and fell instantly in love with—Marcus. Though she never actually confessed her love for him outright, she didn't have to—it was crystal clear.

"It was the Christmas Eve service," she said, "and I was sitting in the balcony. It was my first time back at the Church in many years. I used to come all the time before Paul was the minister."

By this point, I was only half listening. She had been talking for twenty minutes with barely a pause to breathe.

As she continued, her voice gained excitement. "Looking down below at the service, I was intrigued by all the gongs set up onstage! I've always been interested in gongs, and anything new age, really."

Lost in thought about how I was wasting my afternoon listening to her ramble rather than confront her as I'd planned, I didn't know what Alice was talking about.

"I'm sorry," I interrupted. "Are you talking about the Christmas Eve a few months ago?"

"Yes!" Alice exclaimed loudly.

"That's when you first saw Marcus?" I asked, confused. I was sure we didn't meet Alice when I was in Dallas for the holidays. I definitely would have remembered her.

"Technically, I saw Maya first. This beautiful, darling little girl caught my attention. Then up onstage, I saw Marcus playing his gongs. When I put the two together and realized he was the new intern from Hawaii and that was his daughter, it all made sense."

"What about me?" I asked. "I was sitting right there in the front row next to Marcus and Maya!"

"Nope, didn't see you."

"Then what?"

"That's when I decided to come back to the Church. Like I said, I hadn't attended in years. But after seeing Paul and Marcus's fresh, radiant energy onstage and hearing the gongs, I realized that this is where I'm supposed to be. Ever since I came back, Marcus has been amazing."

"What do you mean, amazing?" I asked, bracing myself.

"He gets what I've been through and genuinely wants to help me. I don't think you get it, Courtney. Before I met Marcus, I couldn't get out of bed at all. I didn't want to live anymore. The antidepressants didn't work—nothing worked. My kids never even saw me. I just stayed in bed all day long, numb and miserable. Being at the Church and around you guys has been so healing. I'm a totally different person than I was a few months ago."

Alice finally paused and took a deep breath. As I breathed in the hot Texas air, I noticed she had tears in her eyes. She started to cry, and I thought I might start crying, too. I had judged her so much in the last few months, and after hearing her story about her abusive father, her emotionally distant husband, and her lack of direction in life besides helping Marcus and me, I started to feel guilty.

As much as I desperately wanted to set a strong boundary, I no longer felt capable of drawing that line. Instead, I thought of another tactic to make sure she would keep her hands off Marcus. I would become best friends with her—we were both dying to have a friend anyway—and I'd keep her so close that she would never, ever consider crossing the line. This was my conscious though secret plan, the best one I could come up with at the time. *Keep Alice close, and I'll be safe.*

Twelve Baby Skye

"What could possibly be more educational for Maya than witnessing the birth?" Marcus asked, as we sat next to each other during baby time.

The day's task was finalizing our birth plan, which we'd been discussing on and off for the past nine months.

"I'm sure she'd learn a lot, but I think it's best if it's just us at the birth," I answered. What I wanted to say was, *I'm sure she'd learn a lot, but what does that have to do with anything? This is my birth experience, not hers!*

"Wait a second, so you're saying that your mom won't be there either?"

"Of course, my mom will be there! She's flying in just to be here for the birth. I need her there for support."

"So, it's okay for your mom to be at the birth but not for Maya to be there? That doesn't make any sense."

"Yes, it does makes sense—my mom is my mom!"

"And Maya is my daughter!"

When Marcus got up and left the room, I let out a deep sigh of frustration. *Why was it so hard for him to understand me?* My reasons for not wanting Maya at the birth had nothing to do with excluding her—I was nervous that I'd be too self-conscious to fully relax into the natural birth experience. Our becoming a family unit happened quickly, and the idea of her watching, studying, and learning from me felt like too much pressure.

I was so stressed out about who would or wouldn't be at the birth that

I called some of my close friends in Hawaii to get their advice. Was I being irrational to not want Maya there?

My midwife friend Kaja said, "Courtney, if you don't want Maya there, she doesn't have to be there. This is your birth. You can't have anyone there who will make you even the slightest bit uncomfortable."

My friend Jackie was a new mom who had also used Hypnobabies—a special hypnosis technique for natural birth. Her advice: "Giving birth is the one time in your life that you need to get all of your needs met. This is not the time to compromise."

Despite their advice but in line with my usual pattern, I gave up the fight and compromised my needs in order to keep the peace between Marcus and me. The compromise entailed having no one at the birth—not even my mom, who would have to wait outside the room—so we could do it on our own, giving us an intimate birth experience to deepen our bond.

Somehow, after hours of back and forth, Marcus convinced me that this was truly the best plan, although this plan freaked me out a bit. While the midwives took detailed notes about our desired experience, Marcus said, "Stay as far away from us as possible. If you could leave the room until you absolutely have to be there—like, when the baby's already out—that would be even better."

Given that Marcus was my everything for the birth—my rock and sole support both emotionally and physically—he completely threw me for a loop when he announced that he was planning a church-wide campout on May 27—my due date.

"We've spent months preparing for this! I need you with me the whole time I'm in labor!"

"I have an idea," he said. "If you're in labor during the campout, just come sit in the middle of the drum circle, and we'll drum around you until the baby pops out."

I wasn't sure whether to laugh or cry. Just then, my mom walked in the living room. She had recently arrived from California to stay with us for two weeks. Relieved to have a third party hearing this insane discussion, I turned it over to her, who knew more about having babies than I did.

"Mom, what do you think of Marcus's idea to have a church-wide campout in our backyard on my due date?"

"Can't you move the campout to another date?" she asked.

Marcus shook his head. "The date's already set. The campout's already happening. But I think it could be exciting!"

I threw Mom right in the middle again. "Mom, Marcus is going to let everyone use the bathroom in our house, so for the entire weekend of my due date, people will be constantly coming through the house, potentially while I'm in labor. What do you think about that?"

I could see that Mom was getting uncomfortable, yet her love for Marcus was strong and unwavering despite his strange ideas and constant emotional tormenting of her daughter.

"Is there any way you could move the campout so it's not in the backyard?" she suggested.

"Great idea, Mom!" I chimed in.

Marcus persisted. "I really love the idea of having it in the backyard."

I found myself at the end of my rope. "But what happens if we need to go to the birth center? Or, what happens if we've just had the baby and want the place to ourselves? I just don't understand why you have to organize a campout, in our backyard, on my due date."

After another several minutes of awkward, unproductive dialogue, Marcus agreed to discuss with Paul the possibility of having the campout on the front lawn of the Church campus instead.

May 27 came and went, and I was still pregnant, thank God. The campout took place in the front lawn of the Church, and my mom and I sat next to each other and drummed along with twenty-something other church members in a lively drum circle at sunset, led by Marcus. Sounds fun and exciting, but trust me, it wasn't.

Marcus focused solely on set up and preparation and on the community that he had gathered—he barely spoke a single word to me the entire day. And of course, wherever he went, there was Alice, right by his side. While I appreciated Mom's unconditional love and support, she couldn't fix the fact that I felt ignored and unimportant on this very important date, while Marcus socialized with every other guest at the campout.

While drumming, I asked Mom over and over again, "Is it just me, or is he purposely avoiding us?"

All she could say was, "Let's just be present and each enjoy being with each other. Let him do his thing."

Every day five times a day, as I walked around the campus, church folks commented, "You must be so ready to have this baby!"

I weighed 175 pounds and had a belly the size of a watermelon. "No, I'm good," I replied.

I was in no rush to have the baby. Now that the campout on my due date had come and gone, I faced another problem: Marcus had agreed to give his first-ever Sunday sermon on the first Sunday in June, a week after my due date and a probable day that our baby could be born. This was an incredible and unexpected opportunity for Marcus, who was known not as a minister but as the "intern from Hawaii" who mostly set up tables and chairs, changed lightbulbs, and played a standard array of gongs, flutes, Tibetan bowls, and drums during Sunday services and on Friday nights at the ministry he was building from the ground up.

I was overjoyed that Paul believed in Marcus enough to give him an opportunity to preach in front of hundreds of people, but I was equally confused why Marcus would accept such an offer now, given that we were expecting a baby any minute. Agreeing to preach at both Sunday services would make him unavailable for the entire day, not to mention all the hours of study and preparation beforehand.

"When do you expect me to have this baby?" I asked him. "It doesn't seem like you're leaving her any room at all to come in."

"What do you mean? She can come anytime she wants!"

"No, she can't! She can't be born Sunday because you're giving your first sermon. And she can't be born Saturday because you'll be too busy preparing for the sermon."

Marcus, who usually always had something to say, was silent.

"What happens if we're at the birth center on Sunday when you're supposed to be onstage? Are you still going to give your speech and make me go through the birth alone? How will I even get to the birth center? My mom doesn't even drive!" I fell into such a fretful state I'm surprised I didn't induce my own labor right then and there.

Marcus thought for a moment before responding. "If we end up at the birth center on Sunday, I'll find a way to make it work."

"So, if I'm pushing the baby out at nine on Sunday morning, how would that work?" I probed further, knowing that it was safe to do so since Mom was in the next room. He was always on his best behavior around her.

Marcus smiled. "I'll give my speech through video chat from the birth center. In fact, that would be perfect—I wouldn't even have to give a speech. I'll just show you giving birth, and they'll put it up on the big screen. What could possibly be more enlightening than watching a baby being born?"

My mom, hearing our conversation, came into the room, and we exchanged glances. She shrugged and looked at me as if to say, *Yes, he's a little nuts. But what can we do? You're too far in to back out now!*

In my mind, due to Marcus's unchangeable schedule, the baby had a short window to be born—a few days in his schedule that would allow him to be with me at the birth center without our intimate experience projected onto the big screen on Sunday morning. I prayed that our baby was listening intently to the hours of conversations so that she understood she was on a tight schedule. She had to be born either before Saturday or after Sunday. After Sunday wasn't great, however, since Mom was flying back to California the following Monday.

Baby girl, please come out to meet us this week, for the highest and best good of all!

On Tuesday morning—several days before Marcus's first sermon—I started to roll over in bed to cuddle with him but stopped mid-roll. "Whoa! I think I just peed, but I didn't pee!"

Marcus examined the situation. About eight ounces of something had just flowed out. I definitely didn't feel like I had peed, but there wasn't enough fluid for it to be the water breaking. To my great surprise, the mystery liquid came out again about thirty minutes later. I had no contractions or other signs of being in labor, so we figured it was probably nothing to worry about.

But Mom, with the Jewish worry gene embedded deep in her DNA, insisted we call the birth center for an extra appointment, just to make sure, even though we had an appointment scheduled for the next day. While Marcus sat through hours of staff meetings, she and I went to the birth center that afternoon. I was in a great mood and hoped the surprise liquid was a sign that baby was coming soon, as in, that day.

The birth center, which was only a fifteen-minute drive from our house, was the cutest, sweetest little place. I had been stuck on the idea of having a home birth until Marcus and I interviewed a handful of midwives in the area, none of whom I felt connected to and none of whom we could afford. The cost of a home birth in Hawaii was about a third the cost of a home birth in Dallas. This put us in a bit of a bind.

I believe we were fated to find Blossom Birth Center, where I felt at home from the instant I stood outside the light-blue door, taking in the beautiful view of an expansive park filled with walking paths, wildflowers, and a lake teeming with fish, turtles, ducks, geese, and all kinds of birds—the perfect backdrop to welcome our daughter into the world.

Edie, the owner and primary midwife, was a teeny-tiny English lady who stood only four foot ten but with a personality so big, so delightful, and so hilarious that what she lacked in height she made up for in pure, outlandish charisma. She may have been in her early sixties, but she had more energy than a twenty-year-old.

The first time we toured the birth center, she brought us into the birth room where she demonstrated—with theatrical drama and over-the-top sound effects—different labor positions. She hopped around the room like an Energizer bunny from the tub to the shower to the bed until I was hunched over in uncontrollable laughter. I knew then that Edie had to be my midwife. She clearly had such a passion for her work that her joy was infectious. Yet another sign that we'd picked the right place: Medicaid would cover the bill in its entirety.

That Tuesday, our appointment was with Sarah, the younger and tamer of the two midwives. Sweet, nice, pretty Sarah appeared to be my age, but I later found out she was at least ten years my senior, or at least that's what I assumed when I learned she'd had eight kids. Sarah had me lie on the bed in a lavender exam room, which looked more like a bedroom than an office, and took a swab of the mystery liquid. A few minutes later, she returned to say it wasn't amniotic fluid but probably just watery discharge and perfectly normal at the end of pregnancy. Her lack of concern was a huge relief for my mom and me.

"Does the leak mean I'm going to start labor soon?" I asked.

"No," she replied. "It's not really an indication of that."

The next morning at nine, Mom, Marcus, and I were back again at the birth center for my standard prenatal appointment, now four days past my due date. As we sat close together on the small futon in the lavender exam room with Edie seated across from us in a toddler-sized chair, I began to notice mild cramping, similar to my period. I asked if she could check whether I was dilated, just out of curiosity.

"Zero," she reported.

"What about the cramping? Does that mean I'm starting labor?"

"We'll see!" she answered with excitement, as the three of us marched out to enjoy the hot, Dallas day.

We spent the whole day out, keeping busy with last-minute, before-baby errands. In the midst of so much activity, the cramps subsided. Only back home that evening did they return, this time intermittently. Could this be the start of labor? Without having given birth before, how would I know how to gauge it? The cramping came in waves. Though it was mild, I lost my appetite. While the rest of the family enjoyed Marcus's delicious homemade soup, I had no desire to eat at all.

"Come on, just try to have a few bites," Marcus encouraged.

"I'm not hungry. I need to listen to my body," I answered stubbornly, having no clue how hard I would work during—ironic, I know—labor.

At 9:30 p.m., I went to the bathroom and, to my horror, saw a bit of blood on the toilet paper. Was I having a miscarriage? Was something wrong with the baby?

Marcus was calm and reassuring. "I'm sure everything's fine, but let's call the after-hours number and talk to Edie. She's been doing this forever—she'll know what's going on."

On the phone, Edie responded with enthusiasm. "Sounds great! This is exciting! It's nine forty-five. Either it's going to get stronger or it's going to stop, so just go to bed and relax."

Instead of going right to bed, I stayed up with Mom and Marcus, chatting in the living room and feeling the excitement that this might be it. Afterward, I enjoyed a long bath and went to bed around midnight.

Three and a half hours later, I woke up having a contraction, which in Hypnobabies terminology is called a pressure wave, much stronger than I'd experienced before I went to bed. All I wanted was to keep sleeping, yet every ten minutes, another pressure wave—a tightening sensation deep in my pelvis—woke me up. I gently shook Marcus to wake him up and let him know *it's happening*, but he was curled up in a tiny ball, facing the other way (a sleep position he told me was a remnant of his years in prison) and out like a light.

At the start of another pressure wave, I finally said to myself, *I'm just going to do this.* I put on the Hypnobabies audio track and relaxed into each pressure wave as I was guided to. Several trips to the bathroom closely followed those first pressure waves. I stumbled to the toilet in a sleepy stupor, as my body took over and began dispelling all remnants of food and drink I'd consumed in the last week, or so it seemed. My constant trips to the bathroom finally woke up Marcus, who asked if I was okay.

"I'm fine," I answered, "It's just starting to get intense."

The word intense was about to take on all new meaning.

The next morning, I was full of energy and excitement, despite barely sleeping, and started cleaning the house. Every time I felt a pressure wave come on, I leaned over, held onto a piece of furniture or the wall, and relaxed into the tightening sensation. Once the wave had passed, I stood up and continued cleaning.

Mom couldn't believe the sight. "You're amazing! I've never seen anyone in labor like you."

At 11 a.m., I took a long hot bath, which took the edge off, listening again to Hypnobabies, while Marcus left to pick up Maya from her last day of school.

"I'll be right back!" he said.

I believed him. But more and more time passed, and he still hadn't returned. Sitting in the tub, I wondered what could possibly be taking him so long. An hour after he left, I was no longer able to relax and focus on Hypnobabies, as I was getting more upset by the minute. *We practiced for these moments for months! Where is he when I need him most?* I also realized I hadn't eaten anything that day—I had lost my appetite again, despite barely eating dinner the night before. Around noon, I had a vision of a peanut butter green smoothie—I don't even like peanut butter, and I was pretty sure we didn't have any in our house.

I had the perfect excuse to call Marcus, not only to check on his mysterious whereabouts at this crucial time but also to ask him to pick up ingredients for my smoothie, which I needed as soon as possible so I wouldn't pass out in the bathtub where I was still sitting in the same position when he left an hour earlier.

"I'm out to lunch with Maya," he said. "We'll be back soon."

He seemed to be unaware that I was in labor, or if he did realize it, he didn't care.

By early afternoon, the waves were closer together and I could no longer talk through them. Marcus had finally returned with Maya and some groceries. After a cup of the creamy, decadent smoothie, we brought the yoga ball into the living room and began practicing the labor positions—Marcus put counterpressure on my lower back as I kneeled and leaned forward over the ball. It was a gray, rainy day outside, perfect weather to be inside, in labor. Maya and my mom were both in the house but out of sight and uninvolved, as we had agreed.

After two hours on the ball, I went back into the bedroom, and a pressure wave hit me by surprise as I stood at the edge of our bed. I instantly leaned over, hands on the mattress for support, as Marcus walked in the room and closed the door. He took one look at me bent forward from the waist—very pregnant and with few clothes on—and started getting ideas. I thought he was crazy—*who does this while in labor?*—but he persisted.

"I'm only doing this for the baby, honey. It's for the baby," he repeated.

I had no clue what he was talking about. Every five minutes, I asked Marcus to pause as a pressure wave came on, and we'd breathe together, fully connected as one, as I winced only slightly in pain.

From that point on, my labor was a wild, intense ride. My focus shifted inward, as it took every effort just to breathe through the waves of searing pain. In early evening, we went outside, except that I could barely walk at that point, so Mom and Marcus held me up on either side. Maya walked in front, doing her best to hold an umbrella over my head.

An older male church member saw us walking through the parking lot and came over to chat, not understanding that I was deep in active labor and not out for a casual stroll. I had transported into my own internal world—

everyone and everything around me became one fuzzy, gray blur. After the walk, we returned for another round on the yoga ball. Marcus assisted with more counterpressure on my lower back. It took every ounce of concentration to breathe and relax into each wave that passed, rather than clench and tighten against it.

I sensed someone in the room, watching me. I turned around, and lo and behold, there was Alice, who had apparently been there for ten minutes already, utterly still and silent. She stood a few feet away, completely mesmerized, her expression a rare combination of extreme empathy and extreme envy. She saw me looking at her, but her face remained unchanged, unable to express anything aside from the question emanating from her eyes: *Why not me?*

Alice had stopped by to pick up Maya for a sleepover, but once inside, she didn't want to leave. Her frozen expression finally dissipated.

"Can I stay for a bit?" she asked quietly.

I found it hard to talk given that I had only minutes in between pressure waves, but I did my best to get my answer across. "No, you need to go."

Even after she left, a trace of her presence remained in the room, as if a ghost-like part of her had stayed behind to watch.

By 6 p.m., the intensity and pain were just too much. Incredibly nauseous and burping up peanut butter smoothie every so often, I figured that my body didn't want or need food—a mistake that may have made my labor more drawn out and excruciating since I had no nourishment to draw upon. All I wanted to do was go the birth center and have the baby already.

We called the birth center a number of times, but they continued to advise that I keep laboring at home. The exhaustion from not sleeping the night before finally hit me, and I collapsed on our bed at what felt like the final edge of my tolerance for pain.

Marcus called Sarah, who was on duty that night, and put the call on speakerphone.

"How are you doing?" she asked.

I couldn't even answer. I buried my face in the crook of my elbow and made a low toning sound, as a pressure wave was coming on again.

Marcus answered for me. "She's having back-to-back contractions, fifteen to thirty seconds in between each, lasting for two to three minutes."

Sarah instructed me to lie down on my side, with several pillows propping up my top leg, and allow my body to fully relax. "Take some time in this position, and I'll meet you here in an hour. How does that sound?"

It sounded like an eternity, but I nodded anyway. In my blurry mental fog, I had a disappointing realization that Edie wouldn't be the midwife after all. But it was supposed to be just me and Marcus anyway, so what would be the difference?

Walking into the birth center, my fog lifted for a brief moment as I took in the beauty of the space in which I was about to give birth. Gregorian chanting filled the room, along with dim lighting, golden candles, a beautifully made queen-sized bed, and the calming aroma of essential oils. On the drive over, the sun had miraculously poked through the clouds after an entire day of rain, and sunlight now streamed through the sheer white curtains. In this sacred, holy temple, I felt like I was in some kind of dream.

The next pressure wave—a ten out of ten in pain—brought me instantly back to reality.

In the birth tub, out of the birth tub, over the yoga ball, back in the birth tub, back on the yoga ball, on the bed—the hours of labor and pushing that followed were grueling, unrelenting, unimaginable torture. No one had prepared me for this. And thank goodness—otherwise I would have never chosen natural birth. I did my best to follow the Hypnobabies tracks playing in the room, but the pain was so intense that the positive birth affirmations faded into background noise.

Who does this? Every woman has to go through this *to have a baby? I'm sorry, but this baby is going to be an only child. I am never doing this again.*

And that was before I started pushing for the next three hours.

My body shook violently, and my voice had gone hoarse from hours of emanating sounds like a wild animal, but still I pushed with every muscle I could find. I pushed, and I pushed, and I pushed—sixty freaking times. I was dying for some kind of replenishment to keep me going, but I couldn't even find the words to ask for what I needed.

When the pushing commenced, Sarah and her assistant came in closer, no longer sitting in the corner of the room unobtrusively, as they'd been directed. Now, in between every push, Sarah held a fetal Doppler to my lower belly to check the baby's heartbeat. By that point, any form of touch was agonizing. All I could think was, *Baby is fine. You should be checking MY heartbeat—I'm the one who's dying here!*

I pushed one last time with every iota of strength I could draw forth, certain I was going to die, or explode, or turn inside out—that was the moment when baby's head finally emerged, and with two more pushes, she was born into this world, just before midnight on June 1.

Marcus and I lay together with our new baby girl, all three of us covered in goo, blood, and baby poop. With every sip of placenta smoothie, I began to feel like more of a human being again. I'd now begun an arduous recovery process from the most insane physical exertion of my entire life—and that's coming from a former ballet dancer!

In those first moments of falling in love with my gorgeous baby girl, I couldn't shake an odd feeling of disconnection from Marcus. This was the moment I was supposed to feel even more connected to him, and although he had been by my side every moment since we arrived at the birth center, he suddenly and inexplicably felt like a stranger. I brushed off these scary feelings, unwilling to dig deeper as we engaged with our daughter in these first moments of our new life as a family.

The name we had chosen months ago, Skye, fit her perfectly. Even with a head full of jet-black hair, her eyes were a vibrant shade of sky blue. I loved the name Skye because of the openness and expansiveness it brought to mind. Marcus loved it because it was the name of his deceased ministry teacher, and according to him, she's who our daughter was named after.

Either way, her name was one thing we had agreed on effortlessly.

Two days later, I sat rather uncomfortably in the front row for Sunday service with my two-day-old baby held tightly in my arms. I could barely walk the few feet from the bed to the bathroom without excruciating pain from severe tearing, but I wasn't going to miss Marcus's first sermon for anything. Just one glance of loving appreciation from him that I'd made the effort to attend was well worth every bit of pain it took to be there.

Thirteen The Truth

After supporting me for two weeks, my mom left Dallas when our daughter was five days old. She was needed back at home to care for my younger brother. I was still barely able to move without severe pain. Giving birth had beaten me up—I felt like I'd been hit by a truck a thousand times over. I couldn't understand how nature could do this to a new mom—you're in so much pain that you can't even roll over in bed to nurse your baby?

Unlike a hospital birth where nurses care for you for a few days after delivery, the midwives at the birth center had me shower and leave just two hours after giving birth, their typical protocol. In those first five days of Skye's life, my mom did absolutely everything for me. Marcus went right back to work, and Alice continued to buzz around him, leaving baby and me alone at the house.

"What are you going to do when I'm gone?" Mom asked, worried as ever.

"I'll figure it out," I said, although I was starting to worry, too. The nonstop demands of being a new mother while unable to stand or walk without severe pain overwhelmed me, to say the least.

The day before she flew home to California, Mom said, "I'm going to ask Alice to come and be with you."

"No, no, no. I don't want her here."

"But she's offered to help you. Please, for my sake? I'd feel so much better knowing you weren't all alone."

"Don't worry, I'll be fine. I'll have someone else from the Church come over if I need help." I said that just to make Mom feel better—I had no intention of asking anyone other than Marcus for assistance.

As if on cue, the doorbell rang. Mom and I looked at each other in confusion—we weren't expecting any visitors.

"Go answer the door," I said.

A moment later, the loud voice of a woman with a thick Southern accent echoed throughout the house, all the way to where I was nursing the baby in the back bedroom. I heard laughter and conversation, followed by footsteps. My mom and a woman I'd never met stood in the doorway.

"Courtney, this is Cheryl. She's come to say hello to you and baby!"

I felt a bit annoyed that random strangers thought they had a right to just barge in. Mom, on the other hand, seemed to be ecstatic that Cheryl had come.

"I'm sorry," I said, "Do you go to the Church? I don't think I've seen you before."

If I'd seen her before, I definitely would have remembered—not only because she was the only African American on campus but also because she was relatively young compared to the average age of our mostly retired congregation. She was also jaw-dropping gorgeous and dressed to the nines, complete with jewels, bangles, and thick mascara that I could see from several feet away. She was at least five foot eight and had the slim, super-fit body I could only dream of after just delivering a baby.

"Honey, I would love to help you out after your mama leaves," said Cheryl with a warm smile. "I'm going to write down my cell-phone number, and you call me anytime, okay? I'm here for you, sweetheart."

I asked Cheryl where she'd come from—was she some sort of angel who heard my mom's request and then materialized outside the front door? She did turn out to be an angel for me in many ways. Cheryl had been attending services at the Church for three months, but she went to the early service followed by Sunday school, whereas I only went to the later service and had never set foot in Sunday school. That Sunday morning, she had run into

Marcus at the Church. He thought we'd click, so he directed her to stop by.

And he was certainly right. The following morning, Cheryl transformed almost immediately from stranger to long-lost sister. As a Southern-raised, super-Christian, cursing divorcee and mother of three grown children, she seemed so unlike me, but we both loved to laugh and to talk about boys. As she won my trust, Cheryl became the one person in my life to whom I confided everything about my relationship with Marcus—the good, the bad, the insanely amazing, and the really ugly.

Cheryl had been laid off from her job and seemed to be in no rush to get a new one now that she could enjoy her days for the first time in years, especially with her kids out of the nest. She figured that coming over to help me during the day with relatively simple tasks such as changing diapers, doing laundry, and making meals—at no charge—was a sort of community service since the baby and I were part of the Church. As I continued to heal from the traumatic birth, Cheryl was at our house nearly every day for two weeks, until it was no longer painful for me to resume my housewife duties while wearing a baby strapped to my body.

New mom life prevailed, filled with endless diaper changes, around-the-clock nursing, and visits from Marcus's family. As we integrated a new precious human into our daily routines, I was taken by surprise by how little help Marcus contributed to the care of our baby. I had assumed we were equals sharing equal responsibility, but Marcus continued to live as a free, untethered person while I was on baby duty around the clock. He helped when he felt like it and agreed to watch her while I taught my yoga class two mornings a week at the Church, but other than that, the responsibility was all on me. I completed the Church bulletins and marketing materials late at night, with the baby sleeping in a bassinet we put in my office.

My friendship with Cheryl was my bright light and saving grace during this time, and we met frequently at different classes and events held on campus, where she happily took care of Skye so I could have a break.

My relationship with Marcus suffered quite a bit after our daughter was born. Perhaps it was the lack of sleep, but more likely, it was the lack of sex. The abundance of intimacy we shared in the last months of my pregnancy came to a jarring halt after the birth, given how torn up I was.

Desperately needing to reconnect and craving a change of scenery, we booked a lakeside cabin in Oklahoma for the Fourth of July weekend—just me, Marcus, and our four-week-old baby. On the way, we dropped off Maya at Alice's house. Alice would take Maya to the airport at three-thirty in the morning so that Maya could fly to Hawaii and spend the rest of the summer with Tina. Without Maya, we'd be able to bond, just the three of us.

The long weekend away was beautiful, filled with the real, deep connection and laughter that I so craved. Swimming in the lake and taking our baby on her first boat ride made me feel like we were back in Hawaii again during those days when our relationship was always playful and full of love.

"I think we should get working on baby number two," Marcus said on our first night in the cabin.

I laughed in response.

"I'm serious. This first baby is the Church's baby. She's our sacrifice, really. We're barely going to see her as she grows up. It's already happening now—can't you see it? The old ladies at the Church are practically going to raise her for us. That's why we need to have another."

"I don't think it's even possible to conceive a baby now—she's just four weeks old."

Marcus shrugged. "Okay, we'll wait another week."

The return to Dallas after our three-day lakeside retreat gave us both a bit of a jolt.

"It's so strange here without Maya!" I said. "I'm going to really miss her this summer!"

I felt surprised by my attachment to her, which I hadn't noticed until she was gone. Marcus groaned in agreement while busy on his phone. He hadn't talked to me much since we returned from our trip, which was strange because the whole point of the trip was to reconnect. In the four weeks that followed, I began to miss having Maya around—not because I craved doing her hair in French braids on Sunday mornings, but because I needed someone—anyone—to provide me some kind of protection against the latest development in my relationship: Marcus's consistent bouts of yelling, cursing, and insults.

One moment, everything would be fine—we'd be joking, laughing, or jumping on our new outdoor trampoline. The next moment, something would trigger him—I could never quite figure out what exactly—and the agonizing array of demoralizing and demeaning words would spill so fast out of his mouth that all I could do was sit there, listen, and cry. The more I cried, the more he yelled. And the more he yelled, the more I cried. This cycle went on sometimes for as long as three hours, by the end of which I felt indescribably hopeless, sad, and heartbroken.

The one time I stood up and walked out on his yelling and cursing, it only brought the abuse to a whole new level where I feared for my baby's and my lives. We were in the backyard, and I told him I didn't have time to listen to his yelling. I had to get to the Church to start the bulletin. Skye was in her stroller watching us. He stormed over until he was an inch from my face. He screamed at me and then grabbed my shoulders.

I attempted to push him off. "Marcus, Skye is watching."

He ran to our car, and moments later, I heard the tires screeching. He took off at high speed, driving like a crazy person. I looked to see if anyone had witnessed his craziness, but no one was around. It was ten in the morning, and the campus was empty.

Ten minutes later, he texted something poetic about the full moon making emotions more intense—essentially downplaying everything that had just happened and making me wonder if I was the one who was crazy.

What could I possibly have said to make him so mad? I pondered this question every single day, determined to figure out how to heal our relationship. But there didn't seem to be any logic to his madness.

One time, a simple question such as, "Where in your event lineup do you want me to perform my dance?" led to one particular episode of verbal abuse that nearly trumped all the others. He seemed to think I was trying to steal his spotlight. He went on and on about how I had no right or need to know when I was performing. I was only there to do his bidding.

As far as I could see, there wasn't any reason for Marcus's anger toward me besides resentment that I wasn't a perfect housewife. I personally didn't notice if the floors weren't steam-cleaned every week, so the only reason I knew this was because Marcus told me as often as he could, sometimes with joking flair.

"See, Cozy, this is why I need multiple wives. I think you would love it! Then you'd never have to do dishes or housework. Think about it, Cozy."

And sometimes he said so without joking flair.

Determined that Marcus not go searching for other wives, I knew I had to get it together. I'd take the baby with me grocery shopping—pushing her stroller to the Whole Foods on the corner—and then come home and wear her in a baby carrier as I cooked in our spacious kitchen, calling upon my culinary training from years prior to make healthy, delicious meals that I was sure he'd enjoy.

One particular night in early August, while Marcus was at the Church, I sent him a photo of the gorgeous plate of food I'd made, letting him know that his dinner was ready whenever he could take a break. Instead of a response, I heard the front door swing open, and Alice and Marcus's voices filled the air.

I was sitting at the kitchen table with the baby in my lap and my laptop open, checking emails while I waited for us to have dinner together. The two of them appearing in the kitchen together didn't surprise me since by now I was so used to Alice's incessant hovering that I barely noticed it. Before I could close my laptop, they stepped in closer, giving each other nervous glances.

Finally, Marcus spoke up. "Do you have a minute to talk?"

I'd never seen such an expression on his face before—a mix of dread and nervousness. I was instantly worried. "What's wrong? What happened?"

"We need to talk to you," he said, "about Katie."

"Katie?" I asked, completely baffled.

I hadn't seen or heard anything about Katie for months—she was Alice's friend who came to a few of my yoga classes and who I thought would become a close friend, but she flaked out.

"What does Katie have to do with anything?" I finally closed my laptop and invested into this odd conversation.

"Actually, a lot," Alice answered. Her voice was noticeably shaking.

The two of them stood side by side, shoulder to shoulder, and it appeared they were going to take turns telling me what I needed to know.

Marcus had regained his confidence and was back to his usual, strong self. "Katie's gone crazy. She is totally insane."

"Really?" I cut him off. She had seemed pretty sane to me when I met her, as well as a genuinely nice person.

"She's been having mental problems for years," said Alice with more assurance. "She's been on all kinds of medications, but now she's lost it."

"I'm sorry, but why is any of this relevant? I have dinner ready, and I don't understand why we're talking about Katie, whom none of us have seen in months!"

"We'll cut to the point," Marcus said. "Katie is out of her mind, like mental hospital crazy, and she is supposedly coming here to my event tonight and threatening to say some crazy things, none of which are true. We came to tell you so that you're not alarmed in case she actually shows up."

"Right," chimed Alice. "None of what she says is true. She's a lunatic."

I was dumbstruck. This whole conversation hit me so out of left field that I didn't know what to make of it, and I still couldn't wrap my mind around the fact that normal, nice Katie had gone crazy.

"I don't understand what you guys are talking about. What kind of stuff is she going to say?" I asked.

"I know, this whole thing is really messed up," said Marcus, shaking his head.

"What is she threatening to say?" I asked again, a bit panicked.

The two of them exchanged glances. I watched them with my wriggling baby in my lap, trying to read what they were communicating to each other.

"Why don't we all go sit down on the couch?" suggested Alice.

We moved into the living room, Alice, baby, and me on the couch, with Marcus sitting on the floor in front of us. The vibe between us was so tense we were barely breathing. I still didn't know what was going on, which made this whole confrontation rather terrifying.

Alice's voice began to shake. "When I first met Marcus—" She stopped midsentence, crying and laughing at the same time.

Oh, my God, can't she just tell me what's going on?

Marcus started rubbing her back to console her as I rolled my eyes at him. But now she was definitely sobbing, not laughing.

"Are you okay?" I asked, concerned and even more confused.

Alice composed herself enough to continue. "When I met Marcus, I had this little-girl crush on him—"

"You mean, you *have* a crush on him," I interrupted.

"Whatever," she said. "But back when I met Marcus, I was hanging out with Katie all the time, and I guess I mentioned to her that I sort of liked him."

I flashed back to seventh grade, listening to cliques of girls in my private-school class talking about the boys they liked. Yet here I was, a grown adult, with my partner, my eight-week-old baby, and a scantily dressed middle-aged woman in my living room, confessing her crush to me. How had I ended up in this mess?

"Katie's threatening to come to your event tonight and tell me that Alice had a crush on you?" I asked Marcus, almost laughing. "I've known that since March."

"Well, not quite," he replied. "She's making up all kinds of lies about Alice and me, that we—you know—did stuff. She says she can find it on the security cameras at the Church, and she's threatening to announce all this nonsense over the loudspeaker. She said she's going to find you tonight at the event and make sure to tell you personally. But you have to understand: None. Of. It. Is. True."

My head started spinning. I had started to believe their story about Katie going insane, but it all seemed too strange, too out of the blue. Why would Katie spread lies about Alice and Marcus? Where would she get such wild ideas?

Our conversation continued a few minutes longer, as I interrogated them about the time they supposedly spent working together at the Church. I had started to unravel what I feared was true, but I'd only been given the end of the thread. Now, I had to pull it.

The two of them were packing up Marcus's gongs and Tibetan bowls for his event, which was due to start in less than an hour.

"Alice, do you mind leaving so I can talk to him alone?" I asked.

"Sure!" she said, happy to have her part in this conversation over with.

Marcus stood by the front door, several feet away from me.

"I just have one question for you," I asked softly and sincerely. "Of all that stuff that Katie's making up and threatening to tell me—is any of it true?"

Marcus didn't speak a word but gave me a look that spoke a thousand. He shook his head in disgust, as if to say, *How dare you ever think that of me.* He left, slamming the door loudly behind him.

Dinner was ready. Marcus hadn't even noticed. The efforts of my entire afternoon, gone to waste. But that was the last of my worries. As I changed my baby's diaper back in our bedroom, I couldn't shake a creeping suspicion that the two of them were lying. What if everything this Katie girl was threatening to say was true?

Not knowing what to do, I called my mom. She gave me simple, straightforward advice. "Why don't you just ask Alice? She'll tell you the truth."

My mom's commonsense approach gave me the confidence to call Alice right then. "Can you come back over to the Blue House?" I asked. "I want to ask you something,"

"Sure! Be right over," she answered, back to her chirpy self.

We sat on my bed under the massive framed photograph of Marcus and me from our Hawaiian maternity photo shoot. I looked her straight in the eye.

"Alice, I need to know the truth. As a friend, please be fully honest with me. Did anything ever happen between you and Marcus?"

She paused, and her expression changed into one of deep remorse. She looked down at the bed as she quietly said, "Yes."

Entering a state of shock, I went into denial to buffer myself from the soul-crushing blow of my worst fear coming true. "I'm sorry, I don't think I heard you right. Did you say yes?"

She nodded as if her head weighed a hundred pounds of pure, shameful sorrow. "Yes," she repeated.

"You mean, he kissed you or something?" I hoped in vain that maybe it wasn't bad as I thought. *I can handle this,* I told myself, in an attempt to stop the complete shattering of my heart. *He probably got so caught up in flirting with her that he gave her a peck on the lips.*

But it was much more than that. And it had started long ago, back when I was six months pregnant, closing up my life in Hawaii.

With every detail that Alice revealed, I descended into a deeper state of shock. The whole world stopped—first I couldn't catch my breath, the wind knocked out of me. Visibly trembling and crying uncontrollably, my mind spun round and round.

In between sobs, I repeated the same question aloud over and over, "How could he have done this to me?"

In this dizzying mess, I was gagging, crying, and shaking all at once. The sacred, beautiful bedroom that Marcus and I shared, with framed photos of us covering every wall, began spinning and swirling all around me, our smiling faces circling each time in a manic mockery as I everything I held dear was destroyed, one round after the next.

My helpless infant was screaming now, too—loud, inconsolable screeches. Alice sat and watched the baby and me crumble to pieces in front of her—the trajectory of our lives forever changed. I didn't know how to process what she had told me—those first minutes of shock and grief were like falling into a deep hole, and just when I thought I'd hit the bottom, I continued to fall deeper and deeper into an unimaginable pit of darkness.

"I don't see how he could've done this to me," I said, over and over.

And I didn't. I couldn't possibly understand how Marcus could have lied to me, cheated on me while I was pregnant, and had been blaming *me* all these months, saying things like, "You need to see a therapist for all of your insecurities."

And of all the attractive, beautiful women he could have picked to cheat with, he had picked Alice. My self-worth plummeted faster than a rock dropped from the Empire State Building. Maybe that's what I needed to do—drop quickly from a high place to escape the compounding misery.

Suddenly, what was left of my brain flipped, and I realized this was all Alice's fault. She wasn't innocent at all. She knew I was pregnant, and she knew Marcus was building a life with me, and yet she had the audacity and disrespect to break every unspoken code that exists between women by doing something so purely selfish, so awful, that it would ripple out and forever destroy people's lives. She was just as guilty.

It dawned on me—this woman was still here, sitting on my bed, and I needed her gone. "Alice, you need to leave," I said with as much strength as I could muster.

"I can't leave you and baby like this."

"Yes, you can. Leave."

She began adamantly defending herself, their affair, and repeating to me sickening lies that Marcus must have brainwashed her to believe: "You two were in an open relationship. You had no written agreements with Marcus. You never committed to moving to Dallas—you were going to stay in Hawaii. He didn't even know if you were coming to join him."

"Alice, get out." My anger rising, I was ready to kick her off my bed if she refused to leave another moment longer.

We continued to argue, Alice unwavering in her belief in the lies she had been fed, lies that justified their behavior and were so twisted that I couldn't imagine how I would ever make my way out of this deep, dark pit of despair.

Alice finally left, leaving me to sob even louder once no one was around except my baby who had somehow wailed her way into a deep sleep in my arms. My guilt about exposing my baby to this unstoppable force of emotion was great, and I prayed that she would somehow be strong enough to endure the intense trauma that was only just beginning.

I had to get out of my house. I had to leave Marcus. Whether for good or for the night, I didn't know, but I knew I had to get out before I risked seeing him as this lowly shell of myself. I called Cheryl, the first person I could think of who always had my back, thinking she was probably going to the event and could come pick me up instead.

But she didn't answer. I continued to call her again and again. No answer.

I paced the bedroom, trying to form thoughts even though my brain had turned itself off. Who else could I reach out to? *Is anyone out there?* Mom was the last person I wanted to call—she really loved Marcus. I didn't think she could handle the devastation I was going through.

When no one else came to mind, I walked over to the Church, still holding my baby. It was after seven, so the event had already started. I stood at the door and spotted Marcus, playing his array of gongs in a dimly lit room with dozens of people lying on yoga mats around him. He saw me but gave no sign of recognition. He continued to play his gongs along with his sidekick, Alice. I could tell that she hadn't told him what she had confessed that night. The two of them just did their thing. I watched in pure disgust as they spread their "loving, healing vibes" around the room. Marcus's movements were so slick, so smooth that I felt like I was watching the devil himself.

Bawling at the door, I was about to make a scene and had to figure out what to do. I noticed Minister Paul in the back of the room, sitting in a chair next to his latest girl friend (not to be confused with girlfriend), Nina. I quickly walked over to him and tapped him on the shoulder, waking him out of his meditation.

"I need to talk to you, *now*," I said.

Paul saw that I needed help and got right up. "Okay, I'll meet you in your office."

Sitting next to him on the antique sofa in my office, I questioned whether I should even tell him anything, since he was Marcus's boss. Clearly, if I told Paul, then Marcus would get fired, and I would be a traitor. But Marcus had just proved himself to be the traitor, and at this point, I didn't have any other options. Paul listened, shifting around uncomfortably while I told him what Alice had confessed.

"I need to figure out a way to pack up and head to the airport," I said.

"Where are you going to go?"

I hadn't thought that far. I just knew I had to get out of Dallas and away from Marcus. Seeing my state of intense shock, Paul suggested I not leave so quickly.

"We'll find you a place to stay tonight, away from the Blue House, and I'll counsel the two of you when you've had a chance to calm down a bit, okay?"

"No, I think I need to leave—like, pack up my bags and go to the airport, now," I said, sobbing.

Paul moved closer and gave me a warm, tight hug that lasted more than a minute. "You'll make it through this," he whispered, rubbing my back.

The buzz of my cell phone broke us apart, for which I was grateful. It was Cheryl, finally. She apologized profusely for not being able to answer my calls and asked why I'd called her twelve times in a row. When I told her I needed her, she came immediately to the rescue.

I sat in Cheryl's car feeling completely and scarily numb. I told her what Alice had confessed and didn't even cry. I couldn't make myself cry if I wanted to. All of my emotions seemed to have shut off, drained and overworked after two torturous hours. Cheryl demonstrated the utmost empathy and compassion and was in her own state of shock. Like me, she thought Marcus enjoyed flirting with other women but never to the point of actually cheating on his partner.

"Is it okay if I stay with you for a while, with the baby too?" I asked.

"Of course, sweetheart. You stay as long as you need."

"We'll see what happens after our counseling session with Paul. Maybe somehow—"

Cheryl cut me off by screaming so loud I had to cover my ears. "WHAT? Paul is counseling you two? Oh, my fucking God. Lord Jesus! Is this some kind of joke?"

She went into a state of delirium and so did her driving—speeding up, nearly running red lights, stopping so short my body lurched forward nearly ninety degrees, and landing us mere inches away from a major accident. I forced myself to be calm and composed while Cheryl completely lost it.

"Cheryl, please calm down," I pleaded. "Please don't crash this car. Baby's back there!" I reached back to hold the car seat to keep it steady throughout her downright terrifying driving.

As Cheryl slowed down to a somewhat normal speed, I asked, "What's so bad about Paul counseling us? I know he's not ideal, given his own relationship issues, but he's offering to do it for free. I think he'll be okay."

"I'm sorry, Courtney, but this is just too fucking ridiculous," she said, still yelling loudly, her body trembling just as mine had hours earlier.

"Why?"

"Paul is the last person on earth who should be counseling you two. I've been seeing him for the past three months, but we've had to keep it completely a secret since he's our minister. He's just done the same fucking awful thing to me that Marcus has been doing to you—and I just found out, when he dropped me for Nina, last night."

"What?" I asked in disbelief.

I knew that Paul had multiple women coming in and out of his life—or rather, into and out of his office—because I saw them as they walked by my office when I stayed late to finish the Church bulletin. The latest one, who appeared out of nowhere the night before, was Nina.

But Cheryl was different from the young, naive, pretty girls Paul secretly saw—all against Church rules, of course, since it was "illegal" to have an affair with a congregant. She was older and had been around the block. To be dropped like a dish after her investment into their secret relationship only to hear Paul had offered to help fix my relationship—it was just too much.

"It seems like these guys have a lot in common," Cheryl snarled as we approached her apartment, "and not good things."

Fourteen Counseling the Counselor

Around 11:30 p.m., while I was sitting on Cheryl's sofa, crying, Marcus sent me a text.

"Sorry," it read, followed by a tear-faced sad emoji.

That was it. He knew Alice had confessed, but that one word, one emoji text message was all I heard from him the entire night.

I was beyond exhausted but couldn't sleep for a minute. The brief numbness I experienced in the car was long gone, and a crying spree lasted throughout the night. I felt not only my own pain but what must have been the collective pain of every woman who has ever been betrayed since the beginning of time.

I was dying to respond to Marcus's text or to call and hear his voice or even to drive Cheryl's car back to our house in the middle of the night, but I held back, knowing to do so would be insane. But I wanted to feel that he still loved and cared about me.

I found some paper in Cheryl's living room and began to write, letting my anguish spill across the page. Though at first the journaling helped, my tears were soon flowing so fast that they soaked the page before I could finish my next sentence.

I tried going back to bed, but my crying was so intense that the baby started to wake up, so I moved into the bathroom, where I sat on the floor and cried some more. I went back and forth between the bed for the baby's nighttime feedings and the cold, hard bathroom floor until three in the morning.

In desperation, I called Mom. Although it was two in the morning California time, she answered, claiming to be unable to sleep as well, worried that something wasn't right. Against my original intention, I told her everything. Mom was strong and steady through my waves of emotion and stayed on the phone with me for more than an hour to make sure I was okay. She encouraged me to try and get some rest.

Saturday morning finally came. When daylight broke through, I had to accept that it hadn't been one big nightmare. Cheryl left the house at 7:30 a.m. to attend a full-day workshop at the Church—something she'd signed up for weeks prior—led by a guest teacher from the Church's main headquarters in New York. She asked several times if I'd be okay without her for the entire day, and I told her I'd be fine, and I could use the alone-time anyway.

The day passed much like the sleepless night had, yet I felt even worse than before. I cycled through every stage of grief, going from denial to anger to depression to bargaining, which in my case was more like pleading, and then back again, trying to find a way to deal with the fact that my entire world had been shattered. My heart was so broken I felt like a long, sharp knife had been lodged in my chest.

Deep down, in the depths of my heart, below my daily paranoias and frustrations, I had stupidly trusted him. Deep down, below the surface of all of our issues, I had believed in his goodness, his beauty, his sense of right and wrong, and most importantly, in his strong love for me. If just one day earlier, I'd had to make a bet that would cost me my life, I would have bet that he had never cheated on me since the day he found out I was pregnant and committed to being with only me. I felt so duped, so stupid, so worthless—I was a crumbled, unrecognizable shell of my myself.

When Cheryl returned that evening, I hadn't eaten a single morsel, which would have been expected, given the past twenty hours of shock, except that I was still nursing a newborn every two to three hours around the clock.

"Let's go out somewhere to cheer you up," said Cheryl.

"I don't think I'm up for that." I was exhausted from a whole day of doing nothing except grieving, nursing, and changing diapers.

"Sweetie, I'm a complete mess, too—trust me. I had to see Paul today, with his new, bowlegged twenty-year-old. I wanted to slap him in the face. Do you know he had me pick her up from the airport on Thursday?"

"What?" I asked in shock.

"Yes ma'am. That asshole asked me to pick up his new friend at the airport and bring her to his apartment—where she's now living."

Cheryl was a people-pleaser who had no idea who Nina was when Paul asked her to pick her up. Paul simply introduced Nina as someone who was going to join the Church's team. Cheryl took her turn having a breakdown, telling me about the emotional agony that our senior minister had been inflicting upon her since they started secretly dating three months earlier. He had simply dropped her for Nina, who had flown in from Minnesota and moved in with him—with Cheryl's help. Confused and bewildered, we couldn't wrap our heads around why Nina moved to Dallas—had she met Paul online? But I was too wrapped up in my own grief to care about Paul's complicated love life, besides the fact that Cheryl and I were essentially going through the same thing.

"Come on, we need to get out of here and cheer ourselves up," she insisted. "I'll take you out to dinner."

"I'm not hungry."

"Neither am I, but we need to eat. Let's get all dressed up. You can borrow something to wear. We'll have a night out on the town."

She finally won me over, dressing me in her gorgeous clothes and jewelry, which sadly did nothing for my spirit. She took me to one of her favorite restaurants and ordered for the both of us from the sushi menu, dropping at least a hundred dollars on several platters—picasso roll, sunshine roll, voodoo roll, caterpillar roll, and even a spider roll. Though I typically steered clear of raw fish, I was so beside myself by this point I figured I'd try everything.

We attempted to laugh and have a good time, a painstaking effort.

"Now I understand why people drink and do drugs," I said.

"Amen, sister," Cheryl said, taking a long sip of her wine.

With an eight-week-old baby on my lap, drugs and alcohol were the last possible means to cope with my immense suffering, but in the moment, I felt deep compassion for those who do reach for such coping mechanisms. When all is lost, any bit of relief is better than none.

After another few glasses of wine, Cheryl and I were having a much better time. Although I was only drinking lemon water, I felt vicariously lifted up by her wine-fueled mood, with flickering disassociations from the pain of my situation. As we cleaned every platter of sushi, I suddenly remembered that Marcus and I were scheduled to give announcements the next morning onstage during Church services.

"I have to get out of it!" I exclaimed in a tizzy. "I can't just not show up."

As I pulled out my phone to email the woman in charge of scheduling, Cheryl said in her loud, Southern drawl, "Honey, I think we better get on that stage and give those announcements tomorrow."

"Are you crazy? What are you talking about?"

She stood up, smoothed out her dress, and began an incredibly theatrical rendition of Sunday announcements.

"Welcome, everybody, to Sunday service at the Church, a positive place where we come to worship God and see God at work in our lives. Are some of you out there depressed?" She paused with eyebrows raised—waiting for an answer. "Confused?" She paused again. People from nearby tables were now looking on, amused. "Feeling lost in your life? Well, here at the Church, we have a brand-new program for you, sure to become one of our most popular offerings! What is it, you ask? Truly, it must be experienced. Think of it like this: counseling with a twist, or rather, with a thrust. Our two ministers are at your service."

As Cheryl continued, her language grew pretty dicey. By the end, I was laughing so hard I had tears running down my face.

She sat back down. "Okay, now your turn."

For the next several minutes, we passed the baton back and forth, practicing our most hilarious, most ridiculous Sunday announcements, taking us, for a moment at least, out of our sorrow.

After dinner, I was back to being shell-shocked. "I don't think I can stay another night away from Marcus," I said.

"You want me to drive you back, honey? I'll do it if you want me to. But you need to be sure," said Cheryl.

"No, I'm not sure. I have no idea—I'm such a mess I can't even think straight. The sleep deprivation is probably getting to me."

"Why don't you stay one more night at my place, get a good night's rest, and I'll take you back tomorrow?"

That certainly made the most sense since Paul had set up a counseling session for Marcus and me at 1:30 p.m., after the Church services and potluck. Despite hearing about Paul's unhealthy relationship pattern firsthand from Cheryl, I was still going to use him as our counselor. Thinking back, I can't believe I ever agreed to let him counsel us, but I clearly wasn't using any measure of logic at the time. We had no money for an outside counselor, so I had to settle for the most convenient and cost-free option. I figured any counselor was better than no counselor.

I found it tremendously difficult to stay at Cheryl's another night, especially with Marcus suddenly calling and leaving voicemails over and over. His voice on the messages—begging me to come home and saying he loved me and missed me—caused what was left of my heart to shatter even further. I made a point not to answer his calls or speak to him at all, which was downright torture because I had decided that the next time we talked had to be in the presence of a professional counselor. I had been through too many scary episodes with him by now to know that we needed a third party, especially to tackle a topic as big as his infidelity.

After yet another sleepless night, I accompanied Cheryl to her pool instead of going to Sunday services. My mom, dad, and sister each called me one after another, concerned for my well-being.

Months earlier, Marcus and I had booked a trip to California to visit my parents and so I could teach at an international dance conference in San Francisco. We would be there for ten days, including my birthday, and we were due to leave on Tuesday, which was two days away.

"He absolutely should *not* come with you to California," my sister said in a loving, yet stern tone. "Just come with the baby and stay here for a month or two—or just move here and never go back. You can decide that later, but you need time away from him to heal."

On one hand, I knew she was right, and the timing of this trip was perfect to give me space to recover, but on the other, I couldn't imagine going without Marcus. I needed him, and I still loved him, and just the thirty-six hours we'd spent apart were torturous enough—how could I possibly survive ten days without him and appear put together enough to teach at this biennial dance conference?

With my self-esteem now nonexistent, I was obsessed with my image—how I'd appear in front of all these important dance people, who, due to my mother also being prominent in the modern dance scene, had known me since I was in her womb. I was just going to show up, heartbroken, with a two-month-old baby? As a *single mother*? None of these people even knew I had a partner or a baby. I had honored my agreement with Mariana and Marcus not to post pictures online, even though they never honored their agreement to get divorced.

"I'm not making any decisions about the trip yet," I said. "I need to wait until after our counseling session today."

As I walked into the Church, my heart raced, and my entire body trembled. Being back on campus, where my life had come crashing down less than forty-eight hours earlier, made me feel ill.

"You got this, mama," Cheryl said. She hugged me before heading up the stairs to attend the second day of her workshop, which started at 1 p.m.

Seven minutes later, I looked at my phone. What was I going to do for the next twenty-three minutes? I couldn't go back home in case Marcus was there. I couldn't take a walk—the baby had fallen asleep in her car seat, and

I didn't have a stroller with me. All I could do was sit and get increasingly anxious.

And then there was Marcus, wearing a green Hawaiian shirt and black slacks, looking like the world was in perfect order as he walked right by, glanced at me as if I were nothing more than an acquaintance, and continued on his way.

After everything I'd been through, after a phone full of voicemail messages declaring his undying love, he was just going to ignore me? I embodied pure rage as I stood up and followed him. He went into his office and closed the door. I opened it right back up, the baby's car seat in tow, and went inside. I plopped myself down on the gray couch—which disgusted me given what had transpired on top of it—and sat in silence. Marcus started straightening up his humongous wraparound desk with an amused grin. Neither of us spoke a word.

I started arguing with myself. My head said, *Courtney, you shouldn't be in here right now. You promised yourself you wouldn't talk to him without a counselor.*

Then my heart answered, *But I still love him. I need to be with him.*

My intuition chimed in: *This is not a safe place to be, Courtney. Stand up and leave.*

Before I could decide what to do, Marcus started walking toward his office door as if to leave. I stood up to follow him, and before I could think twice, I blurted out with disgust, "Do you even think you made a mistake?"

Looking me straight in the eye, with a stone-cold voice, he answered, "No."

I swung open the door that led into the bustling hallway—to be sure that the rest of our conversation would be heard by as many people as possible—and yelled at the top of my lungs, "YOU DON'T THINK THAT SLEEPING WITH ALICE GILMAN WHILE YOU'RE COUNSELING HER IS—"

Marcus cut me off by gripping me around the throat. He picked me up by the neck, pivoted, and threw me back down. When my knees hit the ground, I was facing the opposite direction. I let out a loud, high-pitched shriek, and Marcus dashed out of his office. Paul heard the drama from down the hall and ran in.

"What the hell is going on here?" He was furious.

Sobbing and shaking, I could barely answer.

"Get in my office, now," he demanded.

All I could think of was Marcus. "You have to find him. I don't know where he went, but he's lost it. He just tried to choke me. See, look?" I pointed to my neck, Marcus's bright red handprint stamped onto it. "I'm serious—he needs help. I'm scared of what he's going to do next."

Paul took me by the shoulder and pulled me to his office. "Do not leave this room. This is not acceptable. We have visitors from headquarters. We can't have your drama spilling into the hallway! Do you understand?"

He closed the door behind him and left, leaving me with the baby who was now awake and needed to breastfeed. How my body was able to produce milk throughout this ordeal was a miracle.

While nursing in the quiet of Paul's office, I realized that I was done for good. *I had to be after what he just did, right?* A few minutes later, I called Mom, still trembling. "He's lost it. He actually picked me up by my—"

Paul's office door opened, and there stood Cheryl, Paul, and Marcus.

"Mom, I need to go," I said.

"He did what?" Mom gasped. "Are you okay?"

Seeing Cheryl put me more at ease. "I'm fine," I said, already regretting what I'd told her. "Cheryl's here now. Don't worry. I'll call you later!" And then I hung up.

Cheryl gave me and the baby a fortifying hug and then left us to our counseling session.

A cocktail of hormones pulsed through my body as Marcus sat down next to me, both of us sitting on the thick, beige rug with the baby between us. I wasn't sure if I loved him or if I was terrified of him—probably a mix of both. As we waited for Paul to begin, I noticed that Marcus hadn't greeted Skye or interacted with her at all, despite not seeing her for the past two days.

"Don't you want to say hi to her?" I asked. Even after being aggressively choked, I wanted him to love me, and as an extension of me, our baby.

"I think she's probably mad at me just like you are," he answered, his face deadpan. He continued to ignore her.

Paul sat down in a chair in front of us, and we commenced a marathon couples' counseling session that lasted for the next three and a half hours without so much as a bathroom break. Paul asked to hear the whole story of our relationship, one at a time, and without interruption from the other person.

"This will give me a clear picture of your situation," he said, and "help us figure out what went so terribly wrong to bring us to where we are today."

"I'll go first," I offered, "but before I do, can I read something from a book I brought?" I took out *Walking the Noble Path* by Thich Nhat Hanh from the diaper bag. Cheryl had given this book to me when I couldn't sleep the other night, and the passage entitled "True Love," one of the Five Mindfulness Trainings based on Buddhist precepts, seemed to summarize everything I innately knew to be true, yet these men obviously still needed to learn.

The first few sentences of the passage read, "Aware of the suffering caused by sexual misconduct, I am committed to cultivating responsibility and learning ways to protect the safety and integrity of individuals, couples, families, and society. Knowing that sexual desire is not love, and that sexual activity motivated by craving always harms myself as well as others, I am determined not to engage in sexual relations without true love and a deep, long-term commitment made known to my family and friends."

Paul seemed intrigued by what I was reading. "Cheryl gave you this book?" he asked, baffled.

"Yes," I answered, looking him straight in the eye.

"Very interesting," he said. "Could you take a picture and send it to me?"

I said sure and did so on the spot.

Paul was supposed to be the experienced professional counselor in the room, but I was the one counseling both of these men, whose immature and selfish actions had hurt not only me and Cheryl but countless other women. Even though I knew that Paul was a phony, a complete fraud of a minister, in that moment, I didn't care. I needed someone, anyone, to help Marcus and me during this crisis, and I figured that he would put his own stuff aside to help us from a fair and objective point of view.

In retrospect, nothing could have been further from the truth.

As requested, I went back in time to when I first met Marcus at the Sanctuary, and although I thought he was a little over the top, I fell madly in love with him when we started rehearsing for a dance performance. I told Paul of the numerous other women Marcus was seeing in the beginning of our relationship, but that I'd decided to ride it out, play by his rules, and wait for him to realize that he wanted to commit to me.

Just a few months later, after our daughter was conceived, he made the promise I'd been waiting for. Completely unsolicited, Marcus offered up of his own free will, "I will be with only you. I'll divorce my wife as soon as I can so that we can get married."

Besides these words in plain English, he had made dozens of inferences to our monogamous relationship—when he came to my parents' apartment on Roosevelt Island, when he attended my family reunion on Long Island, when I visited his family in Missouri, and when we made our Buddhist vows together and the first one he wrote on the list was "kosen-rufu family," meaning that we were joining together as a family to create world peace. And I had closed up my entire life in Hawaii to move to Texas of all places to support his dreams—something I never would have done if we were in an open relationship as he now claimed.

One of the most memorable discussions on the topic of monogamy had taken place between Marcus and me in Hawaii the November before we moved to Dallas. I was two months pregnant at the time.

"Of all the women I've been with, there hasn't been a single one who was Japanese!" he said one night, completely out of the blue. "I've got the entire map covered except Japan. What am I supposed to do if I need to sleep with a Japanese woman, say, twenty years from now, but I can't since we're committed to each other?"

His question brought out every insecurity I had. "Are you saying you want to cheat on me?"

"What? No! I'm saying what happens down the road if I'm attracted to someone else? What am I supposed to do?"

"I guess when and if that ever happens, you'd tell me, and we would talk about it?" I guessed at a best answer to prevent my worst fear from coming true decades into the future.

"We can't just add another wife into the equation? Down the road, you know, in thirty years or so?"

Horrified, I said something to set a clear boundary, but as Marcus later described in our counseling session, I had given him an ultimatum, one that he never forgot, the equivalent of "sticking a gun down his throat." These words, he said, were the reason he cheated on me with Alice—he had to prove that I couldn't control him.

My boundary and his perceived ultimatum was this: "I don't want to be in a polyamorous relationship. You're a free person, and you can make whatever decisions you want, and you can even sleep with anyone you want. But if you ever decide to cheat on me behind my back, I will leave you, and you'll never see me or our daughter again."

We ended that bizarre conversation back in November with a verbal agreement. If Marcus ever met this hypothetical sexy Japanese girl he couldn't resist when he was sixty-five years old, he'd talk to me about it openly and honestly before anything happened.

The worst had already happened less than a year after that conversation. He had cheated on me, lied to me, deceived and betrayed me at the most vulnerable time in my life—pregnant with my first baby. And as much as I wanted to follow through with my "ultimatum," as he referred to it, I deeply yearned to work it out because I wasn't ready for the devastation of losing the dream I had worked so hard to build. With every fiber of my being, I still wanted to believe in us, despite our struggles.

The counseling session dragged on. Hearing Marcus's version of the story was immensely frustrating.

"We had no agreements written in blood about sleeping with other people," he said. "You've been assuming things this whole time—it was never clear to me what the agreements were."

I wanted to kill him right then and there.

"We also never had any agreements 'written in blood' to not burn our house down," I retorted. "Does that mean I can walk over and set it on fire? You are completely making things up. *Of course*, we had agreements!"

Paul cut me off because I was talking out of turn. To keep from going insane, I focused on my baby cooing in front of me.

By five o'clock, I couldn't sit there anymore—none of us could. We were exhausted and needed to conclude, even though Marcus and I still weren't anywhere close to being on the same page. We'd been going in circles for more than three hours, and Marcus still refused to admit fault or take responsibility for his actions.

"It seems like there's been a lot of miscommunication between you two," said Paul. "It's up to you two to decide how to move forward."

"But what about the fact that Marcus was sleeping with a woman he's been counseling? Is he going to keep his job? Will we have to leave the Blue House?" I asked, completely shocked that there was no punishment for his immoral and unethical actions.

"I'll talk to him about that privately," Paul replied. "Now, we need to end here. I haven't eaten anything all day. I need you to make a decision. Do you want to make this work between you or not?"

I started sweating, my body warping with anxiety, while I wondered how Marcus would answer. *What if he said no?* I would truly fall apart, maybe even die, on the spot.

Paul and I looked at Marcus. I prayed he would give me the answer I needed.

"Yes," he answered, and looked at me with those kind, loving eyes that I'd so missed.

"And what about you, Courtney? Do you want to work it out, together with him?" asked Paul.

"Yes," I answered, with only slight hesitation. And for the first time since Friday night, I felt like I could breathe again.

We walked back to the Blue House hand in hand, like long-lost lovers who had just reunited after witnessing a nuclear bomb destroy everything they've ever known. A strange feeling overcame me. Marcus seemed familiar, but I also had no idea who he was anymore.

Bummed and dazed, he pointed out the special things he'd done in the house to welcome me back—bouquets of flowers, gluten-free chocolate cake, a photo of us with a heart-shaped candle and incense in front of it, and a framed love poem whose last line read, "And forever, I will stay by your side."

Marcus seemed defeated. "I did this all because I thought you'd come back last night," he said, clearly feeling like his efforts were a waste of time.

Even though only one extra day had passed, these special gifts had sat out too long. The flowers were withering, a huge piece of cake was missing ("I felt so bad for myself I decided to eat it without you," he said), the candle had burned down, and the poem was too cliché to be believed.

As we made our way into the bedroom, I felt like crying again, the grief pouring through me in waves. I started asking Marcus a slew of questions about the affair, begging to know more, yet each detail he confessed tortured me, taking the knife still lodged in my heart and stabbing me all over again.

As I lay on our bed in a numb fog, Marcus lowered himself down and gently attempted to seduce me. Without thinking, I pushed him away.

"There's no way I can ever trust you again."

Marcus started crying, which I couldn't take, not now, on top of everything else. *Now I have to feel awful for rejecting him, too?* Out of intense guilt, we flipped roles, and I began comforting and pursuing him. Our physical closeness did nothing to help the lack of connection and chemistry. On every other level of our being, we stood light years apart.

Fifteen Entities

The rest of that night, I kept trying to wrap my head around how Marcus could have been attracted to Alice, which he said had been necessary or he wouldn't have had an affair with her in the first place.

The next morning, he noticed my feelings hadn't subsided. "You have some severe jealousy issues," he said. "Do you want to still be upset about this?"

"No! I can't stand feeling like this. I'm dying to feel better."

"You can't feel better if you're obsessing over what happened. Plus, I already told you—it's over with her."

"Yes, but you slept with her while I was pregnant." I started crying again.

"You have severe jealousy issues," he repeated. "You attracted this whole scenario so you can finally work on getting rid of your entities. They're taking over your whole being."

"Entities?"

"I've never seen anyone with as many psychic entities as you have. That's why you feel so bad and can't stop crying. It's not you—it's the entities."

Six weeks prior, with our newborn in tow, Marcus and I had visited a woman named Sylvie, a respected sound healer with a healing studio attached to her beautiful home. She was in her midseventies but had a face as smooth as a porcelain doll and silvery-white hair down to her waist. In a place like Dallas, this mystical, ethereal woman stood out.

Marcus hoped that Sylvie could become an ally since they were in the same line of "work," though our visit that day was purely social. The two of them had plenty to schmooze about—gongs, bowls, crystals, and all things woo-woo. Only half listening to their conversation, I nosed around the place, admiring the myriad shiny, colorful objects. Their conversation caught my attention, however, when I heard the word "entities." I walked back toward them to learn more.

Entities, I found out, were a type of psychic invasion from spirit beings without a physical body. According to people who believe in this kind of stuff, these unenlightened parasitic energies glom on to people and basically run the show, causing all kinds of pain and suffering—or in my case, as Marcus suggested, extreme jealousy. The whole idea of entities sounded weird and just a little too out there, but in my dark pit of despair, I believed Marcus might be right. *Wouldn't that be amazing if I could get these entities removed, and then I would feel like myself again?*

"How can I get rid of them?" I asked Marcus, as we stood in our bedroom.

"It takes an experienced healer. I could do it for you, but I don't have the time, especially if we're leaving for our trip tomorrow. But maybe you can go see Sylvie, if she has an opening. I'll even gift that to you."

His words shocked me. First of all, he assumed that our trip to California was still on even though we hadn't discussed it, and it was unlike him to remember dates and logistics without constant reminders. Second of all, he was offering to pay for my session with Sylvie, which was probably hundreds of dollars. Marcus was not one to treat me to things, so he must have believed this would work.

He set up a last-minute appointment and handed me a thick wad of cash, claiming he truly wanted me to feel better. I walked into Sylvie's airy, light-filled home later that afternoon. A quick glance in a long mirror in her entranceway revealed that the emotional roller coaster I'd been riding had taken a physical toll. I couldn't remember ever seeing myself look so sleep-deprived, worn out, and depleted. Massive purple bags swelled under my bloodshot eyes, and my clothes hung on my undernourished frame.

Sylvie greeted me warmly and led me into a large, attached studio where her energy-healing sessions took place. Wooden bookshelves covered the walls, holding crystals of every size, shape, and color imaginable—even crystals shaped like skulls in all the colors of the rainbow. In the middle of the room stood an oversized massage table draped in purple silk, and next to it, a smaller set of shelves with at least twenty shiny brass Tibetan bowls that ranged in size and harmonic frequency. These sound-healing bowls were going to remove my entities!

I couldn't wait to lie down on that table and close my eyes so Sylvie could get to work. Instead, however, she asked me to sit down on a small squishy couch on the other side of the room. I grew nervous. What if she asked me details about what had happened to bring me to such a debilitated state? Was I going to tell her the truth and risk her losing all respect for Marcus? I hoped the conversation would be quick so that we could get to the healing without my having to divulge too much.

"What brings you in today, dear?" she asked, smiling sweetly, only a faint trace of the Southern accent I was used to hearing at the Church.

"Marcus told me I have entities and need them removed. He said you would know exactly what to do. Can you do that in just one session?"

Sylvie started laughing—not just a chuckle but full-throttle belly laughter. I attempted to laugh along with her until she composed herself enough to ask, "And what on earth would give him the idea that you are full of entities?"

"He claims I have severe jealousy issues."

"First of all, honey, you don't have any entities." She laughed again.

I was instantly disappointed. "Are you sure?" An aura full of entities was my saving grace since their removal would mean I'd feel better.

"If anyone has entities," she said, "it's him. But tell me why this is coming up. I can tell you're shaken up about something. What happened?"

I barely knew Sylvie, and I didn't feel right about opening up to her, especially because my connection to her was through Marcus. I resisted telling her any details, so I simply said, "I've recently been through a trauma."

She continued to probe, saying that our session would be more effective if she knew what was going on. She handed me a business card and said that one of her many hats was that of a counseling psychologist. On the business card, above the title "Shamanic Guide and Sound Healing Specialist" was "Licensed Counselor."

We spent much of the ninety-minute session talking, but before she heard what had happened, Sylvie offered her perspective on his and my relationship, from what little she saw when we visited her six weeks earlier.

"It was clear from the moment you two came in the room that you're dimming your light for him," she said. "You don't seem like the kind of person who should be dimming your light so that someone else can shine. You need to shine, too."

Nothing had ever rung truer. As I revealed why I was so shattered, I was adamant that she not hold anything against Marcus, out of fear that he would find out and possibly kill me. I tried hard to protect his image and reputation by shifting the focus from what he had done to how I felt. With just thirty minutes left, I climbed on the massage table, closed my eyes and relaxed.

While Sylvie played her Tibetan bowls and recited Native American prayers, I continued to ask her, "Are you sure I don't have entities?"

Driving home, I can't say I felt much better than before. I had hoped for a grand, sudden healing, where light would drop from the sky, shoot into my body, and all of the pain in my heart would instantly dissolve. But that didn't happen. The best part of the session turned out to be the hour of talking to Sylvie and hearing a sane, objective view on my situation—from someone unrelated to the Church. She was brutally honest and said a few things that got me thinking.

One of them was that she couldn't see me happy living in Texas. "You need to go back to Hawaii, and he needs to understand that," she said.

"I can't go back! I have a two-month-old baby, and I moved my whole life here."

"Do you want to stay living in Texas?"

"NO!" I screamed. "But I have to. I'm stuck here."

Sylvie suggested that if I truly wanted to stay in a relationship with Marcus—which she wasn't sure was a great idea but which she saw that I wasn't ready to give up—I had to find a way to get my Hawaii fix.

"You could travel to Hawaii at least four times a year to teach workshops and retreats as you used to do," she suggested.

Her brilliant idea was the best thing out of the entire session, as it gave me an ounce of hope, and I couldn't wait to share it with Marcus.

Another piece of advice she gave me was the same thing I'd already heard from my sister, my mom, and my trusted astrologist, whom I'd called while hanging out at Cheryl's pool the day before: "Do *not* bring Marcus with you to California. Use the trip to get some space for yourself and to heal. Extend your trip and stay at least a month or two."

Although I nodded in agreement, I couldn't see that happening. While I could see the logic in their advice, the thought of his reaction terrified me. He would be so furious he'd either leave me or cheat on me again. If I left on the trip without him, I was certain that would be the end of us, and I wasn't ready or able to deal with that yet.

The long, quiet drive back from Sylvie's house gave me more space to think than I knew what to do with. After going over our entire conversation in my head several times, my mind invented a new sport—one that I would practice daily in the months to follow in the private confines of my own mind.

First, I'd think of all the incredible, beautiful memories that Marcus and I had shared in the last year of being together, reliving them and feeling immense love and appreciation for him. But then, the painful, heartbreaking memories came running in. They'd replay themselves in full detail, bringing up overwhelming hatred and disgust. Back and forth I went. One minute I truly loved him, and the next minute I absolutely hated him.

I hadn't forgotten about Alice either—I absolutely hated her, too. From loving Marcus to hating Marcus to hating Alice to hating Marcus—the pendulum exhausted me. I tried to remain in the loving feelings, but then I'd remember his betrayal. And it wasn't just the cheating that upset me. I was enraged at how he exploited his position of authority at the Church.

According to both Marcus's and Alice's separate accounts, their affair happened by accident when he was counseling her and her husband about their pending divorce. A few times, Marcus counseled Alice alone, and the "counseling" got out of hand, all of which took place in the Church—most memorably, in one of my favorite hangouts, the elegant, spacious Victorian ladies' restroom. The thought of ever going in there again made me ill.

Back on campus, I pulled into our driveway feeling like I'd just run a marathon—my hands slick with sweat, my breath shallow, and my whole body hot as flames.

"How'd it go, Cozy?" Marcus asked brightly, as I walked in.

Our bedroom smelled strongly of marijuana. I surveyed the room. "Oh, fine," I answered.

He was neatly rolling and packing clothes into a large backpack on the bed while the baby slept peacefully in the swing.

"What are you doing?" I asked.

"Packing for our trip. We're still going, right?"

This was my chance. I attempted to assert myself. "I think it may be best if I just go alone with baby. What do you think about that?"

Marcus's blurry pink eyes teared up. *Not again*. I stepped in closer to give him a hug. We held onto each other for what felt like forever while I conjured another round of love-hate in my mind, this time with more emphasis on *love*.

"I think it would be a terrible idea if you guys went without me," he said, crying. "This is when we most need to be together, so we can get through this."

His sincerity seemed so real that I fully believed him.

We left the next morning for the airport, only three and a half days since Alice confessed the affair. While I wanted to be healed, I was still deeply traumatized and unable to function properly—eating, sleeping, and packing were almost impossible. I even forgot to bring a stroller—a most essential item for a two-month-old—which resulted in the great inconvenience of carrying a heavy car seat while Marcus pushed all of our bags through the heavily delayed twelve-hour journey through airports and train stations.

Interestingly enough, during our journey, the Universe gave us a way out, a path that would shift the course of our intertwined destinies if we were ready to take it.

Sitting on the plane next to Marcus, with our adorable, smiling infant sprawled between our laps, I mentioned Sylvie's brilliant idea about my traveling back and forth to Hawaii to lead my own workshops and retreats, which would give me a break from Texas. I assumed Marcus would be thrilled about the idea since, according to Sylvie, it was the only way we could stay together for the long-term.

He wasn't thrilled at all.

"You're saying you're just going to leave me for several days at a time?" he asked. His mood had shifted abruptly.

"Well, this is all hypothetical—it's just an idea Sylvie had. And of course, you could come to Hawaii, too!"

"How could I go to Hawaii if I'm building a life in Texas?"

"Right. Well, you could stay here then. Like I said, it's just an idea. But, if you're not into it, then—"

"No. I'm not into you just taking off and flying to Hawaii to lead retreats," he said. "And how could I ever trust you if you're thousands of miles away?"

Was this some kind of joke? Was he implying that I would cheat on him if I went to Hawaii to teach a workshop? Was this guy truly out of his mind?

A woman's voice on the loudspeaker interrupted my thoughts. "Ladies and gentlemen, pardon the interruption. As you've noticed, we're experiencing heavy delays on the runway."

I looked out the window, then at my phone. No, I hadn't noticed. Our plane had been taxiing for more than twenty-five minutes while Marcus and I had been focused only on each other.

"Please continue to be patient. We will be taking off shortly," said the flight attendant.

This was already becoming the trip from hell. I was trapped in a few cubic feet with Marcus when I wanted to get as far away from him as possible. The plane continued to idle for another twenty minutes. I attempted to change the subject and lift the mood since we were stuck together at this point.

Another announcement came through. "We apologize for the continued delay. Due to an engine malfunction, we will be returning to the gate where we will ask everybody to deplane. A new aircraft will arrive shortly."

"Did you hear that?" I asked Marcus.

"Yep," he answered.

This was my moment—my second chance to tell him clearly and decisively, "I need to go on this trip alone. I need some time to reflect and heal. I don't feel it's appropriate to stay together at my parents' apartment."

I felt that the Universe had provided this opportunity for us specifically so that he could leave the plane, and my life, for good. It couldn't have been spelled out any more symbolically than the plane turning around after Marcus had dismissed the Hawaii idea, which would have met my creative needs. Though I'd forgotten a stroller, I'd brought several suitcases of clothes for me and Skye, packing enough for three months rather than just ten days. This delay seemed meant to be—Skye and I would continue to California while Marcus stayed in Dallas, and our dysfunctional journey would finally come to an end.

But instead of acting upon logic, my mind and heart ran frantically in opposite directions, terrified at the thought of Marcus leaving me. After the announcement, we didn't speak a word, but I studied him carefully, seeking a clue as to whether this was really it. Was he going to take this prime opportunity to leave us and let us move on without him? The thought alone sent me into sheer panic, and I began clinging to him for dear life.

I begged any benevolent Universal force that might be listening. *I'm not ready for him to leave. Please, please, please don't let him leave me.* Marcus and I walked off the plane in silence, and I wondered in horror what was going to happen next. To my astonishment, he didn't even threaten to leave. He didn't seem to notice the symbolism of the deplaning, or we were both going to ignore it and continue to pretend—much to our long-term detriment—that everything was just fine.

The ten days in California were filled with the usual ups and downs with Marcus. Even in this time of shock and grief, the highs were incredibly high and only mildly tainted with the memory of his affair. When I taught at the dance conference, dozens of my former colleagues commented on my "adorable husband." I had a beautiful and only slightly depressing birthday hike with Marcus and the baby through the redwood forest, and we even took a road trip to visit a close friend in coastal Monterey. We also visited my great aunt and uncle in Palo Alto, retired Stanford professors who were most intrigued with Marcus's over-the-top charisma. ("That boy will certainly have a following one day!" my great-uncle later emailed.)

After finding out about his affair, however, my mom and sister weren't thrilled to have Marcus around. My sister later told me she found it hard to keep from slapping him every time she saw him. The excuses I gave to my mom and sister for having him along—*I need his help with the dance workshops. I need him to watch baby so I can teach and participate in the dance symposium. I think this will be a healing trip for us. I think the change of scenery will help our relationship. I think being away from the Church is important right now*—were only partially true.

But I knew the reason I needed him there—my survival.

I hadn't forgiven Marcus for having an affair, but while in California, at least on the outside, I pretended to forgive him, and I did my best to pretend the whole affair had never even happened. I thought of it like a nightmare, a terrifying story that had only appeared real. I begged my family not to mention anything about the affair to Marcus, and they agreed, not saying a word. And while at the dance conference, Marcus, our two-month-old, and I appeared as a perfect, happy family with not a problem in the world.

For my survival, I needed the reprieve of this fantasy world, if only for ten days. I wasn't ready to face what my life would look like without him. I truly think it would have killed me.

"Forever and ever," as we often confirmed with each other, was ingrained into my very cells.

Sixteen Audrey

Dressed in our Sunday best, Baby Skye and I showed up at the Church for services the day after our return to Dallas and sat in the front row next to Marcus, while Paul preached a sermon I'm pretty sure he devised specifically for me, entitled, "Forgive and Forget," on the power of forgiveness, letting go, and moving on.

While I believe in forgiveness, I had barely had a chance to process what happened and certainly wasn't ready to let go. The ten days we had spent in California were a small bandage that covered the icky, sticky mess of my heart that still needed much more time to heal before I could move on.

Paul's speech, however, wasn't what made that day so memorable. We would hear plenty more like it in the weeks to come. What made that first Sunday back at Church stand out among all the others is what happened *after* the service.

While I was in California, I had been messaging Paul, thanks to my sister, who picked up my phone and typed the messages for me. She wrote as me, telling Paul that in order for me to return to Dallas and attempt to heal, Alice could no longer be Marcus's personal assistant or be involved with the Church for at least several weeks. I couldn't possibly heal while having to see her every day.

Paul wrote back, "Okay, I'll see what I can do."

He hadn't done much because, after sitting through his "Forgive and Forget" sermon, I spotted her on my way out of the sanctuary. Smiling and as scantily dressed as ever, Alice hadn't an ounce of shame or embarrassment about her—she walked around like she owned the place, even going out of her way to give Marcus a tight squeeze, not knowing I was standing several feet away.

Watching them hug made me feel sick.

Everyone milled about, hugging and smiling, while I was about to lose it. I made my way to the back door of the Church and ran across the lawn, baby in arms, to the Blue House, where once inside, I collapsed into the worst breakdown I'd had yet. My sister's last words before I left California were ringing in my head: "You're not ready to go back there yet. Stay here a little longer. What's so great about Dallas that you need to rush back?" She was absolutely right. There was nothing remotely great about this place at all, and I feared that harboring this much resentment, anger, and fury would start to affect my health.

Despite numerous messages and even a few meetings with Paul, Alice continued to come to the Church services, events, and classes. One Sunday afternoon, Paul pulled me aside.

"I used to work in corporate America where this kind of thing—affairs between employees—happened all the time," he said. "Do you think people are forced out of their jobs? You think lives get turned upside down? No! Work goes on. Life goes on."

"That's how it works in corporate America?" I asked.

"Yes, that's how it works. People have affairs all the time, and you still have to go to work. Trust me—it's time for you to step up and be the enlightened one here. Alice is a free person, entitled to come to Church, just as you are."

"But Paul," I said, "I live here, I work here. This is my home. I can't just find another place to be all the time. Can't you tell her she needs to take a break? Isn't there another church she can go to for a few weeks? For my sanity? Please?"

"There are people in the world with real problems, Courtney," he replied. "I'm counseling people whose children have cancer, people who've lost everything in floods and fires, people who are battling life-threatening illness—and your issue is so small, so petty in comparison. You need to start cultivating some gratitude."

To this, I was silent.

"Be grateful Marcus didn't cheat on you and then leave you! I know plenty of women in that situation, too. Can you imagine that? Just for a moment, imagine if after cheating on you with Alice, he chose her instead of you. How would that feel?"

"That would feel awful."

"Right. So, be grateful he picked you."

Grateful as I was to be the "chosen one," life in Dallas with Alice lingering around the Church was absolute hell. The sweet fantasy bubble Marcus and I had created on our trip to California burst in one quick pop, and the true colors of those around me were revealed. Paul not only refused to ban Alice from her "spiritual home," as he referred to it, but he also doled out no punishment or consequence to Marcus for doing something against every Church policy and basic ethics.

Paul and Marcus were closer buddies than I'd realized and were clearly committed to saving each other's backs—at any cost to those around them. Cheryl stopped coming to the Church, but I stayed in touch with her, and she told me how Paul called her daily, profusely apologizing for any miscommunication in their relationship and begging her to keep what went on between them a secret. He even offered to pay for her to take personal development courses at the Church, usually costing several hundred dollars, to ensure she'd keep quiet.

The corruption was seeping out, slowly but surely, but my attention remained on Alice. Every glimpse of her stabbed me in the heart all over again. Marcus had spent ten years in a maximum-security prison for stabbing someone. I'm not sure my emotional wound hurt any less than being physically stabbed, such was the intensity of the pain I couldn't escape, even with my strong Buddhist practice and spiritual wisdom. My relationship with Marcus wasn't doing so great either, since all we ever did was argue about Alice and whether or not she should still be buzzing around.

In the midst of this chaos, an unexpected visitor arrived for an extended visit. Marcus's ex-girlfriend Tina had come to drop off Maya at the end of the summer and then, without prior consent or invitation, stayed on at our house for the next seven days.

Her presence was both a blessing and a nuisance. I appreciated having another female around—especially one who not only sided with me but to whom Marcus would actually listen. And yet the two of them still had chemistry, and several times a day I walked in on them practically sitting on each other's laps, laughing and smoking pot in the bedroom.

"Oops! Sorry, I'll come back later," I said, closing the door to give them space.

In the end, however, Tina granted me the best of favors—she made it her mission to get rid of Alice. (And not by whacking her on the head with a giant gong, although we half jokingly considered that as a last resort.)

She confronted Alice in typical Tina fashion, which included lots of yelling, cursing, and drama. Maya, Skye, and I watched wide-eyed from our living room window as Tina and Alice battled it out right there on our front lawn. Tina defended me adamantly, and Alice, of course, defended herself. At several intense moments, I couldn't predict the outcome and wondered if I should join in the catfight.

Several minutes later, to my great relief, Alice had had enough of Tina's harsh words and stormed off. Maya had no clue what was going on—all she knew was that Alice was practically another mommy. Even so, Maya was much amused when Tina stepped through the front door, proud of her accomplishment, and began a theatrical rendition of "Ding Dong! The Witch Is Dead."

With Alice gone for good and Maya back home, we attempted to return to some semblance of normality. We made it a rule not to speak Alice's name, and whenever Maya accidentally mentioned her, she quickly corrected herself. "Look! These are the same socks that Alice—oops! I mean, she who must not be named—wore." Marcus and I did our best to pretend that the woman who was once so involved in our life never existed.

After Tina's departure, Marcus took to using what Maya referred to as "Daddy's medicine" more frequently than I'd ever thought possible. The smell of marijuana permeated the house from early morning to late at night. I brought up my concern that we might get kicked off campus for what amounted to mild but constant illegal activity.

"Where do you think I get this stuff?" he asked, laughing.

"I have no idea. Tina?"

"It's all good, Cozy. Michael from the board sells it to me."

One morning, a few days after Tina returned to Hawaii, Marcus told me he had a surprise for me. I couldn't handle being caught off guard by even one more thing.

"Cozy, I can't do surprises anymore," I said. "Just tell me what it is."

"Cozy, you need to lighten up. This one's a good surprise, I promise!"

That afternoon, I was treated to a wonderful surprise indeed—my Cozy threw me a belated birthday party at our house!

Several months prior, I told him, "It's one of my goals in life to have a surprise birthday party." Of course, you can't plan your own surprise party, but clearly he'd been paying attention. I was blown away by Marcus's thoughtfulness and attention to detail—the guests he knew to invite, the secret Facebook event page, the sparkling clean house, the beautiful birthday cake shaped like a sunflower, the piles and piles of presents, including a colorful tapestry he bought in Berkeley when we were in California without my knowing.

The friends who gathered at the Blue House to celebrate my twenty-ninth birthday showed me I had built a large community in Dallas despite having arrived only five months earlier knowing no one and complaining that this city wasn't right for me. I looked around at a picture-perfect life—

a spacious and beautiful home, a community of wonderful friends, a partner who went out of his way to spoil me, and an almost three-month-old baby who was healthy, happy, and adorable. Everything I'd wished for one year ago sitting on an empty pizza box before a smoldering bonfire with friends in rainy, tropical Hawaii—I had it all and then some.

Underneath it all, however, I was absolutely miserable.

As many gifts as Marcus had given me—and oh, how I love gifts—they couldn't take away the pain of his betrayal. Plus, I was doing practically nothing artistic or creative. My life once full of dancing, directing, and teaching in Hawaii had morphed into being merely a housewife and Church marketer.

I looked happy, I acted happy, and everyone at the party assumed I was happy—but nothing could have been further from the truth. All I could think of was Marcus's affair. More than anything, I wanted to speak honestly and openly with my friends. I wanted to sit down and confide everything that had happened and feel the sisterly support that I so needed instead of simply putting on a façade and a fancy dress. But that wasn't an option. Marcus put his best efforts into planning and hosting my birthday party, and given that my entire life centered around the Church, I had to maintain the image of our "perfect family."

Hours later, everyone gathered round the dazzling sunflower-shaped birthday cake, now lit up with candles, while Marcus and I stood next to each other holding hands.

"Before we sing," Marcus said, "I want to share something with everyone here." A poetic speech of gratitude and praise flowed from him. "Courtney is amazing! She is wonderful. And I absolutely adore the way she brings out the smiles and giggles not only in herself but in everyone around her. Just to see the way she moves with such grace and beauty, the way she dances, and to see her growth over this last year as she became a mother . . ."

He shifted his focus from the crowd to me. "I absolutely honor your dedication and your beauty. Thank you so much for spending your life with me. I thank you for everything. And I just want every dream you have to come true."

By then, many of my friends had started crying, moved by his expression of love for me and by our seemingly powerful soul connection.

"I'm crying! I'm crying!" shrieked our gay friend Ken, while Marcus leaned in to kiss me.

Thanks to Ken, I watched the video of this birthday speech, which caused the most inner conflict. How could I tell what was true? Was this the real Marcus—the man who adored me, praised me, loved me? Every ounce of it appeared real. Nothing seemed forced, fake, or phony. But then why was it so hard to maintain a strong, loving connection? Why did he often say things that were completely the opposite when other people weren't around?

As friends slowly trickled out after the party ended close to midnight, Marcus's love and appreciation for me trickled out the door with them. I had assumed that having Maya around would quell his debilitating tirades, but I was wrong. He didn't seem to care that Maya was anywhere nearby—sometimes he changed victims mid-episode and began yelling at her instead.

Once elementary school resumed in Dallas, I was glad to be back on pickup duty so I could leave the house. By late summer, Marcus had begun heavily monitoring my whereabouts, and my attempts to go anywhere as a free person—a mother's group, the Botanical Garden, a walk with a friend—would instigate an endless philosophical argument about whether I truly needed to leave the house to be happy.

With his newly adopted Southern accent, he said, "I found my happiness living in a filthy, tiny prison cell, so I can tell you for a fact that you're not going to get happy by walking around dem flowers."

"That's great. But I'd like to go the gardens."

"All you ever try to do is leave where you are. You need to learn to just be okay without running to the next pretty place. Look out the windows—there's grass out there! Go take a walk in the backyard. Save the Botanical Garden for when we can go together."

After an hour of defending myself, I no longer had the energy or desire to go out after all. Under the outward façade of Marcus's free spirit and go-with-the-flow vibe, his intent was quite clear: we either left campus together, or I didn't leave at all.

His method of control—so subtle, so sneaky, and riddled with guilt trips about staying home with him for the sake of our relationship—worked like a charm. Friendships paused, outings postponed, activities monitored, whereabouts questioned—my spirit started to die a slow death.

Yet school pickups prevailed. I could leave, as long as I took the baby along for the ride. Being out of the house and away from the Church gave me the space and privacy to call my mom every day. One hot August day, however, I had a more pressing call to make first—I hoped Tina could give me firsthand advice on what I was going through. To my surprise, she answered on the first ring.

"Hey C. What's up?" she said nonchalantly, as if I called her all the time.

"I need to talk to you about something important."

"What is it?"

"When you were in a relationship with Marcus, did he yell at you for hours at a time?"

"What do you mean?"

I explained the current dynamic in our relationship, which had been heavily suppressed while she was visiting.

Tina contemplated my question before answering. "No. I mean, we fought all the time, but I yelled at him just as much."

"Right. Well, I don't yell at him. I just sit and listen. And once it starts, it never seems to end. Even after it does end, I'm unable to do anything for the rest of the day because of how much it affects me."

Tina suddenly sounded concerned. "It sounds like you two need a break from each other."

Her answer surprised me. I expected and almost wanted her to say, *Oh, that will pass. I went through the same thing. Stick it out. It will get better soon!*

"Take a break—like leave Texas?" I had dreamed of leaving him and Texas for months now, but to hear it from Tina was a totally different experience.

"I don't know all the details, C. But I do know that if it's gotten that bad between you guys, you should probably take a break from being together."

The episodes had grown so severe that I started documenting what Marcus said so that if I ever had the courage to leave him, perhaps these hurtful words would ease the heartbreak. Either during or after one of Marcus's episodes, I would escape to the bathroom and sit on the toilet seat with my phone, quickly typing word for word what had just come out of his mouth. While I felt like a traitor, I knew that if I didn't write it all down, I'd try to convince myself that it was all in my head, which it certainly wasn't.

The long list started relatively mild and grew worse as the days passed. The first one: "He calls me 'little girl.'" I found it demeaning when my romantic partner morphed into a stern fatherly figure, replacing my loving nickname with mocking and patronizing, and a slew of insults.

Another line came from a typical argument over his affair with Alice. One afternoon, already past the point of tears, I said, "You're about to lose us! If the baby and I end up leaving you, will it have been worth it?"

Marcus thought about it for a moment before answering in his stone-cold voice. "Yes, I guess it was."

During one of our long, drawn-out daily conversations about Alice, I realized he was manipulating me—right down the checklist of every emotional and psychological technique known to man. Two hours into one such conversation, my head was spinning. I apologized for making his affair into such a big deal, for having such an intense reaction, and for dwelling on it. I felt forced to make these apologies—Marcus was furious that I couldn't just move on.

Bit by bit, he began brainwashing me into believing I was at fault for what had happened. As he put it, I was "destroying everything he came to

Dallas to build." But one day, listening to him mid-monologue, a light bulb switched on in my mind, and I was able to witness the manipulation instead of being engulfed by it. This was truly a turning point, as I would have otherwise followed him down the rabbit hole.

As his manipulative monologues grew wackier and more upside down, I started recording his tangents on my phone instead of trying to write them down during a ten-second pee break. Marcus wasn't aware I was doing this, but Texas is a one-party consent state, so I had a legal right to record our conversations. I had no intention of sharing the recordings publicly—that wasn't the point. I needed a way to prove to myself that the madness was real—that he was, in fact, blaming anyone and everyone but himself for his affair.

Some days, he blamed his former mistress. "Alice made me do it—she practically got down on her knees and begged me. How could I say no? She needed what only I could give her. And look, I saved her marriage! She's still married because of what I did for her."

Some days, he blamed me. "If you hadn't given me that ultimatum about not cheating on you then I wouldn't have had to do it. But you need to know you can't control me."

Other times, he blamed his family. "This has nothing to do with me. My cousin abused me when I was younger."

And he even claimed he had to sleep with Alice because his "healing powers" were too potent to be contained by our relationship. "I've always known I hold the power to heal the world—now if only everyone could have access somehow . . ."

These conversations were neither playful nor light but quite the opposite—heavy, disconnected, and painful—because his ramblings were simply illogical, although always framed as wise, nonnegotiable truths. Adding to my immense frustration was the amount of time wasted—hours every single day—gone and irretrievable. Sometimes while Marcus was on a roll, I'd imagine all the things I could be doing if I wasn't sitting on the couch listening to him. *I could take a ballet class, a yoga class, a barre class. Remember the days when I just decided what I wanted to do and went and did it?*

I tried every excuse I could think of to avoid a lengthy philosophical discussion ("I'm exhausted, it's midnight, I have to work on the bulletin, don't you have work to do?"), but Marcus only grew more furious at these remarks, saying, "Our relationship obviously means nothing to you if you can't take the time to talk."

Though I hardly ever listened to the audio recordings, I needed them after our dynamic flipped so quickly. Just minutes after his devastating rampage, we would be going out for ice cream, shopping for a new bookshelf, or cuddled together in bed, rendering the prior conversation a blur. I wondered if I had imagined it all. The ten-plus hours of his ramblings recorded on my phone gave me a small sense of power, as if I held some kind of asset against him. But they only helped a tiny bit because overall I was sick of the constant roller coaster ride, and I had to find a way out.

One relatively good day in between staff meetings, Marcus, Maya, Skye, and I took a family walk to the corner shopping center about ten minutes away. As we walked inside Maya's favorite bakery chain for a quick snack, I realized I didn't want anything from this place. How many times would I give in to eating unhealthy food just to spend a few more minutes with Marcus? The vegan, herbal tea-drinking Marcus I knew in Hawaii had shape-shifted the moment we landed in Texas into someone with quite different food preferences, which were starting to rub off on me.

"I'm going to Whole Foods instead," I announced. "I'll take the baby with me, get something to go, and meet you guys back here in a few minutes." I felt proud that I was taking ownership of my choices.

"Are you sure, Cozy?" Marcus asked. "Why don't we all just stay together. I'm sure you can find something here you like."

I read through the menu a few times, but the food seemed so heavy. "No, I think I'll go to Whole Foods." With this many people bustling about, he couldn't make much of a scene.

I pushed the stroller quickly across the large parking lot and made a beeline for the salad bar. I was so focused on my mission that I didn't notice my good friend Audrey, a strong, powerful dark-haired woman and self-proclaimed big sister, standing right in front of me. Audrey was a long-time member of the Church and had recently accepted a position as director of programming, which she was due to start the next day. I was thrilled that she was joining the staff. She was the only other woman at the Church besides Cheryl with whom I had developed a close bond.

"Court-nayyyy! Oh, Court-nayyyy!" Audrey called out with her quintessential Southern charm.

I almost didn't recognize her. I spent so much time on Church campus that running into a friend off campus was a rare experience.

"Oh, my sweet Court-nay. Sweet, sweet girl. I'm so glad I'm running into you right now." Compassion oozed from every long, drawn-out word.

Her ultra-warm hello left me confused and even a bit suspicious, as if she knew something I hadn't told her.

She raised her eyebrows. "What on earth is going on with you, sweet girl?"

I laughed nervously. "What do you mean?"

"The other day, I saw you and Marcus out on the balcony over the lobby after services. You had the baby in your arms, and it looked like he was yelling at you or something. You certainly didn't look happy. What was going on? You two okay? I'm concerned."

It took a moment to recall what she was referring to—since that sort of thing happened so often it was hard to keep track—and then I spoke nervously and quickly. "Oh, yes! You saw that? Marcus and I were having a pretty upsetting conversation." I left out the part "about Alice still being at the Church after he had an affair with her." "But everything's okay, sort of. I mean, today, for once, is a good day. And I need to get back to the bakery with Marcus and Maya so—"

"Court-nay! Everything about you is so different from just two weeks ago. Your whole presence has changed. Is your mom okay? Is your dad okay? Is something going on in your family?"

"What? No! They are doing fine! You're right. Something did happen a few weeks ago with Marcus, but I can't tell you about it, although I wish I could. I mean, maybe I could? I don't know."

Audrey leaned in a bit closer. "Sweet girl, you can tell me anything. I give you my word—I will keep it between us."

"Are you sure you won't tell anyone? Because this is super personal information—it could cost me my entire life if this leaked out somehow."

She agreed. And right there next to the checkout line, I told her what had happened, as briefly and to the point as possible.

Just as we were drawing more attention from concerned onlookers, Audrey completely blew up. "WHAT? This is NOT okay. This is NOT okay. At a CHURCH? COURT-NAY, do you realize that what he did with Alice is NOT OKAY?"

She looked like she might explode. I apologized profusely for making her so mad—I had no intention of creating a scene, especially on relatively calm day with Marcus.

"Audrey! Calm down, please. Someone might be here from the Church." I pulled her away from the checkout area and toward the greeting card display while glancing nervously around us.

"First Cheryl and now you!" she continued. "And have you heard about Nina arriving out of nowhere? Did you hear *her* crazy news? This is getting to be too much. I can't believe this is going on at a church, for Christ's sake!"

Seeing Audrey red-faced and fuming, I instantly regretted telling her anything. She wasn't just shocked about my situation but about the culmination of everything different women on campus had all confided—and right when she was counting on her new job for her livelihood.

As a close friend of Cheryl's, Audrey heard all about Cheryl's heartbreak firsthand, and she witnessed how Paul's behavior had crushed Cheryl. And there was more she seemed to know about Nina, too. But what I told her pushed her past the tipping point. She knew Alice well and saw how close she was with our whole family, and she was furious at the manipulative cover-up for the sole purpose of allowing Paul and Marcus to keep their positions of power.

Texts and calls from Marcus were popping up more frequently, as they were ready to leave the bakery and wondering where I was.

"Look, I've got to go. They're waiting for me." I wished I had more time to bring our conversation to a proper close.

I ran across the parking lot, pushing the stroller at top speed back to the bakery, but by the time I arrived, Marcus and Maya were nowhere to be found. I realized the next staff meeting had already started, and I would arrive late and hungry—I never even made it to the salad bar. How was I going to explain this to Marcus?

The next day, I sat in my office attempting to focus on the Church bulletin while Audrey's words swirled in my mind. With an L-shaped desk, I had devised a system to nurse my three-month-old and work on the bulletin at the same time by laying her on a pillow on the desk, using one hand to keep her steadily on her side and the other hand to type. Just as I was beginning my one-handed work session, Audrey walked in and closed the door behind her.

"Court, we need to talk," she said, her tone serious.

In protective big-sister mode, Audrey began to recount her own experience of betrayal by a narcissistic man with whom she was deeply in love and how she wished she had left him sooner. She was almost twenty years older and urged me to not make the same mistake—waiting until I was forty-something to summon the courage to leave.

"I kept waiting for him to change, as he promised, but he never did," she said. "And those years staying with him were the wasted years of my life."

After sharing her story, Audrey finally noticed—and was mightily impressed by—my multitasking. "How do you like working on the bulletin?" she joked.

She knew me well enough to know that sitting in an office designing a Church pamphlet was not my goal in life but rather the most random thing I could be doing on the planet.

"Yeah, I don't love it. But at least it's something."

"Court, I'm sorry, but I have to say it. If you don't get the heck outta here, you're going to be sitting in that same chair, in this same office, working on that same bulletin with not one but two babies a year from now. Mark my words."

My chance encounter with Audrey at Whole Foods spurred her own crisis. As a newly hired employee, she didn't know how to handle the corruption at the Church and was heavily torn about what to do. This job was, as she put it, her "bread and butta." In the end, she decided to confront the board of directors, promising not to bring up my situation but to call their attention to the dichotomy between the Church's values and what happened behind closed doors during "counseling" sessions with Paul or Marcus. And even this confrontation with the board Audrey considered a last resort. She attempted to speak to Paul and other executives at the Church first, but they only brushed her off and twisted things around to make her concerns seem irrelevant.

I found myself in a bind. On one hand, I was elated that Audrey had voluntarily assumed the role of whistle-blower and was determined to expose the truth. On the other, I desperately wanted to heal my relationship with Marcus. Regardless, Audrey was a force to be reckoned with. The next week, she set up a meeting with the board president himself, an older, conservative man in his late seventies.

And then, *poof,* she was gone.

I sat in my office, working one-handedly on the bulletin again, when Paul came in and closed the door.

Geez, how am I ever going to get any work done if I'm constantly interrupted?

Without so much as a hello, he paced back and forth in front of my desk. "You know that Audrey's not working here anymore, right?"

I nodded. Marcus had filled me in the night before—she had been let go.

"And do you know why she no longer works here?" Paul questioned me like a second-grade teacher.

"I think I do. But can you tell me?" I wondered what kind of excuse he'd come up with.

He stopped pacing but couldn't look me in the eye. "Audrey's crazy. She's trying to burn this place down. We can't have someone like her on the team."

"Right," I answered, after an awkward silence. Marcus had used the exact same wording when he told me why she had been fired.

"Do you understand?" Paul asked.

"Yes, sir." I'd never used the phrase before in my life, but it seemed like the most appropriate response.

"If you're going to be fully on board with our team," he continued, "there can be no more communication between you and Audrey. She's gone. She's out of here. Got it?"

"What? But Audrey is my friend—"

"Audrey no longer works here, so I see no reason for you two to communicate," Paul interrupted.

"I can't talk to her at all? Even as a friend?"

"That's correct. I've informed her of this as well. There's way too much for you to focus on here at the Church. None of us have time for people who are not on board with our mission. Do you have the bulletin done yet? I need to review it."

"Almost. I need another few hours," I answered, embarrassed that all of this drama made it hard to focus on my job.

Paul turned around and left as quickly as he came, saying he had a meeting to attend and leaving me with unanswered questions. *Paul had the power to tell me I couldn't speak to my own friend?*

As soon as he was out of sight, I sent Audrey a text, hiding the phone under the desk in case Paul walked by and questioned me. "Were you fired after confronting the board? Did he tell you that we can't talk anymore?"

She wrote back right away. "Yes and yes. But I'm still here for you, Court."

Seventeen Grand Epiphany

In September, my mom came to visit for the fourth time. She'd been a frequent and most welcome guest at the Blue House over the past few months—but this time was different.

I was terrified at what the climate would be like between Marcus and me. In the past, whenever family came to stay with us, he would be on his best behavior, playing the role of World's Perfect Host and giving us all an off-the-charts memorable time together. But that no longer seemed possible. Our relationship at this point could best be summed up with one word: disaster.

My mom would only be staying with us for five days, and then Mom, Skye, and I were headed to New York City for my cousin's wedding. I was excited to return to New York—after my parents sold their apartment and moved to California, I didn't think I'd ever go back. I begged Marcus to come along, but he said he couldn't afford to take any more time off.

To my amazement, despite the emotional rubble that filled every corner of our home, Marcus somehow pulled it together, pretending all was well while my mom was around. He even invited us to perform at an event he was hosting at the Church for World Day of Peace, as long as we chose dance pieces that were "as short as possible"—more specifically, "under three minutes max"—to not take away from his big night.

The dance I planned to perform was *Revolutionary Etude,* choreographed in 1924 by Isadora Duncan, the pioneer of modern dance in America. Isadora Duncan is best known for forging a path of freedom, feminism, and expression through dance at a time when dance was purely for entertainment. *Revolutionary Etude* couldn't have been a more appropriate piece to perform that night, given my circumstances. The choreography depicts breaking free from the chains of destiny and transforming from victim to victor.

Though I'd be performing a dramatic dance to intense music by Russian composer Alexander Scriabin during a Church service about peace, I managed to convince Marcus that in order to have peace, sometimes you have to break through oppression first. He liked the strong, aggressive movements and agreed to the performance, although he put up an argument saying he should be the one dancing this piece onstage. "This dance was clearly made for me!" he said.

After the performance, I made my way to the front row for the rest of the event. The more Marcus preached about peace, the more ill I felt. He discussed peace within homes, peace within families, peace within ourselves—yet nothing he said did he embody during our daily life together as a family. Every well-chosen word contradicted what went on within the confines of our house. And I was supposed to sit there in the front row smiling and looking pretty?

Who am I anymore? Why am I spending my Saturday night sitting in a Church when I have no connection to this place whatsoever? And who is this well-dressed man preaching onstage about peace? He seems like a great family-oriented guy I'd like to get to know. I wonder if he's single! Oh wait, that's my partner. Or is it? I have no freakin' clue who this guy is.

I glanced around the spacious sanctuary at the mostly gray-haired people around me. They were all smiling and laughing at Marcus's effervescence and cute jokes. Completely sucked in, fooled, and mesmerized.

If they knew he'd had an affair with Alice, none of these sweet old people would be here. If only they knew what he did in their favorite Victorian ladies' room, they would be horrified. If only they knew the hours and hours this cute, smiling man in front of them yelled and cursed at me, for no apparent reason other than to purge his deep internal rage, they would all stand up and storm out, circling around me in support and protection.

Interestingly enough, one woman did stand up and storm out, and she continued to support and protect me for many months to follow. Not Cheryl, she was a rare guest at the Church these days. Not Audrey, she never stepped foot on campus again. And certainly not Alice, who stopped coming to the Church as well.

The woman who stormed out that day was a woman named Samantha, or as I called her, Sam. She had hosted our ladies' night at the Blue House months earlier. Like my other friends, Sam was part of the small but slowly growing group of younger people Marcus and I helped recruit—she was nearly double my age but not retired yet, which made her part of the "young" crowd. Sam and I bonded over our love of healthy food, juicing, and cooking. Before I found out about the affair, I had lent Sam one of my favorite recipe books, and she finally returned it a few weeks before the performance.

What I didn't know was that when she knocked on our front door and heard no answer, she stepped inside to leave the book on the bench in our entranceway, as I had instructed her to do if we weren't home. Once inside, Sam heard what no one else from the Church community was privy to, as she happened to walk in during one of the most intense episodes of verbal abuse that had ever occurred in our house—spurred on by the fact that I hadn't folded Maya's laundry. It was always about the laundry.

Marcus and I were far from the front door—in the back bedroom with the door closed—and had no idea that Sam was in our house. When she heard his nonstop yelling and cursing, Sam stood frozen in shock in the entranceway for several minutes, not sure what to do, until Maya came out of her bedroom, eyes puffy and bright red from crying.

As Sam later described to me, Maya attempted to hide her tears to greet her. "Now's not a good time. Daddy's busy."

Sam was worried for Maya, the baby, and me, but she didn't say a word, unsure of how to bring it up. One night a few weeks later, after Marcus had strangely disappeared, I called her looking for him, and we had a heart-to-heart about what she had witnessed.

The World Day of Peace service took place a few days later. In the text message conversation that ensued, Sam wrote, "Courtney, you have to understand that this is domestic abuse." She had to get up and leave in the middle of the service, she said, because she couldn't sit there for one more second—the whole thing made her want to throw up.

"That's how it made me feel to sit through his peace service, too," I said, "but I forced myself."

She continued to text me links to articles in an attempt to help me understand the harsh reality, and even danger, of my situation. In case Marcus read my messages, she wrote things like, "My friend was married to a narcissistic sociopath. You won't believe the kinds of things he did. Read this article!"

Each time she sent a link with her commentary (and she sent plenty), I skimmed each one for only a few seconds, heavily in denial. I didn't want this to be my reality, nor did I want to admit to myself that what Sam was saying might be true.

Going to New York City for my cousin's wedding in mid-September—six weeks since the affair came to light—gave me a welcome break from the emotional intensity of life in Dallas. Even though I was surrounded by my entire extended family for the celebratory occasion, my mind raced constantly. I stressed about whether to leave Dallas, and even though I was fifteen hundred miles away, I felt like I was still back in Texas. On a pre-wedding family walk through Central Park, I felt my phone buzz and saw Marcus's photo pop up on my screen, making me both anxious and relieved at the same time.

"Mom, I need to get this." I frantically handed the stroller over to her and walked away from our large group.

I could hear from the first hello that he wasn't happy. His voice was so quiet I had to strain to hear him over the children, street performers, and tourists passing by from every direction.

"Are you okay?" I asked.

"Not really," he replied, in his now-typical stone-cold voice. "Things are not okay over here."

"What happened?"

"A lot has happened since you left—"

"But I only left two days ago!"

"Right. Well, the entire board now knows what happened, and this whole place could crumble, thanks to you. Because you committed triangulation against Church policies, both Paul and I could be fired, and everything we've worked so hard to build—destroyed."

I began to sweat all over, my heart racing in my chest. Hundreds of feet behind my family, I looked ahead to see my mom at the tail end of the group, pushing the stroller. She happened to turn around at that moment, waving and smiling at me. I couldn't even force a smile in return but motioned for her to keep walking. I was trying to process what Marcus was telling me. How was any of this my fault? He was the one who had an affair!

As he continued, his tone changed dramatically from cold to warm and kind. "I need you to do something for me, and it needs to be done ASAP."

"Oh?"

"I need you to email Paul by the end of the day—preferably right now if you have time—saying that you're doing fine after what happened between me and Alice and that you won't go around committing triangulation anymore with Audrey or anyone involved with the Church. After he reads it, he'll forward it to Audrey so she knows she no longer needs to be involved in our personal matters. This letter will also be presented to the board for their review."

"For their review of what?"

"To see if we can continue staying here. Triangulation is against Church policies, and you are guilty of that. You really messed everything up by getting Audrey involved." Marcus's tone had gone icy again.

"Audrey hadn't even started working at the Church when I told her, and I told her as a friend, not to cause problems! How is talking to my friend privately considered triangulation? That doesn't make any sense!"

"The two of you talking about Church employees behind their backs is triangulation, which is taken very seriously. I need the letter as soon as you can, so we don't lose our home and life together."

I ran quickly to catch up with my mom and filled her in on the conversation. "I need to write this letter right now."

Mom seemed concerned by my frazzled state. "Why don't you just enjoy the rest of the walk and do this tonight? We're only in New York with family for a few days."

"No, I should just do this right now. I'll catch up with you guys later. Just go on without me."

I sat down on a bench and drafted a short email:

To Whom It May Concern:

I am beyond grateful for the support I have received in dealing with an intense emotional shock. As this is not a simple matter, I am taking my time in meditating, chanting, and getting counseling to come to the best possible decision for all of those involved.

I appreciate your support in giving Marcus and me space to work through this without getting any additional people involved or giving any strong opinions since this is something I need to come to on my own in order to truly feel good about my decision.

In Gratitude,
Courtney

I purposely made the letter as vague as possible given that my own close alliance and "big sister" would be reading it. I didn't plan on cutting Audrey out of my life as Paul insisted, but I needed to at least comply with writing the letter to keep things as peaceful as possible back in Dallas. For the rest of the walk, I put my phone away, considering myself unavailable if anyone from Dallas tried to reach me, and attempted to stay present while walking through Central Park with my relatives.

The next day, while strolling through a beautiful garden with my mom and aunt in Sands Point, Long Island, we stopped to admire the expansive views of the bay, and I made the mistake of checking my email. Paul had responded to my letter, and he certainly had a lot to say. I felt extreme anxiety just looking at the length of his email, which he had written with minimal punctuation.

> *This is an excellent letter. Thank you for writing and sharing it. Also I am asking [whether] you can assure me that you will not talk to any congregant of [the Church] anymore about this situation or other personal situations, even if you are pushed by Audrey or anyone?*
>
> *I encourage you to seek outside therapy as you did before in Hawaii.*
>
> *Is this your plan?*
>
> *Everyone involved now knows that if there is any further triangulation that I will have to implement the board policy of no triangulation and let the person go, because in triangulation not everybody is getting to say their side of the story and it is causing a lot of drama . . .*
>
> *There is absolutely no benefit [to] these other people knowing your situation because they are not trained in counseling or psychology or familiar enough with your past or anyone's past including [Marcus's] or mine to make judgments or give advice from a helpful place.*
>
> *With all that said I understand why you seeked helped* [sic] *from Audrey and am giving you the benefit of the doubt as you*

didn't know of that triangulation policy before this all started but we have to have an agreement moving forward.

Paul wanted to know to whom I would be sending the letter, which confused me. I thought he would be forwarding the letter to Audrey. I figured I would have to tell her in advance that he forced me to write it.

As if Paul had read my mind, his email continued:

> *If they ask you if you were forced to send it, which you are not, are you telling them that you wanted to send it? If they press, say I'm sorry this is mine and [Marcus's] business. I don't want them coming to me and saying that you told them you had to write it.*
>
> *I truly want us all to be in peace and move forward and to have learned from this very difficult challenge. Like I've said there are children at stake and other people [who] are trying to have healing in their life that this drama does not need to spill over into.*
>
> *I hope all is going well for you in New York. As always I want the best for everyone involved. Our work is a big work to promote peace and we need all hands on deck and all of us to be heathy and happy and prosperous to accomplish this sacred mission!*
>
> *Blessings!*

"Mom, can I talk to you for a minute?" We fell a few steps behind Aunt Beth. "You're not going to believe this."

I handed over the phone so she could read the email herself. My hands quivered—all communication with Paul had a way of sending me into a panic, especially when he threatened to let me go from the only community I had.

"This is getting out of hand, Courtney," Mom said. "Why are they so obsessed with this whole triangulation thing? I've never even heard that word before. They're the ones who had affairs in the first place—not you! It sounds like they're just trying to find a way to shift focus off themselves and not assume any responsibility."

"You're right." I put my phone away. "I'm not writing him back."

My cousin's wedding took place the next day at the Queens Botanical Garden—a beautiful day, tainted only slightly by a follow-up email from Paul, who wanted to make sure I agreed with everything he said. He said he was waiting eagerly for my response so that we could all move forward together.

I pulled my mom aside and told her I had to make a decision. Should I agree to cut off my entire support system at the Church, as Paul wanted? Or should I risk being let go?

"I think this whole thing is crazy," Mom said.

"Of course, it's crazy! But what should I do? Should I agree?" Like a broken record, I continued to say, "Should I agree? Should I agree?"

Should I agree to something that I absolutely don't agree with at all, in order to keep my job, my home, and my life together with Marcus, whom I love despite his issues? Should I agree so that I can stay on good terms with Paul—my employer and "CEO of the place" where I lived and worked? Should I agree to the male domination and abuse of power I don't know how to stand up to because every time I try, I'm knocked down?

In the midst of my discussion with Mom, Audrey called. We couldn't believe the irony—Audrey would most certainly say not to agree to anything Paul asked of me. I let the call go to voicemail but listened to her message right away, which was four minutes of yelling until the message got cut off.

She was fired up. "These two men are so messed up! You need to get out of there, Courtney! Just pack up your stuff and leave. You won't believe it—Paul has been calling me nonstop to reiterate that I'm no longer allowed to talk to you. So please, I beg of you, don't tell anyone I'm calling you right now. But I want you to know I'm here for you, and I will help you in any way possible. You've got to get out of there. Those two men are very, very messed up. Call me back, when you can—"

After I listened to Audrey's lengthy voicemail, Marcus's smiling photo popped up again. I answered on the first ring.

"We need to hear back from you in writing, right now, to show the board," he said, without so much as a hello. "You need to agree to what Paul wrote in his email—that you won't commit any more triangulation or talk to anyone at the Church about your personal problems. The board is meeting now. Everything we've built together is at stake—you need to send it right now."

Without giving it another thought, I opened up Paul's previous email and wrote back, "Yes. I agree to the above."

As much as it pained me to agree to things I felt were entirely wrong, I had to keep the peace so Marcus wouldn't kill me—figuratively and perhaps even literally. Giving in to the corruption was my only option. Paul's master manipulation techniques weren't lost on me—he had mentioned in one of our counseling sessions that he was a former CIA agent—and he seemed to know exactly what he was doing.

My mom couldn't believe that I responded yes to giving up my entire community of support at the Church. It had never been in my nature to be so subservient. She expressed her concern over how different I seemed lately—the strong young woman she'd raised had been reduced to mere pieces, a ball of nerves, startled whenever my phone buzzed.

On the drive to the airport, we began to seriously discuss the possibility of my leaving Dallas. We agreed I should leave sooner rather than later, before things got any worse—just pack up my and the baby's belongings and go. I didn't have to leave forever, but I needed a break from Marcus. And I could use the time to be with my parents and siblings in California before returning to Hawaii to pick up where I left off. In theory, it sounded like a good plan. Why would I want to stay in Dallas and live in such a treacherous environment if I had somewhere else to go?

My mom and I said our goodbyes at the airport, and I spent the plane ride wondering how I'd even begin to pack up and leave. Would I tell Marcus or just leave quietly while he was hosting one of his Friday night events? And what about the framed photos of us all over the walls that I'd put so much time, energy, and money into making? Would I have the emotional strength to take them down? And then what? Bring them with me? Those photos were every hope and dream I had for my life—just the thought of taking them down made me tear up.

But Mom and Audrey were right—I needed to get out. Why let such a toxic relationship drag on any longer?

Several hours later, however, when I arrived at the Dallas-Fort Worth International Airport, something incredible happened.

Marcus changed. And I mean, he *really* changed.

Unbelievable and yet true. From the moment he picked me up, he was back to being the man I fell in love with in Hawaii, showering me with endless adoration and praise. Coming home was like walking into a bubble of bliss.

"I had a grand epiphany while you were away," he said lovingly. "I really missed you and the baby. It took us being apart for me to realize how much I love you and how important it is to me that we spend the rest of our lives together—forever and ever. So, I've spent the last few days consulting lawyers about getting divorced. Soon, we'll be married! I was thinking we could get married right here at the Church, in the sanctuary."

I practically fainted. "Really?" I was truly amazed at this new and improved Marcus.

He had hidden surprises and sprinkled gifts throughout our home, just like he had when I moved to Dallas six months prior. All the thoughts I had on the plane dissipated as he gave me the tour of our "new" home where are "new life together" would begin, from this moment onward.

Of all his surprises, what impressed me most was a to-do list he wrote on a huge whiteboard he wheeled into our living room. I have a thing for to-do lists—I always have, for as long as I can remember. As soon as I learned to write words in preschool, I was writing to-do lists, attempting to organize my daily life into a routine I could see on paper. When Marcus and I first met, I amazed him with my list-writing abilities—I made separate lists for each life category and organized each one by priority, repeating the process every day as things got completed. He called me a list-writing expert and even asked to take lessons.

So, he must have known I'd be ecstatic when he wheeled a giant whiteboard right into our living room, entitled "The Cozy Family Checklist," and sectioned it out for everyone in our family, writing weekly lists of what he guessed was most important to each of us. Next to each item was an empty checkbox for us to mark off as we completed each task.

In addition to our individual lists, the biggest chunk of the massive whiteboard was reserved for "Cozy Projects," under which Marcus and my collaborative ideas were listed, with detailed tasks under each heading. There was the Hawaii retreat we were planning to host next winter, the cooking classes we would be teaching together at the Church, and the workshops we were creating to combine dance with sound healing.

The tiny section at the bottom of the white board for Skye read: take a bath (one checkbox), baby massage (three checkboxes), Mommy-baby yoga (three checkboxes), Daddy-baby drumming (two checkboxes), play with Sissy (five checkboxes).

The best part was what he had written under my list, as if he knew me better than I knew myself. I read aloud as Marcus stood beaming next to me. "Chant (five boxes), meditate (five boxes), Pilates exercises (three boxes), jump on trampoline (four boxes), green smoothie (five boxes), Marcus (five—). Wait, why are you listed under my to-do list?"

Marcus smiled a big cheeky grin, waiting for me to figure it out. He wrapped his arms around me. "You can adjust the number of checkboxes to your liking, but I thought I'd start with five for now."

The next morning, I called my mom to tell her that things were different. "Marcus really changed while I was gone. I'm not going to leave so quickly. I need to give it more time before I can make a decision about whether to leave or not."

Mom was relieved that things were going better for us.

In fact, things were getting better every day. The day after I returned to Dallas, I received a call from a director of a dance company who was looking for an additional dancer for an upcoming performance at a large and reputable theater—the same stage that hosted Broadway tours. In all the months I'd lived in Texas, I hadn't done a single thing for my dance career besides dancing in Marcus's events at the Church, nor had I taken a single dance class, which was something I did regularly throughout my life.

The director, a woman named Roma, had heard about me from an elderly friend of mine at the Church who knew I used to be a professional dancer. Roma wanted to choreograph a solo role for me. Things were clicking into place! I agreed to perform that December and to attend regular rehearsals beginning in early October.

Excited as a little kid, I jumped up and down with joy in our front yard. Marcus and Maya jumped along with me, ecstatic over "Mommy Courtney's great news."

Eighteen An Exit Plan

And, of course, the bubble of bliss burst in a matter of days.

The drama on campus went from bad to worse—now Marcus's job was truly on the line. In early October, entire board meetings were devoted to reviewing his unethical actions. The extreme stress on Marcus led to extreme rage and resentment toward me, day in and day out.

My sole focus became survival—keeping the baby and me safe while maintaining the image of our "sweet, perfect family" whenever I went into the Church. Every day, I woke up and told myself, *This will be a good day. Please let this be a good day.* And then I'd do my best to avoid Marcus or at least avoid being alone with him lest I face another explosion. According to him, everything going down was my fault. If only I hadn't told Audrey, none of this would be happening.

If he had never slept with Alice in the first place, none of this would be happening either.

Marcus refused to take an ounce of responsibility for his actions, dumping all of the blame on me at every opportunity. I needed space away from him and our house to think. Since we lived and worked on the Church campus, we were in close quarters all the time. I wasn't the free person I was back in Hawaii, and I couldn't just get in our car and drive somewhere, although I often tried. Marcus always wanted me to stay on campus unless we left together. School pickups weren't until the afternoon—I wanted a way to leave earlier.

Sam sent me one of her typical texts, saying, "I'm worried about you—how are you doing?" She suggested we meet for a walk. We made a plan for her to come to the Blue House at ten on Thursday morning, and we'd take a brisk walk around the neighborhood together. It didn't occur to me to check in with Marcus. It's not like I needed him to watch the baby because she was always my responsibility anyway.

On Thursday morning, when I mentioned that Sam was coming over for a walk, he wasn't happy.

"So now you're making plans behind my back? Trying to sneak off without me knowing?"

I wished I'd had my phone handy so I could start recording. "No, I'm not trying to sneak off without you knowing. I'm going on a walk—for exercise—with Sam. And I'm telling you about it right now. We just made this plan a few days ago."

"How come you didn't invite me on the walk? I'm the one who recruited Sam to the Church, not you. Since when are you even friends with her?"

"Of course, I would've invited you, but I know how busy you are, and you're always telling me I'm a huge distraction. So, I thought I'd just get some exercise with a friend. And yes, Sam has been my friend since she joined the Church. I'm sorry this is so upsetting, but it's just a walk."

Marcus and I continued to argue about whether it was in "our best interests" for me to go on a walk with Sam without him. Underneath his guilt trips for leaving him out, I perceived clearly why he didn't want me to spend time alone with her. She was smart, she was strong, and she could see right through Marcus—he didn't fool her one bit. She had my best interests at heart, while Marcus had only his.

Sam showed up right at ten wearing yoga pants and sneakers, and I was dressed the same, with the addition of a baby strapped to me. Marcus gave her a brief hello, obviously still annoyed at my disobedience, and then headed over to the Church. Sam and I walked along the immaculate tree-lined streets amid the ginormous mansions of the wealthy neighborhood until the stifling heat made us turn back around.

Sam was an incredible listener, and because she no longer attended Church services after what she had witnessed at our house, talking to her couldn't be considered triangulation. Rather than tell me what to do about my relationship problems, she posed questions that helped me come to my own conclusions.

"Would you be fine if the dynamic between you stays the same, if he continues to yell at you daily for the next, say, thirty years?"

"No! Of course not."

"What if he continues to have affairs with other women? Would you be okay with that?"

"Are you crazy? No!"

"How would you feel if he never actually marries you? Are you okay staying with him and not being married?"

"No! We need to get married if we're going to stay together, but he knows that. He knows how much marriage means to me."

"If he knows how much marriage means to you, why hasn't he proposed?"

"Everyone at the Church already thinks we're married."

"And you're okay with that?"

"Well, no. You're right. I'm not."

I went on to tell Sam about my dream—the beautiful, harmonious life that Marcus and I were building together, at least in theory. A part of me still believed in the dream and couldn't handle the devastation of letting it go—not until I truly was certain I couldn't make it work somehow.

I continued to meet Sam for walks around the neighborhood, except I had to disguise them as walks for exercise, just me and the baby. Sam would meet us several blocks from our house, and we'd find back roads to walk on. She thought this was nuts but agreed to keep our meetups a tight secret.

Another person I was meeting secretly was Audrey. Her advice often felt too forceful, too fired up, and just too much in general, but she was so insistent on meeting that I gave in a few times, breaking my agreement with Paul. Trips to the "chiropractor" turned into top-secret lunch dates with her. After learning of Marcus's ten-year stint in prison, Audrey was so worried about my safety that she was ready to buy my plane ticket right then.

But I wasn't ready to go. Almost, but not yet.

I vacillated every ten minutes. One minute, I was resolved: *I need to go. I need to start writing a list of what I need to do to leave.* But then, while I was writing the list, Marcus would switch back to his over-the-top kind and loving personality. *This may actually work, thank God, because I don't have the strength to leave anyway.*

I couldn't think clearly—I was wrung out from adjusting to being a new mother, to being in a new city, and to being a victim of severe emotional and verbal abuse by the person I trusted and loved most in the world. I kept telling myself, *I don't want to rush into a bad decision. This decision is going to affect my entire future. If I'm going to leave him, I need to be sure it's the right thing to do.*

Many other things hinged on my decision, one of which was the upcoming dance performance. I had started rehearsals and was so happy to be dancing again. Roma invited me to take company class, and if I stayed, I could be a part of a dance company again. She was counting on me for the December performance. How could I just abandon her? Maybe the best choice would be to stick it out until after the performance.

I also had to face the issue of how heavily involved our family was in the Church. Baby Skye was not just my baby—she was the Church's baby, too. Everyone considered us a model of a loving, tight-knit, churchgoing family. If I left with the baby, the entire Church might be affected. Was I even allowed to leave?

I decided to call my trusted elderly Buddhist leader for her advice. I was embarrassed to tell her about Marcus's affair since she'd seen us so happy together. I must have taken on the belief that his affair was my fault after all because I found myself apologizing for what happened as if I'd been the one who'd cheated.

She didn't sound one bit shocked. "I've been practicing Buddhism for over fifty years. Trust me, I've heard everything."

Her advice was simple and true. "Courtney, you need to chant to make a decision. Until you can come to your own decision about whether to stay with him or leave, your whole life is on hold, and that's not beneficial to anyone. Chant to be so clear about what to do that you have no question you're making the best decision for your life and your baby's life. This can't come from anyone else. It has to come from you. And whatever you decide, you have to fully commit to it."

That evening, as Marcus wrapped up work, I sat on the dreaded gray couch in his office nursing Skye to sleep. Maya sat next door in my office watching a movie on her iPad. Classes had ended for the night, and the four of us were the only people in the building. This is what our evenings had come to—Marcus, Maya, and me, all doing our own thing, completely disconnected from each other—a stark difference from the days in Hawaii when we lived in my apartment, laughing, playing, and spending hours of quality time together.

Marcus had begun tidying his desk to perfection, which meant we were about to head home. Maya was up past her bedtime, and neither of us had even checked to see if she'd done her homework. I started to gather my things, but then Marcus did something strange. He walked over to the gray couch, sat down without a word, and stared blankly at the wall in front of us.

"Are you okay?" I asked him, concerned.

He didn't speak but continued to stare, the whites of his eyes blurry and yellow from staring at the computer screen. Unsure of what to do, I transferred sleeping Skye into her car seat and then left to use the bathroom, figuring that Marcus would bounce back soon enough. When I returned, he hadn't moved an inch. He wasn't blinking—I wasn't even sure he was breathing.

"Hey, Cozy, are you okay? You're freaking me out!" I gently shook his shoulders. "Move! Say something!"

In a trance, still staring at the wall, he spoke in a slow voice that sounded like Eeyore from *Winnie-the-Pooh*. "I'm feeling really sad, Cozy."

"What are you sad about, Cozy? I'm here for you."

Thanks to his suggestion, I had just completed a five-day course in nonviolent communication at the Church where I learned important communication skills, one of which was being fully present for someone else and their needs and desires. I decided to use this conversation as good practice. He was always the one counseling me in our relationship, and maybe this time I could finally help him. God knows he desperately needed some help.

Still staring at the wall, Marcus said, "You should just leave me, Cozy. Then I'll be alone and depressed again."

"What?" I asked, shocked. *How did he know I was thinking of leaving? I thought I was keeping all of that a secret.*

"Just go. Leave. Be like all the other women I've ever loved and leave me. Then I'll be alone again. And I'll just disappear. I'll vanish into the ether, and no one will even notice I've gone forever."

His statement freaked me out. I'd never heard him quite this depressed before. I tried to lighten the mood.

"Oh, Cozy, stop being silly. I'm not leaving you! Where did you get that crazy idea? Plus, you have Maya, remember? Who will raise her if you just disappear? You're everything to her."

"Tina will take her in. I'm having a vision as we speak. Maya will go back to Hawaii and live with Tina—that's where she wants to be anyway. You and Skye will go live in California with your parents, and everyone will be so much better off without me. You'll be busy with your dance career, and your mom will raise Skye, and that will be the best thing for her. Your mom is amazing. I can see it in front of my eyes. Everyone is happy without me."

Tears were now streaming down Marcus's face, yet the rest of him remained frozen. I watched as the weight of each tear, one after the next, dropped off his chin and onto his lap. For a moment, I thought his "vision" was pretty accurate—we probably would be happier without him. And my mom would love to watch Skye during the day while I went back to my career. But it absolutely killed me to see him this sad.

"Look, I don't want to leave," I said quietly. "I want to stay together and make it work. That's what I truly want, deep in my heart. But it hasn't been working, so I don't know what to do anymore."

Marcus began an all-encompassing philosophical monologue—one that went on for the next two and a half hours. I wish I could remember every topic he touched on, but most of what he said went in one ear and out the other. For a good hour, he spoke about whether or not we truly have callings and why he didn't believe in callings, and so everything I've ever felt was a calling in life—living in Hawaii or pursuing a dance career—was merely my ego running the show. I couldn't disagree more, but I couldn't get a word in during his endless tangent.

Every half hour, I interrupted him. "Shouldn't we get Maya to bed? It's getting late."

But Marcus said our conversation was more important—though I wouldn't have called his nonstop rambling a "conversation" at all. By 11:15 p.m., all I wanted was to go to sleep. His ideas were so bizarre he seemed insane. By the end of nearly three hours, I knew I needed to leave him as soon as possible.

Knowing he was about to lose me, Marcus asked something he'd never asked after one of his tangents. "You still want to marry me, right?"

Was this some kind of joke? I didn't respond but just stared at him, confused.

"You do still want to marry me, right Cozy?"

No, not really.

Then I looked at his face, so sad, so worn, and strangely, so *old.* He looked like a sixty-year-old man rather than the young, charming, sparkly guy I once knew. Or maybe it was just the lighting. Either way, he looked so depressed, and we were obviously so incompatible—and I had just wasted three hours of my life listening to him ramble—why the heck would I ever want to marry him? Just to torture myself?

Scared of the consequences of a wrong answer, I shocked even myself by answering, "Yes."

Marcus seemed pleased, even a little cheered up, and we finally scooped up Maya, locked the building, and made our way back home.

The promise of marriage had kept me hooked, a prize to be awarded when I finally earned the status.

Months earlier, Marcus told me flat out, "You have to earn being my wife. You have to show me that you know how to be a wife before I can propose. And don't you think for one second that having a baby with me means I'm going to marry you. Just look at the evidence—that's never happened before."

He'd had at least three children from at least three different women, and he had yet to marry any of them. I liked to think I was the closest to being married to him—he already had the ring after all—but though I'd honed my towel-perfecting abilities to perfection, I was no closer to wearing my great-grandmother's diamond ring. A carrot on a string, dangling right in front of me, just out of reach.

Marcus knew how much marriage meant to me—stability, commitment, and security. Most of all, it meant I was finally good enough to be chosen and worthy of his public devotion. Our baby was now four months old, yet Marcus adamantly refused to post photos of us all together on social media, and the "rules" I'd agreed to on Mariana's balcony almost a year earlier hadn't changed. Skye and I were virtually invisible. The hope of marriage had been the glue that kept us together, but now everything had come apart at the seams.

Two days later, I woke up on a tiny cot with Skye's head tucked under my armpit in a dark, closet-sized room with thick dust and dirt covering the walls and carpet. *Where the heck was I?*

After a moment, I recalled what had happened the night before. I was staying with one of Cheryl's friends who was giving me refuge from the Blue

House. I'd made the mistake of telling Marcus that I wanted to go back to Hawaii. Infuriated, he screamed at me that I might as well pack up and leave right then.

"Really, just get out of here this fucking minute!" He stormed toward me, morphing into the version of Marcus that had picked me up by the neck a month prior.

Terrified to be alone with him, I ran into the bathroom with the baby in my arms and locked the door. I texted Cheryl, who was still one my closest allies, to see if I could stay at her place, but she was out of town at a spiritual growth conference and didn't have a spare key. Her friend Susan, however, would take me in. I creeped out of our bedroom through the back door, climbed into our car—I still had the key after picking up Maya from school—and drove to the address Cheryl had sent me, chanting and crying the whole way.

While the outside of Susan's house resembled the surrounding suburban area, the inside looked like it hadn't been cleaned in twenty years. I'm not sure why Cheryl thought this was a good option for me and my infant, but at least I had a place to go. I left the Blue House so quickly, grabbing just a handful of diapers and nothing else, that I didn't think to call any of my other friends or a domestic violence shelter for refuge.

Susan was a nice woman who had her own set of troubles. She was gracious and apologized profusely for the state of her house, which I helped her clean during the two days I stayed there.

While I was busy vacuuming, sweeping, and nursing, Marcus left me a handful of messages saying he was worried about me. He couldn't understand why I left when he clearly told me how much he supported my going back to Hawaii—he would even try to get his job transferred to a branch of the Church in Honolulu.

None of what he said made any sense. Everything was completely flipped around. He'd had a massive, angry explosion! But according to him, I was the one with the issues. It was truly crazymaking.

I returned to the Blue House two days later to a kind and calmed-down version of Marcus who expressed his concern about my "erratic behavior," refusing to acknowledge that his violent rage was what had compelled my departure in the first place.

Back at the Church, annual Personal Growth Week, which took place every fall, was underway. Marcus stayed busy keeping the snack table stocked and moving around tables and chairs for the various classes, so I barely saw him that week at all.

Paul had granted me a scholarship to attend as many classes as I wanted, so I signed up for everything I could squeeze in, bringing along four-month-old Skye to every class, including "Healing and Wholeness," "Prosperity," and "Finding Your Purpose." During these classes, I realized something profound. Unless I left Marcus, this would be my life—live on campus, act as though all is well, suffer from various forms of abuse, go to an array of classes and events to heal, suffer some more, attend more events, and so on. If I stayed with him, I was signing up for this cycle.

One more emergency stay at Susan's and I made up my mind—I was leaving Marcus for good. I couldn't live like this anymore—the constant state of terror, the emotional roller coaster, the escapes with Skye to random people's homes out of fear that Marcus might kill us.

Some of my friends painted this as an all-too-real possibility: "You know, Courtney, if you stay with him, he will eventually kill you. And he'll walk away completely innocent. 'She slipped and fell,' he'll say."

I thought back to my life in Hawaii when I could wake up, feel good, and have a happy, normal day. My life had become so out of control. *I just need to get away from Marcus and back to Hawaii.*

But leaving required the board's approval. Our family was so entrenched in the Church that I couldn't just buy a plane ticket and go—that would upset hundreds of people. Instead, I had to submit a "plan of leaving" to Paul so he could show the board, which meant my exit would be twisted, turned, and fluffed as much as possible to avoid waves within the community—or even better, so my exit could be strategized in such a way that loyal churchgoers wouldn't even notice that Skye and I were gone.

Paul, however, supported my leaving. I'd sent him way too many emergency text messages when things were getting out of hand at the Blue House, and the last thing he wanted was a domestic violence blowup on Church property, which would make him look terrible for hiring Marcus, whom he had just promoted—in the midst of all this chaos—to assistant minister. He even told me that although he thought I was probably safe with Marcus, in all his years working for the CIA, "double homicides always happen when you least expect them."

I often wondered why Paul didn't step up in his role as senior minister to help me, despite knowing what was going on in our house. The best explanation I came up with is that he and Marcus were out to save each other's backs at any cost. They both had affairs with church congregants and knew that if news continued to leak, they would be instantly fired, their careers and reputations forever ruined.

Besides submitting an exit plan, I also had to tell Marcus that I was leaving him. I was way too scared to tell him alone, so I asked Paul if we could have a counseling session to address the matter, to which he agreed. The session itself was both torturous and plain ridiculous—both men blamed me for "breaking agreements" by involving outsiders in my personal problems.

As it turned out, breaking the news to Marcus wasn't as bad as I expected. In fact, he agreed that it was best for us to take some time apart. Paul helped us figure out how to minimize our time together until I left in order to avoid any more drama. Marcus and Maya would leave for a ten-day trip to the church's Houston branch on October 31, which was six days away. While they were gone, I would pack up. I would still teach my bimonthly cooking class and lead a full-moon women's circle—two events that already had paid sign-ups—plus I'd continue working on the bulletin until November 10. My mom would fly to Dallas to help, and I'd fly to

California where I'd spend a month visiting my immediate family before returning to Hawaii to restart my life.

The few days after Marcus found out I was leaving him were some of the strangest days of my life, including a spontaneous family trip to the Texas State Fair, where we went all out, skipping and dancing through the overcrowded stadium, one last hurrah. Knowing we were about to separate made us both suddenly so in love with each other in the most bittersweet and nostalgic sort of way.

"Cozy, I don't know if I can really do this. I'm going to miss you so much," I said, as my eyes welled up with tears.

Marcus held me tightly for a good five minutes as the bright lights of the fair swirled around us. I closed my eyes and went back a year and a half to the first time he hugged me like that after we'd just met. I smiled as I remembered how much he creeped me out at first, and how deeply I fell in love with him when we danced together in the moon piece, and then how it had all wholly fallen apart.

I nuzzled my head into his shirt like a puppy, trying to soak in every last bit of him that I could, crafting a sensory memory of his smell, his skin, his spirit that I could store inside of me, already anticipating the heartbreak I was about to feel in every fiber of my being. And still, I wouldn't budge—my plan of exit was in writing and in the board's hands. I couldn't change my mind even if I wanted to.

Nineteen The Crucial Moment

One weekend remained before Marcus drove to Houston. According to a previous discussion in Paul's office, Marcus and I were supposed to spend as much as time as possible away from each other to avoid any more emergency situations. As it worked out, I had enrolled in another intensive personal growth seminar for the weekend at a hotel ballroom in downtown Dallas.

The weekend workshop, which drew several hundred people, was about designing a life you love and featured a well-known expert in personal development. This intensive three-day immersion promised to help me gain clarity on my goals and dreams and how to achieve them. Cheryl, Sam, and a number of others from the Church were also in attendance.

I asked Cheryl if Skye and I could sleep at her house and ride with her to and from the event during those three days. A day before the workshop began, however, she announced she'd be staying at a friend's house within walking distance of the hotel, but there wasn't enough room for all of us. I would have to stay with Marcus and find a way to and from downtown Dallas. We only had one vehicle between us—the old black Volvo SUV that belonged to the church, which Paul had been renting to us—so I couldn't keep our family car from seven in the morning until ten at night.

My best idea was to convince Marcus to attend the workshop with me so we could ride together, to which he immediately agreed. He also agreed to let me stay the weekend at the Blue House. His mother was visiting from Missouri—I figured he wanted her to see the baby, which is why he didn't give me a hard time about altering our agreement to stay away from each other.

As we walked down the wide, carpeted hallway into the hotel ballroom, Marcus let me know he was going to "do his own thing" this weekend so that he could get as much as possible out of the workshop and focus on building his dreams—without me. In response, I began crying, and I barely stopped crying for the next three days.

Marcus sat far from me and Skye for most of the workshop, as if we were strangers. During the sessions, we were given assignments to write out our dream lives in detail and then share them aloud with the person sitting next to us at least a dozen times over the three days. I couldn't get through the first sentence without starting to cry. Our loving family was such a major part of my dream, and now it was clear as day that my dream had crumbled.

During the three days, Marcus never once offered to help with Skye despite not paying for a ticket to attend the workshop in the first place. He just blended in with the crowd and let himself in, and not only that, after the first morning session, he used his overflowing charm to worm his way into the VIP section.

On day three, Maya tagged along with us because her grandmother had gone home to Missouri. Marcus went to the VIP section, leaving Maya, Skye, and me on our own again. We parked ourselves on the floor in a back corner—diaper bag, toys, and blankets sprawled across the carpet. All I wanted to do was sit there on the dirty, uncomfortable floor and eat. I was ravenous. I kept munching away on snacks I'd packed for the day, listening as best I could to the inspirational stories and lessons. Though I'd paid a hefty sum to attend, I was getting nothing out of this workshop, despite filling an entire notebook, because I couldn't seem to absorb the motivational content while my relationship was falling apart.

When the lunch break started, willing to try any tactic to get Marcus's attention, I brought Maya and Skye with me to tap on his shoulder and surprise him from behind.

"How about we all go for a walk?" I asked.

Seeing Maya and Skye's eager, adorable faces, he agreed. We walked down the street together but separated by a massive chasm. Marcus's body seemed made of ice, sending a rush of freezing air that shocked me to my core. But then, like a light at the end of a dark tunnel, Cheryl appeared, walking toward us. I was so relieved to see her.

"Well, hey y'all!" she called out.

Fabulous as ever, Cheryl wore a black-and-white patterned dress and jewelry galore. She walked right up to Marcus, locked her eyes with his, and kissed him on the lips. And as if that sort of thing happened every day, she continued her walk back toward the hotel.

"I want to get back early to get a good seat!" she said, waving goodbye.

I stopped dead in my tracks. Cheryl, too? Though only a peck—a long, drawn out peck—this was my closest friend and confidante. *How could this possibly be happening?*

I confronted Marcus right away, which launched him into another fiery tirade. Onlookers seemed concerned. I imagined what must be going through their heads: *Why is she staying with this crazy man? What is wrong with her? Why is she putting herself and her baby through this? Should I try to intervene or call the police?*

Back at the hotel, I skipped the afternoon session and sent Cheryl a text message. "Why did you kiss Marcus? I'm incredibly hurt. You know how fragile I am after what happened with Alice. Why would you do that?"

Cheryl wrote back an apology. "Oh sweetie, I'm so sorry! I kiss all men like that. I didn't mean to upset you. That's just my style."

When I later asked Marcus if what she said was accurate, he answered, "Yeah, she kisses me all the time. It's just a friendly thing—I told you you're paranoid."

"If that's true, how come I've never seen her kiss you before?"

"She only does it when you're not around."

"And is it ever more than just a peck?"

"Usually just a peck, Cozy!" He chuckled.

"Usually?" I asked.

"Well, there was that one time . . ." Marcus smiled. "But it was just once."

I had reached rock bottom. I could trust no one. Even my closest friend had betrayed me. How could things possibly get any worse?

After the workshop concluded on Sunday night, I asked Marcus to drive me straight home, skipping the celebratory dinner. I was so exhausted that I couldn't imagine sitting upright at a restaurant. All I wanted to do was collapse on our bed.

Once inside our house, I did just that. Skye was unusually quiet while she watched me with curiosity from her car seat. I lay on the bed, arms and legs outstretched, took a deep breath, and closed my eyes. Sprawled out, I took stock of the past three days. I snacked nonstop all day. I rode crest after crest of an emotional roller coaster, crying nearly constantly. And although I hadn't done anything but sit all day, I was thoroughly exhausted. A crystal-clear inner knowing arose. *I'm pregnant.*

As soon as the realization hit, I started freaking out. *How could this be?* Marcus and I had continued an intimate relationship in the month since I returned from New York, but we had been careful 90 percent of the time. I tried to remember every instance over the past few weeks to pinpoint when I might have conceived, but everything blurred together. My period hadn't yet returned, and I was still nursing a four-month-old around the clock. How could I possibly be pregnant, especially now that I was leaving him? Was this some kind of joke?

I walked into the bathroom, searching for a pregnancy test in the cabinets. I had picked up a few from the Dollar Store. Like extra hair ties or menstrual pads, pregnancy tests seemed like a good thing to have in stock. I unwrapped the small test, which looked so cheap and dinky it resembled a toy more than a predictive tool. I peed in a cup, dipped the little pink and white stick, and waited. The instructions advised taking the test in the morning when hormone levels are higher, but I needed confirmation right away.

Sixty seconds later, two parallel pink lines. Pregnant.

I called Marcus. "You have to come home right now. I need you here, now."

"We'll be back soon."

Ten minutes, twenty minutes, thirty minutes. He still wasn't back. When I finally heard the front door, I ran to him and pulled him into our blue-tiled bathroom, our favorite hangout back when we still liked each other.

"You have to see this for yourself." I motioned to the small test on the counter.

Marcus glanced at it but didn't say anything.

"I'm pregnant!"

Still, he said nothing, his expression unmoved.

"Don't you have anything to say?" I asked, completely exasperated.

"No, not really." He turned to leave.

"Where are you going?" I asked, anger rising.

"Maya's waiting for me. I told her we'd watch a movie."

A few minutes later, the two of them came skipping into the bedroom and climbed onto our bed to watch a movie on a laptop my dad had given Marcus. Maya didn't know what I'd just found out, and I certainly didn't tell her.

"Mommy Courtney! Mommy Courtney!" she called cheerily. "Come and join us!"

I sat on the bathroom floor and googled "abortion Dallas."

Sit and watch a movie—now?

I joined them not because I had any desire or capacity to watch a movie but because I desperately needed some kind of support—and sitting next to Marcus was the best option I had. Though I inched myself closer to him, he remained distant and unaffectionate, as if I were that homeless person on a subway car from whom everyone recoils due to the unimaginable stench.

Even Maya noticed. "Daddy, why don't you put your arm around your Cozy?"

"I'm comfortable just like this, sweetie." He wrapped both of his arms around her instead.

The next morning, I took another pregnancy test. Still pregnant. When Marcus came strutting past me into the bathroom, I showed him the second test, desperate for some kind of response.

"Look! I'm pregnant," I shoved the plastic stick into his hand. "I took a second test to confirm it. I'm not making this up—it's real!"

"Interesting," he muttered, more to himself than to me. "This baby will be born a few months after Paul's baby."

I nearly fell over. Paul was having a baby? With whom?

"Nina's pregnant," he said, reading my mind.

"WHAT? Nina's pregnant?" I couldn't wrap my head around this one so quickly.

"Yes, and I have to run now. I need to pick up his camera—I'm going to be out at the Botanical Garden all day to photograph his proposal to her in the pumpkin patch so I—"

"What?" I interrupted. "Paul is proposing?"

"Courtney, come on. Yes, he's proposing to her at the Botanical Garden, and I need to go. I've been helping him plan this for weeks."

"But what about me? I'm pregnant, too!"

Marcus shook his head. "I've never had that happen twice with the same woman."

He turned to leave, but I had to teach my yoga class that morning at the Church and had been counting on him to watch Skye. Afterward, I had a full day of appointments and needed the car, including a final meeting with Roma, the director of the dance company. Part of our written "plan of leaving" gave me the car for the whole day.

"Wait! Marcus, I need to talk to you about—"

But he was already out the front door.

I went into a panic. I couldn't deal with the unanswered questions and painful emotions flooding my system because I first had to figure out the yoga situation. Thankfully, the Church receptionist agreed to watch Skye while I taught.

The moment class ended, I resumed researching my abortion options. I refused to allow myself to consider keeping the baby given our imminent separation. But besides that, Marcus had given me an additional reason to end the pregnancy. The night before, I'd woken him up to ask him something important.

"Since I'm pregnant, maybe we should rethink our plan. Maybe I should just stay here and not leave after all. What do you think?"

"No, that's not possible," he said. "You can't stay here anymore. You need to stick with the plan and leave."

"But I'm pregnant! I have a baby growing inside of me, right now!"

"Deal with it." He rolled on his side and went back to sleep.

So, deal with it I would. I booked an appointment for the next available opening on Thursday and the required second appointment on Friday. There was only one problem—an abortion cost seven hundred dollars. I texted Marcus to ask if he'd pay half, but he didn't respond.

Without Marcus's support and in the midst of a nervous breakdown, I still had to figure out a way to get to several important appointments. I continued to text him to ask him to bring the car back. Though he said he would, he never showed up.

One of my appointments was therapy at 3 p.m., the first and only session I had scheduled during the entire time I lived in Dallas. After Marcus's detached response to my second pregnancy, I needed to talk to someone. Because my therapist was a woman named Margaret who taught Bible classes at the Church—and whose husband sat on the board of directors—this session was technically "illegal" and went against my agreement with Paul. But Margaret happened to be a licensed counselor by profession, and she promised to keep whatever I told her confidential.

Without a car, I was still pacing our driveway at 3:04 p.m. After Marcus continued to decline my calls, I called Margaret to tell her I was trying to figure out how to get to her office. She kindly responded that I would need to arrive by 3:30 p.m. to have the session.

Marcus, who was still devoted to Paul and Nina's fairy-tale proposal, sent me his final word on the car issue: "Take an Uber."

I hadn't even thought of Uber.

I walked into Margaret's office at exactly 3:30 p.m. When she saw what a ball of stress and anxiety I was, she offered to drive me and Skye home after our session, which could run late so I would have the full hour I needed. I was beyond grateful—I considered Margaret to be my last and only lifeline.

Though my original intention had been to address my grief over Marcus's betrayal with Alice, I could only focus on what felt most pressing. I told her I was leaving Dallas on November 10—Marcus and I were splitting up because I found him impossible to be with, despite trying as hard as I could to make it work.

"I'm planning on having an abortion in a few days," I admitted, "because there's no way I could have another baby if I'm going to be a single mom."

Just saying those words—single mom—made me shutter.

Margaret agreed with my decision. In her slow Southern twang, she replied, "Having just one baby will make you more marriable."

"Oh, really?" I hadn't considered that.

During the hour, I sensed Margaret was on my side and that I could trust her with anything. She was exactly my mom's age and even called herself "Skye's bonus grandma." Thanks to her, I felt that somehow everything would be okay. She even offered to drive me to the abortion clinic and watch Skye during and after the procedure. *Finally, someone who truly has my back.*

Once in Margaret's car, Skye started screaming at deafening decibels. As soon as Margaret turned into the Church parking lot, I unstrapped Skye from her car seat and held her in an attempt to calm her down. I assumed Margaret would drive me right to the Blue House driveway, but instead she stopped at the edge of the Church parking lot, several hundred feet from our house.

"I can see Marcus is up there near the house," she said. "I'd feel better just dropping you off here. Is that okay with you? Can you walk from here? I don't want anyone seeing you getting out of my car or knowing you just had a therapy session, given the circumstances."

I agreed and plopped Skye back in her car seat and left the car quickly, holding the clunky seat with two hands since Skye wasn't strapped back in.

As I walked across the massive parking lot toward the Blue House, a strange sight unfolded before my eyes.

Marcus and Maya were sprinting from the house to the car and back again, carrying huge duffle bags with them to the car. Once they saw me, they started running back and forth even faster, laughing as if they were playing a game to pack the car and drive away as quickly as possible. *Where are they going? And why are they so desperate to get away from me?* The trip to Houston wasn't until tomorrow, and they'd be leaving in a car supplied by the Church, not our family car, which I needed for the ten days he was gone. Everything was planned out and in writing. But here he was, trying to take off like I had some highly contagious disease.

I was determined to stop him from leaving, and he was determined to drive off without a word of explanation. The race between us ended in an exact tie—to the millisecond. The moment Marcus jumped inside and revved the engine, as Maya scurried into the backseat, I stood directly in front of the hot, humming SUV. We locked eyes. I'd never seen such a malicious look, as if he were possessed.

"Where do you think you're going? You can't take the car!" I shouted.

"Yes, I can. Move out of the way."

"You can't just leave! You've been avoiding me all day. The car is mine to use, and you know that. Where are you going with all those bags?"

Calm, yet icy cold, he replied, "I need to leave now. Get out of my way."

For the first time in our sixteen-month relationship, I finally lost it.

Every ounce of built-up anger, hurt, and frustration poured out of me in copious quantities. I yelled, I cursed—for the first time in my life—and I continued standing directly in front of the car.

"You can run me over if you want to, but I'm not budging." I placed Skye in her car seat on the ground next to me—there was no way he could leave now.

Underneath my outburst was a potent cry for his love and attention, which he'd been withholding since I showed him the positive pregnancy test the night before. All I wanted was for him to step out of the car, give me a hug, and have a simple conversation about this latest pregnancy. We didn't have to get back together on the spot—although I would have loved that—but I needed to feel some sort of humanity from him. I had never witnessed Marcus so cold, so devoid of any emotion, and so determined to have nothing to do with me, the woman he once loved who was now carrying his baby.

To my horror, instead of getting out to give me a hug, Marcus started backing up. He turned the wheel to put the vehicle at a slight angle but still facing me and our front lawn. Seeing the uncannily malicious look in his eyes, I bent down to snatch up Skye's car seat and then ran to the right.

Marcus drove straight toward me where I stood in the grass.

"Nooooo!" I screamed.

That's when I felt the force of the car. I became completely powerless against the fast-moving SUV that knocked my body to the ground. My will, my muscles, my strength, my ferocious determination to not lose this battle—none of it mattered. *I can never win a fight with someone in a car. This was a very bad idea.*

Time slowed and each moment expanded. I still remember every thought in this strange, hyperaware state. First, while falling toward the ground, I felt my right arm twist and crunch—a sudden, intense pain shot up to my shoulder. As Marcus drove toward me with increasing speed, I had stuck out my arm toward his open window in one final attempt to stop him from leaving. (It didn't work.)

After being hit by the SUV, I lay face down, my head buried in the damp, squishy grass. *Am I in heaven now?* But then, just as I was wondering whether I was dead or alive, I felt a strong pressure—the weight of an entire car—roll onto the right side of my back, then the pressure released, and then it happened again. *So, this is what it feels like to be run over.*

I was instantly brought back to when I was four years old, standing next to my mother in the elevator in our New York City building as she pushed my baby brother in his carriage. The elevator was small and cramped, and the carriage took up most of the space. Although I was little, there wasn't much room for me, and when the doors opened, I took one step too soon and felt the front wheel, and then the back wheel, roll over my toes. My mom expressed great concern and apologized over and over.

"It's okay," I said. "It doesn't hurt. Feels like the wheels ran over me." I didn't fully categorize it as pain but as a new, intense sensation. And that's how I felt after the left wheels of our car skimmed over the right side of my back. *It doesn't really hurt. It just feels like the wheels ran over me.*

I lay completely still, unable to move, until my baby's shrieking cries forced me to try. As I lifted my head, I saw Marcus drive through the Church parking lot at lightning speed.

Desperate, I screamed, "Help! Help! Come back!"

But he continued to speed off, turning right out of the parking lot and zooming out of sight, leaving the two of us helpless on the front lawn.

Twenty Church or Cult?

Despite the excruciating pain in my right arm and shoulder, I had to make sure Skye was okay. Her car seat had overturned and lay upside down in the grass a few feet away.

Marcus's clear, wide track marks had completely flattened the grass, proving that he had driven through our front lawn, looping around trees and passing where both Skye and I now lay. I looked around, desperate to know if anyone had witnessed this or could help us, but there wasn't a soul in sight.

When I reached Skye, I breathed a sigh of relief and gratitude—she had been protected during the accident—Marcus hadn't run over her. When he hit me, the force of the blow sent the car seat flying out of my hands, and she landed about three feet away. But the car seat had landed on top of her, shielding her like a helmet. Her greatest trauma was the shock of being dropped in the grass upside down. Within a few minutes, she calmed down, and her crying ceased.

I reached for my bag, cringing in agony with every movement of my arm, to call the first person who had come to mind—Cheryl. Her kissing Marcus the other day now seemed entirely irrelevant. I needed help.

She blew up. "Have you called 9-1-1?"

I hadn't even thought of that.

"I'm calling for you right now," she said, "and I'll be there as fast as I can."

I tried to reach Paul, but he didn't answer. Left-handed, I wrote him a text message, letting him know 9-1-1 had been called. "I'm in the grass in front of Blue House with the baby. He ran me over with the car. I can't move my right arm. Emergency."

"Call you in a minute," he responded. "I'm around people at my celebration."

Celebration?

Minutes later, the shriek and glare of sirens filled the air, and the Blue House transformed from a sweet home into a crime scene crawling with police officers, paramedics, and other officials. Paul had ordered Marcus back to the scene—his big rush off the property had been to get to Paul's "celebration"—where he now stood with his hands cuffed behind his back, talking to two fierce-looking police officers.

I wished this weren't happening—I just wanted to go back in time and take back the outburst that had triggered Marcus so dangerously. *Why couldn't I just let him go without trying to stop him?* I was living through my worst nightmare. *This can't be happening.* But the searing pain coursing through my body reminded me I was, in fact, wide awake.

Cheryl held Skye while we took in the scene swirling around us. As soon as Paul arrived, he began speaking fervently to a third police officer, exuding the authority and gravity of a king about to lose his kingdom. Three male board members appeared, including Margaret's husband, joined moments later by Margaret herself. Seeing me sitting on the lawn, Margaret rushed over to me, finalizing the gender divide—the men hovered nearer to the Church while Margaret, Cheryl, Skye, and I sat on the front lawn of my house.

"Oh, my gosh, honey, I'm so sorry," said Margaret, her face shrouded with concern. "I had a feeling I shouldn't have dropped you off when I saw Marcus outside the house." She kneeled down to whisper with great urgency. "Do *not* tell the police you were hit by the car."

"What?" I asked. "But that's what happened!"

"Sweetie," she said quietly, "if you say what really happened, they'll consider it a domestic dispute and call Child Protective Services. Trust me—they'll take Skye from you."

"But what do I say? You want me to lie to the police?" I couldn't imagine being separated from Skye for even a minute.

A pair of male paramedics walked toward me.

Margaret whispered, "Just say you tripped and fell down in front of the car or something. I'll hold Skye and pretend to be Grandma—they're less likely to take her if Grandma is here. Please trust me on this. You don't want to lose Skye."

Cheryl passed baby Skye over to Margaret's open arms just as the paramedics kneeled down to talk to me.

During their checkup, I asked the younger of the pair at least three times, "Can't you just tell me now if anything is broken? If not, I'm not going to any hospital."

My mind-set heavily steeped in fear and lack, I was terrified by the idea of losing Skye to CPS if I went to the hospital. Margaret had planted a ridiculous idea in my mind, but I couldn't take any risks. And my pregnancy Medicaid had just expired days earlier. How would I ever afford an emergency room bill? I still had to figure out how to come up with seven hundred dollars for an abortion—if I was, in fact, still pregnant after being hit by the car. In my foggy, nonsensical state, I figured whatever injuries I had would heal on their own, as long as nothing was broken.

The paramedics continued to insist that Skye and I be taken to the hospital. They said they weren't able to diagnose anything on the spot—we needed X-rays and scans.

While I argued with them about whether it was in my best interest to go to the hospital, Paul walked over and interrupted our conversation.

"You broke our agreement," he snapped, without even asking if I was okay. "You weren't supposed to be around Marcus." Then he called out to one of the board members, motioning to the track marks in the grass. "We gotta get this cleared up right away. We've got classes starting at six."

"On it," the older man replied.

Six? That late already? I'd lost all sense of time. I shivered as the sun disappeared behind the Church. The paramedics had placed ice packs around my right arm, shoulder, and ribcage, and they were waiting for me to make a final decision about going to the hospital.

I turned to Margaret, who was attempting to soothe a fussy, cranky Skye, ready to trust her guidance. "What should I do?"

"Just come back with me," she replied, her voice warm and comforting. "You can stay at my house tonight. I'll give you the master bedroom. You could always go to a doctor in the morning."

The paramedics made one final attempt to convince me to go to the hospital, but I declined. They prepared a clipboard so I could sign documents stating that I was going against their recommendation and that I voluntarily assumed all risks involved by declining appropriate medical care. They handed me a pen, but I couldn't lift my right arm to take it.

"What do you want me to do? I can't even hold the pen to sign this." The two paramedics exchanged nervous glances. I attempted to minimize my dilemma. "Oh, I'll just scribble something with my left hand."

After the paramedics left, three policemen walked toward me, notepads and cameras in hand. Just their presence alone intimidated me. A long and drawn out interview followed, but I didn't know what to say—the truth or what Margaret had advised. The policemen wanted details and weren't satisfied with what I offered up in an effort to protect Skye from being taken away and Marcus from going to jail.

"I don't remember exactly how I got to the ground," I lied. "One second I was having an argument with him about whose turn it was to have the car, and the next thing I knew I was lying in the grass."

"Yes, we know about that," said the officer. "He played us an audio recording."

"What?" I asked, shocked.

Marcus had recorded me? All of a sudden, the whole thing made sense—his unusual quietness while I lost it, his simple and direct remarks, the look in his eyes. An entirely new set of fears wracked me. If he had a recording of me sounding crazy and daring him to hit me, then could I be the one going to jail? I didn't know the rules. Maybe I risked having Skye taken from me based on that recording alone. Plus, even though Marcus hit me with the car, I basically told him to when I refused to move. *That lets him off the hook and shifts the blame to me, right?*

All I wanted was for the policemen to leave and for this whole thing to be over. A part of me expected Marcus and me to simply make up like we always did, with the usual gifts, extraordinary flower bouquets, and romance. But this time, that was physically impossible. Marcus stood in handcuffs talking to the police, and I sat on the lawn, unable to move.

I had already fallen victim to so many intense and aggressive moments with Marcus that the car incident seemed no worse than what I'd already experienced. Running me over wasn't worse than cheating on me. Given everything that had led up to this encounter, it didn't feel at all out of character for Marcus to hit me and drive off. In the moment, his hitting me with our car seemed like a logical progression, not something that should involve police officers and paramedics. Only later would I understand that these types of thoughts are hallmarks of abusive relationships.

After my incomplete answers to their questions, the police went back to speak with Marcus one more time. I watched from across the lawn, and although I couldn't hear his words, I had a perfect view of the show he performed. He animated his explanation with grand arm gestures, radiating such charm, confidence, and assurance that I knew his version of the story wouldn't look anything like mine.

The night grew longer and cooler, and I was beyond ready for this ordeal to come to an end.

Finally, one of the policemen walked back to me. "I've got some news for you, and you're not going to like it."

My stomach twisted into a tight knot. "What is it?" I clutched onto Margaret's and Cheryl's hands as they kneeled on either side of me.

He hesitated for a moment. "We're not pressing charges on your boyfriend tonight. You two have very different accounts of what went on, and we don't have enough evidence to know exactly what happened. So, we're going to dismiss this. But please stay far away from this guy, okay? We don't want to be called out here again for another domestic dispute."

I let out a huge sigh. "I'm free to go, with my baby?"

"You're free to go."

Free to go sounded better in my mind than it felt in my body, especially as I made my way up to stand and tried walking a few steps. While sitting in Margaret's car, the pain began to settle into my body, and I felt worse by the minute. The entire right side of my body started seizing up.

Once inside Margaret's home, I wished I had gone to the hospital after all. When I mentioned this to her and her husband, they remained quiet and showed no sympathy. Although they were cordial—giving me the ibuprofen I requested and inviting me to eat dinner with them—whenever I said things like, "Oh, my gosh, I can't move my right arm. I'll have to eat with my left hand," they didn't say a word.

Given my injuries, I attempted to sleep sitting up with Skye lying beside me. As I waited for sleep to come, a long message from Paul arrived first. He was furious that I had ruined what was supposed to be a special day for him and Nina. "Staying at the Blue House is not an option anymore," he wrote. "I will meet you there in the morning to pack."

I began to panic. *He can't kick me out of my own home!* But then I realized I had several friends in Dallas who would take me in: Audrey, Cheryl, Sam, even the old ladies from the Church. They all loved me and Skye. Of course, they would be there for me in a crisis.

The next morning, feeling truly like I'd been run over by a car, I asked Margaret, "You don't think Paul expects me to leave today, do you? I can't even move my arm. I need to get to a doctor. I can't possibly pack up my house. I need at least a few days to do that."

"You need to stand up to Paul and tell him that, then," she responded.

"Really?" I asked.

"Yes, be assertive! I told him I'd drop you at the house, so we'll go there this morning, and then tell him what you just told me. If you want, you can stay here the rest of the week. My husband left this morning for a business trip, so I'll be all alone."

I was overcome with gratitude both for her kindness and for her husband's trip out of town. Margaret was a kinder, more gracious person without him around.

She dropped me off in the Blue House driveway and went on to teach her morning Bible study. I turned the doorknob, but it wouldn't budge. *Strange,* I thought, as I dug through my bag to find my keys.

Paul walked up a minute later, pulling out a key. "This door must now remain locked at all times. I'll let you inside to gather your belongings, but that's it."

"Is Marcus here?" Of course, that was the first thing on my mind.

"No, Marcus is already on a plane to Hawaii."

"Hawaii?"

"You don't need to worry about him. You need to get your stuff and go."

I cowered like a child.

"I've called a few people to come help you pack," he said. "Vincent and Michael from the board should be here soon. We've got to be as efficient as possible to get you out."

I didn't understand his massive rush, especially if Marcus was in Hawaii. I had a notebook full of to-do lists for my move on November 10—detailed lists with timelines of things to sell, things to mail, things to pack. How could I possibly be out any sooner than I'd planned, with a tiny baby, a pregnancy, and significant injuries?

Minutes later, I found myself in a tight alcove in the garage that had built-in shelves from floor to ceiling, each holding the empty suitcases Marcus and I had used to move to Dallas. Paul had followed me into the garage, so I passed them to him one at a time with my left hand.

I figured now was as good a time as any to "assert myself," as Margaret had encouraged, not considering that a dark and isolated alcove might not be the best place to do so.

"Paul, there's no way I can leave today. I need at least two or three days. I need to go to a doctor, and I can't possibly pack or get on a plane if I can't even move my arm."

He set down the suitcase I'd handed him and walked into the tight alcove, cornering me against the white cement wall.

"You need to leave today. I already told you, no one is staying in this house anymore."

"I don't need to stay here," I said nervously. "Margaret said I can stay with her this week, and I can just come here during the day to pack."

"You don't understand." His voice was harsh. "I was up all night talking to the police. I didn't get any sleep, thanks to you. The police want to reopen your case and press charges against you for lying, since your account doesn't match Marcus's. They also plan to contact Child Protective Services because you endangered your baby. They're asking me for more information about you, and I've been doing my best to put them off. I'm doing you a huge favor, so you really owe me one. If you leave the state today, I'll tell the police you're already gone, safely with your parents, and there's nothing to worry about. Hopefully that will be enough for them to close the case."

"But what happens if I don't leave Texas today? What if I stay to go to the doctor and take the time I need to pack up all my stuff?"

Mere inches away, he towered over me. "Then you'll be sitting in jail tonight without your baby."

That was enough for me to follow orders. My whole body trembled as we entered the living room. *I just need to do what he says. What I believe is right doesn't matter anymore. I just need to keep Paul on my side.* Nothing in the entire universe could possibly be worse than sitting in a jail cell with my baby taken from me. Just imagining that scenario made me want to get out of Texas as soon as possible.

"Go, go, go!" shouted Paul, a mantra he repeated over the next three hours as I scrambled to gather my belongings. When he wasn't patrolling the house, he laughed with the other men and helped himself to the food in my fridge. Rather than being in modern-day Texas, I felt transported back in history to Eastern Europe during World War II, living out my final hours in a concentration camp, a powerless victim of intractable corruption.

At various times, I tried to call my sister and my Buddhist leader for advice, but each time I walked into another room or out to the backyard for some privacy, Paul followed me to remind me that I needed to "go, go, go" so I'd make the plane, which was leaving that afternoon. He'd already purchased my plane ticket to ensure I would get out.

"If you don't get on that plane," he repeated, "you'll be sitting in jail without your baby."

The amount of stress I felt was so intense I'm not sure how I kept breathing, but I felt I had no choice other than to follow his plan or else face potentially worse consequences.

The two-minute phone conversation I had with my sister before Paul forced me to hang up made a strong impression on her. Months later, she said, "I was so worried about you. It all sounded so messed up, like you were part of a cult. I kept telling you over and over to call a lawyer and not to believe his threats. But you were adamant about doing whatever he said. I had never heard you like that. It completely freaked me out."

If I had known anything about the legal system, I would've realized that nothing Paul was saying was true. He had no right to threaten me in an attempt to make me flee the state. There were no late-night conversations with the police, and despite his being the senior minister of the Church, he didn't have the right to kick me out of my home in a mere three hours.

But in my absolute ignorance while facing off with a former CIA agent, I believed every word he said. I was petrified. I thought getting hit by a car was bad enough. Now I had to deal with being forced out of my home.

My elderly Buddhist leader, however, had a different take. Eve was a sweet, gentle British lady. In sheer panic, I called her from the blue bathroom. With the deepest compassion, she said, "Please know that you are so protected. Everything that has happened is all for your protection."

I didn't know what she meant at the time, although her words rang true on a deep level. I *was* protected. I was alive, and so was my baby. That alone was miraculous.

Three hours later, the group of men encircled me and escorted me out of the Blue House. I had no opportunity to say goodbye to Cheryl, Sam, Audrey, or the other women who had befriended me during the last eight months. In fact, there were no women around at all. Skye and I were tightly enclosed in a domineering cocoon until we were in the car that Paul had hired, as if the men were trying to shield any potential onlookers from witnessing my exit. That way, *poof*, I could just disappear, another addition to the growing list of women who disappeared from the Church and were never mentioned or heard from again.

I spent much of the plane ride to California sobbing and scribbling a ten-page letter to Marcus, a bittersweet, nostalgic, love letter that flowed straight from my soul. I recounted all the blissful, amazing times we shared together and detailed every single thing about him and about our relationship that I would deeply miss. I wasn't sure if I'd actually give it to him, but I had to write it anyway.

My sister Leandra picked me up from the airport on Halloween night. No one had expected me to arrive for another ten days, so no one was prepared for my arrival. Leandra was in the middle of moving—her house was full of boxes, and she had no extra beds. My parents and brother lived in a small two-bedroom apartment. By putting us on a plane unprepared, Paul had rendered my baby and me homeless.

Because we'd used a cloth diaper service in Texas and I was obsessed with being as eco-friendly as possible, I didn't have a single disposable diaper on hand to pack for the trip. I also didn't have Skye's clothes—although I had directed one of the board members to pack them, he must have forgotten or was too busy socializing, laughing, or raiding my fridge. My family was willing to do anything to help. My parents set up a makeshift bed in their living room, and my sister gave me diapers and baby clothes for Skye.

Seeing me in such disarray, my sister recommended I work on getting my belongings back. She advised I do this before Marcus returned from Hawaii—a two-week "suspension," I learned from eavesdropping on Paul, rather than his volunteer work in Houston—as he'd probably make everything more difficult.

Getting my belongings back should have been relatively simple. I emailed Paul that my parents and I would be hiring a professional moving company to take from the house the things I needed—most importantly Skye's clothes, stroller, crib, organic crib mattress, car seat, and many more items I wasn't able to pack. In the three-hour rush, Paul also refused to let me go into the Church building to retrieve my yoga-teaching supplies and things I'd left in my office. He claimed that he'd send them later.

The email I sent him was straightforward and direct and as professional as possible. My request didn't sit well with him, however, and the process of getting my belongings back was nearly as traumatic as getting hit by the car.

I spent my first days in California not only in extreme withdrawal from Marcus but also in a constant state of heightened panic. Paul continued to threaten me over email and text message—the police were coming after me, and CPS was preparing to take my baby. According to him, the only ways to stop them were "to pray" and to follow his strict guidelines: speak to no one from the Church about what happened and ask no one for help getting my belongings back. The only person I was allowed to communicate with was Paul, the self-appointed point person. The only problem was that he didn't actually want to help me.

On the day the movers arrived at the Blue House, Paul denied them full access, therefore stopping them from retrieving many of my belongings, including the brand-new and incredibly sentimental crib for Skye that had been a gift from a former Pilates client in New York. When I called the movers, I was astonished to learn that even they were scared of Paul and were unwilling to speak up on my behalf—despite that I was a paying client.

According to the movers, Paul reviewed the inventory I had given them, took a pen, and crossed out several items, saying "Nope, these aren't here. She must have packed them herself." Unless he had already gone through the Blue House and stolen the crib, stroller, and other large items, those were there indeed.

The incident with the movers kicked off a charged email thread with Paul. He wrote that I should be thankful that I got any of my stuff back because the board wanted to take everything I'd left in the Blue House and throw it in the dump in retaliation for how I "lied about being hit by the car." Although he had counseled me and Marcus for hours, he noted, I had never donated any money to the Church, which demonstrated a lack of gratitude, and he had no reason to help me out.

I couldn't believe he actually put this stuff in writing. I forwarded his emails to my sister, who advised me to immediately hire a lawyer and stop all direct contact with him.

In the midst of hiring lawyers and taking steps to protect myself and my baby, Marcus reached out unexpectedly after no contact in six days. I was at an outdoor café having lunch with my parents when his message came through, so I quickly stood up and ran into the women's restroom. I had to watch the video message by myself because I didn't know what to expect.

I pressed play, praying that Marcus wouldn't be furious with me. A rugged, disheveled face appeared against a backdrop of turquoise water and swaying palm trees, yet he was practically unrecognizable. He looked like he hadn't slept, shaved, or stopped crying for six straight days. His eyes were red and swollen, and he could barely speak for crying so much—gasping, stuttering, and wallowing like a toddler mid-tantrum in between repeating the phrases "I love you" and "I'm sorry."

The emotional charge in his video could have fueled a rocket ship to outer space fifteen times over. When I later showed the video to the lawyers who were helping me secure a restraining order, even they were taken aback, unsure of how to respond besides wide-eyed stares at the video and a single word, "Wow."

Still standing in the café restroom, I watched the video again. This time, the desperation of his plea for forgiveness brought tears to my eyes and jostled my feelings of love for him once more.

I didn't respond to his video message. How would I have responded to something of that intensity? Yet I spent days mulling it over. *Do I forgive him because he's truly sorry? Do we just make up like old times?*

My family formed a bubble of protection around me, doing their best to stop me from responding to Marcus, or worse, getting back together with him. And yet, I was dying to do both.

My mom, dad, sister, and brother-in-law continued to remind me, "Courtney, he hit you with a car and drove off. It doesn't matter that he feels bad about it, and it doesn't matter that he's sorry—he can't take that back. You can't be with someone like that."

Meanwhile, despite hiring a lawyer in Texas, I remained unable to retrieve all of my belongings from the Blue House, thanks to Paul's interventions and excuses. I knew these things were just "stuff," but I couldn't let go of my deep sadness and anger over losing Skye's crib—a beautifully crafted piece of wooden art and an emotional totem filled with memories and hopes. I'd spent months picking it out, and we'd put it together as a family. I couldn't fathom replacing it—I decided instead that Skye didn't need a crib after all. She'd slept with me since she was born anyhow. It took a year to get over that loss, and I still wonder whether Paul stole that crib for his own baby.

When I shared everything I'd been through in Dallas—to my family, my lawyers, and my new therapist in California—each response was exactly the same: "What is this place, some kind of cult?"

I'd laugh and brush off their comment as if it were just a joke. "Really, the bad stuff was only a small percentage of what I experienced."

But then I remembered something strange that happened in one of our

Tuesday staff meetings at the Church. I was sitting at the large mahogany table with the others but bouncing on a yoga ball I'd recently purchased for my office and wearing Skye in a carrier trying to get her to fall asleep. I was also trying to not fall asleep myself. These meetings were long and could get very boring.

Someone knocked on the open door and stood nervously waiting to be acknowledged. I recognized her as a volunteer in the nursery on Sundays, a place that Skye had never been because as a first-time mom, I was too nervous to hand over my baby to relative strangers. Instead, I always brought Skye to sit with me in the front row during services.

This forty-something woman looked extremely disheveled, and we could tell that something wasn't right. It looked like she hadn't slept, brushed her hair, or changed her clothes in days. In Dallas, unlike Manhattan, you notice those kinds of details.

Paul told her we were in the middle of a staff meeting but had her come in and sit down anyway. We had to adjust ourselves to bring an extra chair around the table.

"What can I help you with today?" Paul asked.

"I have a major problem, which I'm very embarrassed about, but I need your help," she replied.

"Well, what is it?" Paul asked.

The energy in the room perked up. The woman, whose name I later learned was Sonia, gathered her words to speak. "I love this place so much. And I love you all so much. This church means everything to me. I can't imagine my life without it. But you know, I moved two and a half hours away a few months ago, and the commute has been killing me. I'm up here every single day organizing the nursery and planning for Sundays with the little ones. But when I get home at ten or eleven at night, I'm exhausted. I don't know what to do because I can't imagine going to any church but this one."

Everyone at the table smiled, clearly relieved, and congratulated her on her incredible devotion.

Meanwhile, I stopped bouncing and looked at her in shock. "You drive *five hours* every day to volunteer here?" I asked.

"If there's no traffic, yes. But in traffic, it could be over six hours every day in the car. The gas, the time . . ."

Paul cut her off. "Well, Sonia, we all applaud your efforts and work here, and we'll pray for you to find a place closer to eliminate the time in the car."

"Oh, actually, the time in the car isn't an issue right now. I haven't told you the real problem yet," Sonia said, fidgeting. "I'm just so embarrassed to say it."

We all just stared at her.

"You can tell us anything, Sonia," Paul said. "We're your family, remember."

"The truth is, I rented one of those small storage units just off the freeway, and I've been sleeping there so I can be closer to the Church. I'm worried they're going to kick me out, and then I'll have to go back to living hours away. Is there any sort of housing you can offer me so I can volunteer here all day, every day? I'm fully devoted. I just need a place to live."

That wasn't the worst of it. My so-called friend Cheryl returned to the church after I left, as did Alice. The whole lot of them "forgave" each other, and Cheryl continued to cover for Marcus. If anyone ever asked details of what happened to me, she told them, "They were in an open relationship." I had trusted her, but in the end, she was more loyal to the Church and to the Church's success. She told me she "reframed" what happened with Paul and was even going to help Nina raise the baby.

Only after a second professional counselor pointed out all of the characteristics of a cult within the inner workings of the Church did something click. I had been controlled using extreme fear, I had been forced to keep quiet, I had been lied to then deceived about and then blamed for countless incidents, and I had lost every ounce of confidence, assertiveness, and strength I once had—all in a mere eight months.

After I finished telling my therapist how Audrey was immediately fired for speaking up, she asked slowly, "Church or cult?"

Twenty-one The Diamond Ring

"The best thing you can do is move on with your life," said my sister, several times a day.

Moving on and letting go sounded like vague, distant, unattainable concepts. I couldn't just "move on" if I was newly pregnant and a single mother of a five-month-old. No one in my family knew about the pregnancy, not even my mom. How could I possibly tell them? They were already worried sick without that extra bit of news. I didn't plan to keep the baby anyway, so I figured it was better they didn't know at all.

In those first days, weeks, and even months after leaving, I craved Marcus like a hard-core drug addict jonesing for a hit. I knew that our relationship was unhealthy and that getting back together would be a terrible idea, but deep down, I was still holding out hope that he might change and that we might reunite as a loving, happy family.

As hard as it was to be in an abusive relationship, leaving Marcus was insanely, unimaginably harder. I would have stayed with him for another twenty years if I had known how difficult it would be to give him up. The withdrawal symptoms I experienced were unbearable. I couldn't sleep or eat, and I cycled through every stage of grief, round and round again, unable to process the shock of my unraveled life. Since I thought about Marcus all the time anyway, I reasoned it might make more sense just to get back together with him—the real, live person rather than the character in my imagination.

While I fantasized about reuniting as a peaceful, blissful couple, I continued the process of cutting him out of my life, with the help of my parents and a team of lawyers in California who wanted an account of every incident between Marcus and me, as well as tangible evidence. I spent days gathering everything I could find and reliving each episode in vivid detail.

My greatest wake-up call came when I stood alone in my parents' bathroom, naked, taking photos of the massive purplish-black bruises along the entire right side of body—the last outward evidence of the vehicular assault. I wanted to cry, but the tears wouldn't come. The magnitude of everything I'd been through hadn't fully hit me. Only when I came out of the bathroom and saw the pain in my dad's eyes and the worry in my mom's face did I begin to grasp the ripple effect of what I'd been through.

A week had passed since I'd arrived in California, and I still hadn't had an abortion, although I was trying to arrange one. I didn't have anyone to watch Skye, and I was told she couldn't come with me.

"I have no one else to watch her!" I said to the receptionist on the phone. "She only just turned five months. Can't she just stay in her stroller, as long as she's quiet? Please?"

"I'm sorry, but babies aren't allowed in our facilities," the receptionist repeated, "and we can't make any exceptions."

It took me a moment to realize why they were so strict about this—the last thing women waiting to terminate their pregnancies want to see is an adorable little baby.

There were other obstacles, too—I didn't have a car and wasn't staying anywhere near the BART train, and to top it off, my family members were watching me like hawks, even when I tried to go for a walk by myself. How could I possibly leave for several hours without anyone noticing?

Every day, as I got a little more pregnant, I got a little more worried about going through with an abortion. I regretted missing my opportunity back in Dallas. I kept calling various abortion clinics for information, and I even scheduled appointments for the procedure, but I always ended up cancelling at the last minute due to the logistical issues.

After enough internet searches for "abortion near me," I started to pay attention to the sponsored ad on top of the page that advertised free medical-quality pregnancy tests, confidential ultrasound exams, and "options counseling." The clinic didn't offer abortions, but they offered free ultrasounds, which would confirm how many weeks pregnant I was. Once I knew how far along I was, I would know how much more time I had to go through with the procedure. Once I had concrete dates, I could relax a little.

The next afternoon, I took an Uber to the clinic with Skye next to me in her car seat. I prayed that my mom and sister wouldn't call me repeatedly asking where I was—they hadn't left me alone for a few hours since I arrived in California. We pulled up to a small house with a large banner out front that read "FREE PREGNANCY TESTS." Inside, an overly kind woman named Kayla greeted me. She was blonde and in her late thirties, and she had a bigness to her both in stature and personality. Kayla not only shook my hand but came out from behind her desk to give me a warm, welcoming hug.

As soon as she saw Skye, Kayla practically jumped for joy. "Oh, my gosh, is that the cutest baby on the planet? I've never seen a baby that beautiful! Oh, my goodness! What a lucky mama you are." She called down the long hallway behind her. "Christina, Becky! Come out here right now. You've got to see this baby!"

A minute later, the whole staff stood over Skye's stroller, gushing and cooing in silly baby talk. Once the baby party subsided, Kayla led me into an office and handed me a clipboard of paperwork. I surveyed my surroundings, wondering if I'd come to the wrong place. The posters on the walls and pamphlets piled high on the coffee table conveyed the risks and potential complications of abortion and the right of every woman to give birth. Annoyed, I didn't want to be counseled out of having an abortion—I just wanted to get a free ultrasound.

Kayla and I talked for a while about the recent events in my life. She listened with compassion and free of judgment, even as I admitted I felt desperate to reunite with Marcus. After twenty minutes of conversation, I was ready for my free ultrasound, but Kayla hesitated.

"Remind me when you first had a positive pregnancy result?" she asked.

"On the thirtieth of October."

"Right, I see. We usually don't give ultrasounds unless we're sure that you're at least seven or eight weeks pregnant—otherwise it's too soon for an ultrasound to tell us anything. My guess is you're probably only four or five weeks along. We're also about to close in twenty minutes, which wouldn't leave us enough time anyway. How about you come back next week?"

"Next week? I don't think that's possible. I came here in an Uber with my baby. I can't come back again. It was hard enough to find an excuse to get here today—my family thinks I'm out on a walk. Can we please do the ultrasound today? I need to know how pregnant I am so I know how long I have to get an abortion."

Kayla left to speak with the ultrasound nurse, and when she came back, she said, "We'll make an exception for you since you probably can't come back again. But be prepared—you likely won't see anything on the ultrasound, and you may not hear the baby's heartbeat either."

We crowded into a small, closet-sized exam room—Kayla, the ultrasound nurse, me, and a stroller with Skye now fast asleep. Lying back on the exam table, my feet in stirrups, I looked at the screen with an eagerness I hadn't anticipated. Even before I saw anything, I had a warm, fuzzy feeling like a kid on Christmas morning.

Why am I feeling this way? I'm not even keeping this baby! But then I started thinking things that surprised me. *I hope the baby is healthy.* And then I reminded myself, *Courtney, you just had a baby—you can't have another one!*

Still, I was glued to the screen, waiting for my little white blob to appear. As the nurse poked the cold, plastic stick around, Skye suddenly woke up smiling.

"Perfect timing!" Kayla exclaimed as she scooped her out of the stroller and held her up toward the screen where my uterus was on display. "She woke up to see her little brother or sister!"

"Oh, it's a boy. I already know."

"You do?" said both the nurse and Kayla in unison.

"Yes, it's definitely a boy. I just know. I knew Skye was a girl from the first moment, too. And this time it's a boy, I'm a hundred percent positive."

Seconds later, my little boy appeared on the screen—except he didn't look like a boy, nor the typical white, oval-shaped blob either. I knew exactly what the tiny embryo looked like—goosebumps broke out across my body—but I didn't want to say anything because it was just too weird.

The nurse spoke up first as if announcing I'd won the lottery. "You've got the diamond ring! Oh, my God, that's so cool! Courtney, do you see it?"

Did I see it? How could I miss the perfectly shaped diamond ring on the black screen in front of me: a white circular shape with a large diamond on top. And the diamond appeared to be *glittering.*

"Why is there a diamond ring on the screen? Is that my baby?"

In awe, the nurse replied, "I've never actually seen this before—I've only heard about it. There's a short window of only one or two days at about five weeks pregnant when the embryo appears like this. That ring is the yolk sac—it's nourishing the baby since the placenta hasn't formed yet—and the embryo is the diamond. See that fast flickering inside the diamond?"

"Yes," I replied.

The nurse zoomed in on the diamond, and in sync with the rapid flickering was the sound of a strong, steady heartbeat.

It was just too uncanny to be real. The diamond ring I had wanted for so long—the ring Marcus had taunted and teased me with for more than a year—was finally mine. But rather than a shiny inanimate object, this was life itself, its value truly infinite.

Marcus had given me my diamond ring.

I knew this was a grand, otherworldly sign that this baby was meant to be, not some kind of mistake. What's more, my due date was the Fourth of July—Independence Day. Freedom from Marcus, freedom from an unhealthy relationship, and freedom from all things not serving my highest good. *I can do this, even if I'm alone.* True freedom at last.

Except that I remained determined to go through with my initial decision—I wasn't going to keep this baby.

The nurse printed a set of ultrasound photos and put them inside a small greeting card, the cover of which had tiny baby feet and said, "Better than a thousand words. Sacred, Precious, Life." I had to smile. For a place that advertised as an "options" center, they were obviously pushing for only one option.

As I wheeled Skye's stroller toward the front door, Kayla handed me one more pamphlet to add to the five antiabortion and adoption pamphlets I already had in my bag.

"I was thinking this group home might be a great fit for you since you need a place to live," she said. "Call me if you're interested. I know the woman who runs it."

During the Uber ride home, I skimmed over the pamphlet—a small group home for women who've "chosen life," free rent and utilities, counseling, and other services to help single moms get back on their feet. Given the fact that only a handful of women lived in the home, it wasn't a shelter per se but more of a selective communal environment.

A few weeks later, I grappled with two major decisions. The first was whether to keep the baby—such a significant choice I didn't feel I had the authority to make it. I reached out to close friends, intuitive guides, and finally my mom to help me decide.

When she heard the news, my mom went into hysterics. She cried over and over, "You have to keep this baby!"

Beyond Mom's strong reaction, a phone call with my friend Sam in Dallas helped me gain the clarity I needed.

"Close your eyes right now," she instructed. "Imagine you've already had an abortion. You're living your life with Skye, just the two of you. How do you feel?"

As I breathed deeply and imagined the future without this new life, a sadness and emptiness came over me. "I feel like this is a loss I would never recover from."

"Then you have to keep the baby."

The second decision was whether to leave the safe confines of my parents' apartment for the services in the group home for single moms. I was so wrung out from what I'd been through I hardly felt ready to leave, even though the home was only an eighteen-minute drive away.

In the end, I decided to go because I was taking up the master bedroom in my parents' small apartment, and I wanted to give them their space back. I thought being at the home would help me get back on my feet, though I missed having my family's support. The short time I spent in the single moms' home gave me a wonderful level of support—baby clothes, diapers, camaraderie, and counseling, among many other things.

The home also provided cover since I was still hiding my pregnancy from my dad and sister—my mom had promised not to tell them until I was ready. I was incredibly embarrassed and ashamed, and I feared they would judge me for being pregnant. I imagined them thinking, *What's wrong with her? How could she have gotten pregnant if she was in such a bad relationship?* That's what was always so hard to explain—it wasn't all bad all the time. When it was good, it was really, really good.

I continued to wish I could restart my relationship with Marcus. I felt extremely conflicted about who he truly was. Almost every night, I had wild and vivid dreams in which we'd get back together and then he'd betray me again—I woke up each time in a cold sweat. Adding to my confusion, several mutual friends of ours from Hawaii, including Kealoha, wanted to help us "heal our relationship" and encouraged me to give him another chance. Letting go and moving on seemed impossible.

Around the same time, my sister called about joining her on an international television segment highlighting the now grown-up children who were conceived from the "genius sperm bank," or as it's properly named, the Repository for Germinal Choice. The media has always found our unique conception intriguing, and my siblings and I have been receiving these requests for interviews since we were toddlers.

The thought of being interviewed about my genius-sperm origins struck me as so ridiculous that I burst out laughing. "Leandra, are you crazy? What would I possibly say during an interview? This whole 'genius sperm bank' experiment clearly didn't work because look what happened to me! Let's see—I'm twenty-nine years old, a single mom living in a group home, no jobs, no friends, no direction, and no purpose. In sum, my life is a big mess."

By now, Leandra was chuckling too.

"I think I'll skip this one, but thanks," I said. "And if they ask any questions about me, just try to be vague. Don't hint that my life has completely fallen apart."

At twenty weeks pregnant, I finally told my dad and sister. I had a small belly that I'd been doing my best to hide, but I couldn't delay revealing it any longer. After several minutes of stalling, I was finally able to speak the words. Waves of relief washed over me as soon as I said, "I'm pregnant." After they recovered from their initial shock, my dad and sister were genuinely supportive and happy for me.

Adding to everyone's surprise, my sister announced that she was pregnant, too! Her due date was four weeks after mine, which meant that our babies would be born around the same time.

"Two new grandbabies!" my mom exclaimed, ecstatic that she no longer had to keep my secret.

"So, you're not mad or upset?" I asked my dad.

"Honey, I'm thrilled."

In a further attempt to help get me back on my feet, my dad even rented me an apartment nearby so I could finally unpack and settle after the whirlwind past few months, while having my parents a three-minute walk away.

Despite my family's supportive reactions, I continued to hide my pregnancy as much as possible in the weeks that followed. I found it difficult to make peace with my bizarre situation—brand-new to California, mother of an infant, pregnant, and without a partner. My constant fear of other people's judgment was merely a reflection of how harshly I judged myself—I was angry at myself for all of the "mistakes" that had brought me to this point. I wished I'd reacted differently to Marcus's affair with Alice. *If only I had been okay with the affair, we'd probably still be together.* And in passing conversations with strangers, I continued to nod along and pretend that I still had a "husband" (despite never having had a real husband in the first place) because it was too embarrassing to correct their assumptions.

In the midst of this turmoil, I had to pull myself together for the court hearing for my domestic violence restraining order. It was now early January, and in the two months since I left Dallas, Marcus hadn't communicated much besides his shipwreck of an apology video and a handful of emails—complete with photos of us in our happiest times that tugged painfully on my heart—trying to convince me and Skye to "come home."

In several of his emails, Marcus accused me, in a patronizing tone, of being "unstable" and said he was worried I was putting Skye in danger. His accusations were so flipped around I was tempted to set him straight—he was the one who had plowed into both of us with his car—but the lawyers advised me to communicate with him as little as possible.

As the court date approached, what little confidence I had vanished, and I began to panic. One night, after weeks of paperwork and preparation—not to mention thousands of dollars—I sent this text message to my lawyer:

Hi, I've decided to cancel everything including the hearing on the 11th. Please do not serve him and cancel all attempts to have him served. I do not feel it is a good idea. Please confirm that you received this.

Thank you,
Courtney

Within a minute of my sending that message, my attorney called me. "I think canceling would be a very, very bad idea," she said. "Don't you remember why you came to me in the first place?"

"But what if for some reason I don't get the restraining order? Then I really will be in danger because he'll be furious with me!"

"Look, you have a strong case. You have concrete evidence. You have every reason to get this restraining order. Please don't stop now. You've already come this far."

Perhaps my attorney didn't realize what emotional torture this court hearing would inflict on me. I still loved Marcus. Yes, he had endangered my life, but in my weak state at the time, I longed for a miracle so that we could be together again. The price of protection was much more than the three thousand dollars my parents lent me to retain the lawyers—it was the cost of crushing all of my dreams forever.

This was it. If I chose to go through with the court hearing, there was no turning back. The thought of never running back into Marcus's arms crushed my soul—and yet a small part of me knew it had to happen.

I called my mom two days before the court hearing. She had been absorbing my stress, so I was surprised to hear her in such good spirits.

"Courtney, I want to tell you about this new planet that's been discovered!" Mom bubbled with excitement. As a lifelong lover of astrology, she always shared her insights with me, which sometimes piqued my interest but oftentimes didn't.

"That's great, Mom."

"Really, Courtney. I think you'd resonate with this new planet, Eris, all about the feminine warrior. Everything about Eris reminds me of your situation. You should look it up."

"Okay, Mom, when I have time," I said, knowing I had no extra time.

My mom continued to mention Eris so frequently that I decided to skim a short article about the new planet in hopes she'd stop bringing it up. The more I read, the more I felt connected to Eris after all. The article by astrologer Henry Seltzer is summarized below.

Often referred to as a dwarf planet because of its size, Eris represents the archetype of the feminine warrior defending the soul's purpose. A vital female force, Eris is called to fight a potentially crucial battle for continued existence and for making a stand for what one believes in. In the same way that nature can be both gentle and serene as well as harsh and unrelenting, Eris possesses an intensity that continues to fight for what is right, even if it calls for violence. Her influence is especially related to the feminist struggle for rights in a patriarchal society.

Everything I read rang so true that I decided yes, Eris was my archetype, as my mom had suggested. The night before the court hearing, as I lay with Skye tucked under my arm, I said a prayer to fully embody Eris's feminine warrior spirit so that I would be able to rise to the challenge in court.

Whether thanks to Eris's magic, the prayers of my Buddhist friends around the globe, or simply a strong enough case, the court granted what I'd requested: a three-year restraining order and full custody of my daughter. I was elated. I had never felt so relieved about anything in my life. I could finally breathe. I walked out of the sleek courthouse building with a newfound sense of safety and hope, as if I were enclosed within a golden bubble. For at least three years, Marcus would be out of my life. Hallelujah!

The often-disturbing emails from Marcus ceased. But was I truly free? I desperately wanted to be, but I wasn't, at least not yet. The sixteen-month whirlwind—from coming together in July, conceiving a baby, moving to Texas, conceiving another baby, to the violent ending at the end of October the following year—had taken its toll.

As I walked along the quaint downtown street of my parents' small California town, pushing Skye in her stroller on a warm fall day, vivid memories erupted without permission or warning. Suddenly, I wouldn't be in California any longer—I'd be sitting on my perfectly made bed in Texas, Alice across from me, sharing detail after detail about her affair with my partner. I continued walking along the street with tears streaming down my face. *Stop, stop!* But the scene progressed, skipping to the most painful moments and replaying them over and over.

These flashbacks haunted me daily and at the most random times—browsing the bookstore, taking a shower, or feeding my baby. I sought out counseling and ended up in a traditional therapist's office where I talked about my problems for exactly fifty-five minutes and walked out feeling worse than before.

During these trying times, I decided to devote myself more fully to my Buddhist practice, as I needed something to support me through the healing process. Chanting and prayers became a prominent part of my day, and I connected to a local Buddhist group. Better than therapy were the home visits by Buddhist leaders who listened to me share what was going on and then offered guidance based on their many years of experience. Of all the guidance I received during those months after moving to California, the advice from a leader named Karen stood out from the rest. She shared an important tidbit of wisdom, although in the moment, her sentiment only aggravated me.

"You need to surrender to your new reality," she said. "Stop trying to find a way out of here and just accept that this is where you are right now. I don't see you realistically getting on a plane and going back to Hawaii tomorrow. You need to chant to embrace your new reality."

A part of me wanted to slap her. How could I embrace my new reality if I hated everything about it? And if I embraced it and accepted it, wouldn't that keep me stuck? Only in hindsight could I fully grasp what she meant. I was terrified that if I surrendered to my current life circumstances, they'd be set in stone.

"It doesn't mean you have to stay in this small town forever," said Karen. "But there's a reason you're here. And until you know what that reason is, running to the next place isn't going to make you feel any better. Focus on all the benefits you have here—for one thing, you have your family as solid support. Not everyone has family like you do. They truly have your back."

I could agree with that.

"The first step toward healing is acceptance," she said. "You need to make peace with where you are."

I struggled with this guidance and even flat-out rejected it for a while. *No! I will not accept this. Never!* But whether I accepted it or not, my new reality persisted, and I had plenty of preparations for another baby due in July.

The best and strangest thing about being pregnant again was that I didn't even notice I was pregnant. I had no symptoms of any kind—no morning sickness, no headaches, no tiredness, no extreme hunger, nothing. I felt great, which I found surprising given the emotional trauma I'd endured. After I made peace with keeping the baby, I began to connect to him frequently, and I knew this soul was immensely strong, brave, and resilient. He had purposely chosen me to be his mother, and he hadn't made a mistake.

Months earlier, when I first learned I was pregnant, I found myself thinking, *Why would this baby choose to come in now? Couldn't he see from his place of all-knowing wisdom that my relationship with Marcus was about to fall apart? Was he just not paying attention?*

I came to realize that this soul didn't care if the relationship was falling apart—he had a mission to fulfill on this planet. His soul wasn't distracted or inattentive when he volunteered to come into human form. In fact, he arrived at the last possible moment, the last chance to have the DNA that would make up the person he would become.

And everything had conspired for him to be born, including the dramatic and traumatic way I left Dallas. If I hadn't been hit by a car and forced to leave my home in three hours, this baby wouldn't exist.

And that is indeed an act of grace.

Twenty-two An Ocean of Strength

Against all advice from my friends and family, I planned a home water birth at my parents' apartment to bring my new baby boy into the world, assisted by a midwife and a doula. I had wanted to move back to Hawaii before he was born, but for myriad reasons legal and otherwise, I had to stay in California.

The pushback against my birth plan was immense. From my sister, to distant relatives, to family friends—everyone had an opinion about why home birth wasn't the best choice. Even I wasn't sure a home birth was the best option. All I knew was the experience I had in Skye's thirty-hour labor less than a year earlier; that torturous experience was still etched clearly in both my mind and body. I couldn't believe I was choosing to have another natural birth after the sheer hell I went through the last time. But given my alternatives—hospital, epidural, and medical interventions—I felt compelled to try again.

Above all else, what I feared the most was going through with a natural birth without a partner. As far as I could tell, Marcus had been the reason I made it through the excruciating labor process the last time. How could I possibly do this without him or someone else to take his place?

My mom suggested I hire a doula. I interviewed several, each time asking questions to find out exactly how much they could help me in the same ways Marcus helped me during Skye's birth. For example, could they support my entire body weight if I needed to lean on them? Could they make me a raw placenta smoothie right after giving birth? Could they provide counterpressure on my lower back with true Herculean force?

Finding a doula who agreed to basically be my stand-in partner was not an easy task—most were quick to say no to handling my placenta—but eventually I found a young, eager, and newly certified doula named Verana who bubbled over with excitement to step into the role. Her tiny frame and shorter height wouldn't be a problem, she assured me, as she was also a yoga and fitness instructor.

July 4 came and went without any signs of labor. I was still pregnant. I couldn't believe it—I had spent the last nine months envisioning my baby being born on Independence Day, hoping I could will it into reality. I'd told everyone my plan—the baby would be born in the evening, after which I'd look through my parents' bedroom window to see fireworks heralding his arrival! But July 4 just felt like a typical day. I had to trust that my baby had a different plan in mind.

The subsequent days passed slowly because I had mostly cleared my calendar thinking the baby would have arrived. I continued to teach yoga classes at a nearby studio, swim every day, and spend quality time with Skye since our time with just the two of us was coming to an end. I also practiced setting up the rented birth tub in my parents' living room just in case the doula didn't arrive in time to do it (my parents claimed they were "too old" to set it up). It was in those moments—kneeling on the floor with my huge belly while piecing together my birth tub—that I missed having a partner the most.

Almost every day, I considered abandoning my well-established home birth plan and just walking into a hospital and asking for a C-section. I was terrified of being in labor, even though I had spent the past six months practicing Hypnobabies once again and working on releasing my fears. I wished I could just skip over the painful part and hold my baby in my arms.

My highly experienced midwife, Pearl, and I met regularly for hour-long appointments. She was Asian with short black hair, a round face, and a huge smile. She loved to laugh, and her laughter was contagious. Pearl was easygoing and down to earth, and she confidently told me that women are the stronger sex—men could never give birth. She continued to believe in me even when I doubted myself.

I kept telling her the same thing: "I wish I could have amnesia and not remember anything about Skye's birth. Then I wouldn't be scared at all! I'd be ignorant and confident like the last time."

"But you did it last time—you got through it!" said Pearl. "You had a typical first-time mom experience. And this time, it's going to be different because your body's already done this before. I can't guarantee it, but most likely your labor will be significantly shorter than with Skye."

Her words were comforting, but I didn't want to get my hopes up, in case it didn't turn out that way.

The days dragged on. Ten days past my due date, my midwife sat across from me in my parents' living room. Skye, now thirteen months old, toddled happily around the room, while my parents stepped in and out to keep an eye on her so I could focus on my appointment. Today was an important meeting—we had to discuss alternative ways to help my body start labor because my time was literally running out.

As I was learning for the first time, in the state of California, it's illegal for a home-birth midwife to deliver a baby more than two weeks past the due date. As much as my midwife disagreed with this law and actively lobbied to change the legislation, she gently suggested that it would be best if I had the baby in the next few days.

"Consider seeing an acupuncturist tomorrow morning," she said. "Hopefully that will start things along. If not, we'll take further action with herbal tinctures." As a last resort, I would drink castor oil under her supervision. "Castor oil never fails."

I listened attentively, and once my dad was out of the living room, I asked her a burning question I was incredibly embarrassed to ask.

"Do you think the reason I'm not going into labor is because I have unfinished business with the baby's biological father?"

"No," she answered bluntly.

"Really? I mean, you don't think I need to make amends with him so that my body can relax?"

"Absolutely not."

I went out on a limb. "What do you think about inviting him to the birth?"

Pearl looked at me like I was speaking Greek.

I quickly spoke up again. "Okay, maybe that's going a little too far. But I don't know. It's just so weird that I have no contact with the father whatsoever, and I'm about to give birth to our baby."

"Courtney," she said kindly, "You can do this. Your body knows how to do this. As powerful as your mind is, you can't stop yourself from going into labor. No one's ever been pregnant forever."

Her last statement made me laugh. "Right. I just had to ask."

Though I would never verbalize it, I often wished I could send Marcus a text message like old times and invite him to support me during the birth. After a blissful birth experience, I envisioned we would just slip back into being together again as if the whole nine months of silence had never happened. I couldn't believe my own thoughts—after all these months with no communication, I was still holding on to him, and a tiny part of me was still in love with him. Having the support of my immediate family was the only thing stopping me from inviting him right back into my life.

On the evening of July 14, a few days before my home-birth cutoff date and several hours after my morning acupuncture appointment—which seemed to have had no effect—my sister asked if I'd like to go out for "prego" pizza. I'd never heard of prego pizza before, but it sounded exciting, especially because I had nothing else to do that night. My sister, her husband, their two young children, Mom, Skye, and I met up at an Italian restaurant called Skipolini's where the infamous prego pizza was first conceived.

As I walked inside, I was bombarded by a series of plaques and awards all over the wall, hailing the great prego pizza, one of which read, "Since

1981, Prego Pizza has been giving hope to pregnant mothers who are just ready to put a happy ending to a long nine months." I liked the sound of this place already.

We sat in a beautiful outdoor garden as the sun went down. Something about that night felt so profound—our whole clan together, my sister and me both about to give birth. Small lanterns strung over the large swaying trees lit up, and the whole garden came alive, buzzing with the excitement of new life.

My sister went inside to order as the rest of us chased toddlers around the garden and wrestled them into high chairs.

"Please get me a salad, too," I called out, as Leandra walked inside. "I can't only eat pizza. Oh, and make sure mine is gluten-free!"

She must not have heard me because twenty-five minutes later, three large pizzas (and no salad) were delivered to our table. All I could do was stare wide-eyed at the massive pies, complete with every possible topping covering every square inch and piled high. I noticed several types of meat—sausage, ham, pepperoni, meatballs, to name a few. This is the prego pizza? I hadn't even glanced at the ingredients before my sister ordered. Who needs to read a menu when you've already read twenty testimonials about how prego pizza is the Holy Grail for moms-to-be? I was certainly not prepared for this. I hadn't eaten meat in over a decade.

Eventually I gave in, wincing in preparation for the first bite. "I can't believe I'm going to eat this. All I can say is this better work."

Surprisingly, the meat-and-jalapeño-laden pizza was out-of-this-world delicious, and three slices later, I was in a great mood, confident that my labor would begin soon. "Maybe all I needed was a little meat to get things moving."

I woke up the next morning feeling awful—and not because of labor pains. I was now twelve days past my due date. I had gone to bed praying sincerely to begin labor. If my prayers and the pizza had worked as I'd envisioned, I would have started labor in the middle of the night. At

6:30 a.m., I felt incredibly defeated. *The pizza was a huge waste.* That stupid, crazy pizza I ate seemed like a good idea in the moment, but now I was feeling the brunt of it—extremely bloated, gassy, lethargic. My parents agreed to come over and watch Skye that morning so I could have some time to myself.

An hour later, I realized I didn't have time to mope around—I had a baby to get out! After scouring the internet, I made a long list of everything that could possibly start labor and decided to spend the entire day going down the list, doing one thing after another. Something had to work, and after coming across several terrifying accounts of other people's experiences with castor oil, I was determined to avoid that route.

I started by putting on my sneakers and taking a walk. After only a few minutes of speed-walking in the scorching midday sun, I found a bench on which to rest and closed my eyes to meditate. Tears came to eyes as I connected to my baby boy whose name was still undecided.

You will be so loved by me and Skye and Grandma and Grandpa. It's safe for you to come now—I'm ready to meet you and become a family of three!

I felt my love for him so deep my heart seemed to break open! I welcomed him and told him there was more love for him here than he could imagine.

After my meditation, I went up to my parents' apartment to pick up Skye so she could join the rest of my walk. On my way inside, I noticed a propped-up mini-trampoline—also known as a rebounder—which I hadn't used during the entire pregnancy. I brought the rebounder inside, thinking jumping might help start labor. Plus, I could stay inside and not overheat. Skye got a real kick out of watching Jumping Mommy bounce to upbeat songs I thought my baby boy would like.

After jumping on and off for about forty-five minutes, I began to feel what I assumed were practice contractions—Braxton-Hicks—pretty strongly. I'd been getting Braxton-Hicks contractions for the past few weeks and had been told they weren't an indication of labor. Still, I was excited to feel these sensations, so I kept jumping.

Next on my list was climbing the stairs. I played Bach's Brandenburg Concertos on repeat while I walked up and down the steep outdoor stairs leading to my parents' apartment. Though the sun was beating down on my back, I enjoyed the stair-climbing and felt like I was truly preparing for a marathon.

At around 5:30 p.m., after checking off several more items, I drove to a health food store to buy herbal tinctures and organic pineapple. It seemed unlikely that eating pineapple would induce labor, but at this point, nothing was off-limits. I was willing to try anything to get this baby out before the two-week cutoff.

While shopping, I began to feel contractions, but I was positive they were Braxton-Hicks—practice rounds for my body to get prepared. Although they were intense, I didn't feel any pain. I could still walk and talk through them, and strangely they felt good, like my uterus was getting a nice warm-up. Yet these practice contractions, as I called them, were getting stronger by the minute.

Back at my parents' apartment, I continued to go down my list—determined to see it through to the end—although now I was finally admitting to myself that I could be in labor. But I didn't want to make a big deal of it, since it would probably be another twenty-four hours before my baby was born.

Around 7:30 p.m., my sister gave me a reality check. When she timed my pressure waves, they were consistently three minutes and thirty seconds apart, lasting thirty to forty seconds each.

"Courtney, you're definitely in labor!" she said. "And you're going to be in active labor soon. You need to call your doula and midwife *right now!* And you need to get a good meal in you. You don't have more than thirty minutes, and then you won't be able to eat anymore."

I tried to protest, thinking back to Skye's labor when I felt exactly like this, but I still had twenty-four hours to go. "Leandra, the pressure waves don't even hurt yet. I can easily breathe through them—"

"Oh, they will. Don't worry."

"Right. So, I'm going to try to sleep through the night, and I'll have the baby in the morning. I'm not staying up all night tonight—no way. I did that last time, and it was a huge mistake. I need to get a good night's sleep."

"Courtney, you're having this baby tonight! Come on, let's call your midwife and doula now. Do you want me to do it for you?"

"Fine. Call the midwife. But let me talk to her. I don't want her coming over for nothing! Where is she going to sleep all night?"

Leandra called both Pearl and Verana, who rushed over. My doula, Verana, arrived first at 8:45 p.m., as I was at the kitchen table finishing a bowl of Indian food. I felt incredibly silly sitting there eating samosas when I was supposed to be in labor. I didn't even want any food, but I had learned from Skye's birth that eating before the marathon of natural birth was crucial. Each time a pressure wave came on, I stopped chewing and sunk my face into my hands, breathing deeply while my doula rubbed my back.

While I appreciated Verana's support, what I wanted was my own space. I asked her to set up the birth tub and rearrange the living room as we'd discussed while I went into the back of the apartment, away from my family members as they scurried around packing up their things to leave.

I had set up an aerial yoga sling in the doorway of the bedroom, from which I hung in a deep squat. For a long time, no one bothered me. I was deep in a trance, hyperfocused on breathing and repeating positive affirmations. I squatted low during each pressure wave and then stood up, stretched, and moved my body. The amount of power surging through my body terrified me, but I continued to remind myself, *I am safe, and my baby is safe, no matter how much power flows through my body.*

With eyes closed, I continued to praise my body, my uterus, and my baby. I was vigilant that every single thought that entered my mind be positive and encouraging because that was the only way I was going to get through this. There was truly nothing and no one else who could intervene to help—it was all me.

I heard the sound of soft footsteps approaching, and the next thing I knew, I was jolted out of my trance and conversing with Pearl, my midwife.

She placed her hand on my shoulder. "How's it going?"

"Well, it's going," I answered, my voice shaking slightly.

She smiled at my yoga-sling setup. "Why don't we get you on the bed? The birth tub is almost filled, but for now, I think you'd benefit from a more passive position."

Pearl helped me transition to the bed. The pressure waves were getting to the unbearable point I knew so well from Skye's birth, except something was vastly different this time—it wasn't painful! I was experiencing a massive pressure sensation—one truly unimaginable unless you've given birth—but I just didn't associate it with pain. Along with this incredibly intense pressure sensation came uncontrollable, full-body shaking, which distracted me from the breathing and low vocal toning I was attempting to do.

Pearl sat next to me, her voice confident and calm. "It's okay—the hormones are causing you to shake. Just let it happen." Her next words came as such a shock that I wasn't sure I heard her correctly. "Courtney, you're going to have a few more intense contractions, and then you'll be pushing him out."

Pushing? I thought I had several more hours before beginning to push. I couldn't believe what she had said and kept looking at the numbers on the digital clock on the dresser. *Could my baby really be born tonight? How is that even possible?*

What happened next Verana later described as one of her favorite moments of the birth. After she told me the birth tub was ready, I waited for a pressure wave to pass and then simply stood up from the bed and walked down the long hallway into the living room, where I stripped naked and stepped into the tub without any assistance whatsoever—not even a hand to hold. I didn't think anything of it at the time, but Verana described how I transformed into an Amazon. The sheer strength and confidence I embodied made it seem like I wasn't even in labor, especially not the end of labor.

All that I remember of that long walk was being greeted by pure sacredness. Verana had outdone herself in transforming the living room into a true palace—calming music filled the air, candles glowed amid the dim lighting, and essential-oil diffusers and crystals graced every shelf and countertop. Beyond the physical adornments, the supportive and loving energy cultivated in that room greeted me the most warmly. My all-women birth team, which included my mom, stood at my beck and call, ready to give me space or active support while repeating their own silent prayers and mantras to themselves.

For the first time since I'd left Marcus, I truly felt like a queen.

Pearl's calculations were right. Within minutes of entering the warm, soothing birth tub, I endured a moment of pure agony as my body started pushing the baby out. That first push came out of nowhere and felt like the stab of a knife. I resisted it with everything I had. I writhed and screamed and, for the first time, completely lost my peaceful, focused demeanor as otherworldly pain shot through my entire body.

Pearl came over to me, whispering gentle words of wisdom. "You need to work with your body with these pushes. Remember, it's just stretching."

Those two simple sentences changed everything for me. *It's just stretching.* I knew how to stretch; in fact, I spent my whole life working on stretching and flexibility as a dancer. *If it's just stretching, then I can do this.* Plus, what was my other option? Resist and be in pure agony? I had to work with my body to get my baby out. I began mentally preparing myself for the long haul—the maddening journey of endless, torturous pushes that I remembered from Skye's birth. *Here we go. I got myself this far, and now the only way out is through.*

Nothing shocked me more than hearing Pearl's calm voice say, about four intense pushes later, "Okay, his head's out. Now keep pushing."

I was on all fours in the birth tub, focused on one essential thing to stop myself from dying: breathing. I certainly hadn't felt my baby's head pass through me, and given my position, I couldn't see anything either. Yet with another three give-it-everything-you-have pushes, I felt his body slither out, and Pearl told me to reach down and catch my baby.

I cried in a mix of shock and joy as I held him to my chest, a squiggly, slippery miniature human being with a head full of jet-black hair—my apparent baby trademark. I began talking and singing to him, so enamored that I didn't notice the water in the tub had shifted from clear to a deep, dark red.

Pearl spoke with a measure of urgency as she told me I needed to get out of the tub and lay on a little nest she'd prepared for me on the floor so she could check to see whether I was hemorrhaging. The next thing I knew my baby boy was lying on my chest attempting to nurse while a large needle went into my thigh. I don't remember feeling any pain, but I do remember worrying that this entire scene had been a dream, and I would wake up with contractions and have to do this whole thing over again. How could this not have been a dream? It all happened way too fast. It wasn't even midnight yet. Just three hours ago, I was sitting at the kitchen table eating samosas. And now I had a baby? *I didn't even have to do any real work! That was so easy! I ate all that Indian food for nothing!*

After Pearl brought my initial bleeding under control, we all slowly transitioned to the bedroom. Two hours after my son's birth, Pearl asked if I'd like to cut his umbilical cord. By now the blood had stopped pulsing, and it was time to officially detach him from my placenta, the organ that my body had grown to sustain his life over the last nine months. Pearl directed me where to cut, and I took a deep centering breath, filling my body with strength.

As I cut through the thick cord, I sang out, "Welcome baby!"

"Do you realize you've birthed a three-month old?" Pearl joked.

"Huh?" I asked.

"I'd say he's at least nine, maybe even ten, pounds. Plus, he came out with both fists next to his head, making him even bigger to push out!"

He seemed so teeny-tiny to me that I didn't know what she was talking about. Yet Pearl's assumption was soon proven correct. My baby boy, after a hefty two-ounce poop all over my leg, weighed ten pounds and five ounces! I'm certainly glad I didn't know he would weigh that much or I never would have attempted a home birth. The truly incredible thing was that I barely experienced any tearing. Even the initial bleeding, it turned out, wasn't a hemorrhage but blood from the placenta detaching at the same time as I pushed the baby out. The whole experience was a textbook home birth and ran considerably shorter than I had ever imagined possible.

The bubbling, oozing excitement of this new baby entering the world kept me awake until 4 a.m. when the midwife, doula, and their assistant finally gave their last goodbye hugs. Upon their exit, I found myself in a completely silent apartment, apart from the sweet, soft breathing of my angelic baby lying across my chest. Besides my mom, the rest of my family was staying at my sister's house. I closed my eyes but wasn't ready to sleep—that would require letting go of this perfect, silent, predawn moment.

I did it.

And not only that, but I did it *without Marcus*. The empowerment of that realization—I could birth a baby without a man by my side—seeped in deeply. The difference between this birth and Skye's birth couldn't have been more pronounced. Aside from the fact that both babies were born a few minutes before midnight, there were no similarities between the two experiences whatsoever.

Over the past nine months, I'd been holding onto the belief that I had been able to get through the intensity of Skye's birth thanks to Marcus, but after birthing my son without him, I realized that the strength had been inside me all along. In fact, after the quick, relatively pain-free birth of my son, I'm convinced that Marcus actually hindered and lengthened my labor with Skye because he didn't allow the midwives to be involved.

Although Pearl's coaching wasn't excessive, the things she said were exactly what I needed to hear to get in sync with my body. With Skye's birth, I hadn't been given the advantage of having the midwives coach me because Marcus was so adamant that it be "just the two of us." The midwives sat in the corner and remained silent, as he had requested. I now can see how ineffective and counterproductive that was.

Thanks to my ten-plus-pound baby boy—my shining diamond amid the darkness—I was changed. It took birthing him without a partner to finally realize I have everything I need inside of myself.

Twenty-three Letting Go at Last

My ten-pound baby with the jet-black hair remained nameless for quite some time. Every day, I tried out a new name on him—Gabriel, Aiden, Kainoah, Kai—but none seemed to fit. I came to the conclusion that I wanted his name to represent the vastness of the ocean because of his endless blue eyes, but I still couldn't make a final decision.

When he was about five days old, I asked my sister, "What if I just name him Ocean?"

She laughed. "No way. Everyone will make fun of him with a name like that."

I listened to her and ended up going with the name Ayden, a "good, solid name," according to my family. I threw the "y" in there just to make it unique, but the name Ayden never seemed to fit him either.

When strangers asked what my baby's name was, I answered aloud, "His name is Ayden," while concurrently thinking, *but his name is actually Ocean.* This went on for quite a while. On several occasions, I vented to whomever would listen—my mom, a friend, or my weekly women's group—about the fact that I had named my baby the wrong name.

My regret was deep. "I've made a mistake that will impact the rest of his life." I knew in my heart that his name was meant to be Ocean, as odd of a name as it may be, but I had succumbed to outside opinions and given him a socially acceptable name no one would question.

One day, six months later, I realized that the power to change his name rested in my own hands. Thanks to California's complicated rules, the effort required a complicated mess of paperwork, multiple trips to the courthouse, and even an actual hearing, but I could undergo the process if I wanted. I decided the hassle was worth it. After two months, my baby's first name was legally changed to Ocean.

While changing my baby's first name may seem insignificant, it represented another small victory in my life—owning my power. I was still new to going after what I wanted without my family's full support. I had to become conscious about why I picked Ayden in the first place rather than honor my own intuition as the mother of this baby. Why did I put my sister's choice of name above my own? And what were the consequences? What was so great about my son having a normal name—so he could fit into societal standards? I faced those questions every time someone asked me my baby's name and the voice inside my head and the voice that emerged from my mouth recited two different things.

Other times when people asked about my baby, I had to occasionally reference the father of my children but discovered I had no way to do so. I wasn't comfortable with the phrase "my ex" since Marcus had never been "my" anything. Throughout the time we were together, although most people assumed we were married, I never was formally given the privilege to say he was so much as my partner, which was extremely awkward and upsetting. Was he my husband? No, because he was married to another woman he refused to divorce. Was he my boyfriend? Definitely not. We were way more than just a couple. Was he my fiancé? Sort of. He promised marriage every other day. But he never gave me the ring.

Now that Marcus and I were no longer together, I got to claim him as mine. *My ex*. For more than a year after the breakup, I found it extremely difficult to speak this strange phrase. *The* ex felt better but sounded funny and often solicited confused looks. Could I really claim Marcus with a possessive pronoun after barely having done so when we were actually together?

I tried alternate names for him. "The father of the babies" was one option, but it was inaccurate. He was not a father to the babies since he had no contact with them at all. Baby daddy was short and sweet but inaccurate for the same reasons above. That's when my mom chimed in with her humorous phrase, baby donor.

"Baby donor?" I asked, chuckling.

"Yes, that's exactly what he is! He donated some sperm, and his job was done."

We laughed for about five minutes straight.

A full year after the breakup, I found myself curious about Marcus's whereabouts and decided to look him up on social media. Even as I typed his name in the search box, my stomach tightened, my hands became clammy, and I felt like I was going to throw up. And that was before his picture had even loaded.

My original intention was to take a quick peek to find out where he was living, but I gave in to curiosity and continued to pry. I soon found the photo I was unconsciously looking for: Marcus with another woman. Just one look at this younger attractive girl helping him with his sound-healing events and my eyes filled with tears. Anger poured through my body. I was furious at him for replacing me so easily, leaving me to raise a toddler and infant with no support.

Beyond that, I was deeply saddened that he had clearly moved on, but I hadn't. How could I move on? I didn't have the luxury of simply meeting a new guy—I was a single mother of two babies! While I was drowning in dirty diapers, nursing, and pumping, all while working multiple jobs, Marcus was off doing his thing—putting himself out there as a single, unattached guy. And I was sure the new young girlfriend had no idea he had sired a two-month-old and fourteen-month old!

The hurt I experienced from a relatively quick look online was enough to put me into a major funk that lasted for days. Seeing how Marcus had moved on, I remembered the multitude of times he accused me of wanting to "play house" while not truly loving him at all.

"You couldn't care less about me," he often said when he was in one of his moods. "All you care about is having a husband. It could be anybody. I'm just a pawn in your game, completely replaceable."

Those words stung. When he said that, which happened many times over the months we were together, I would question myself, wondering if his accusation held any truth. Yet the sadness of seeing him with someone else made me realize that while Marcus accused me of using him, the exact opposite was true. I was the replaceable one and had been all along. His endless rants about how I was only "playing house" were him describing his own desires, not mine. I loved Marcus so intensely for who he was and for his uniqueness—not for being a stand-in for a husband—and he never married me anyway!

It shocked me to see how much I was affected by finding out that Marcus had moved on. After all, I'd had no contact with him for an entire year. What was I expecting—for him to stay single in case I decided to rescind the restraining order and jump back into his arms like no time had passed? So much had happened in the year apart. I'd gone through pregnancy and given birth, and I had a full life in California with multiple jobs, a growing community of friends, and two babies.

Yet just as Pearl had guided me in cutting my son's umbilical cord when the blood stopped pulsing through it, it was finally time to cut my cord to Marcus—for good. The life-blood pulsing through it was long gone.

This exorcism of sorts would begin with the physical object I used and looked at every day without fail—my cell phone—where I'd stored the photos of our time together. Having his presence locked inside an object I used every day was another way his energy was following me around, albeit electronically. But I had my reasons for keeping the photos and videos—for one thing, they served as a last lifeline and connection to him. After the photos were deleted, I'd have nothing left—only fading memories of all those beautiful times. I'm not talking about twenty, thirty, or even fifty photos I wanted to keep for good measure. My phone held more than a thousand photos of us, and every single one was of the "good times." We never documented the ugly.

While these photos existed on my phone, it's not like I reminisced over them on a daily basis. I preferred to avoid them, since I was still so emotionally fragile. But deleting them would require actually facing them. And I didn't want to do it. I considered hiring someone to delete the photos for me to relieve me of this daunting and possibly heart-wrenching task. I imagined the feeling of a clean slate—and the freedom I experienced was immense.

So, I added it to my to-do list: "Clear old photos of Marcus off my phone," and after three more months of rewriting that phrase on subsequent to-do lists, the photos were finally gone. The liberation I experienced was very real. With each smiley selfie of us that I deleted, a piece of myself was restored. Photo by photo, I was getting my power back.

Around the same time, a little more than a year after leaving Marcus, I booked an appointment for a haircut. I thought back to a conversation with my friend Rose, a single mom who cut her beautiful long hair very short after her twins were born. Now that I was a mom of two babies, I totally understood. Long hair and little babies don't mesh well, unless you're okay with living in a ponytail or having half your hair yanked out on a daily basis.

"If you chop all your hair off when they're young, you won't regret it. Trust me," she said.

As I drove to the hair salon, I considered doing something radical. I'd had hair that hung several inches past my shoulders for my entire life. I didn't know any other possibility. On the few occasions I decided to cut my hair short, my mom always stopped me: "You have such beautiful hair. People would die to have your hair! Keep it long while you can."

Every time, I'd change my mind, despite being perfectly capable of making my own hair-length decisions. I know we're not talking about major life issues, but at the time, going through with my plan to have my hair cut short was nothing short of revolutionary.

As inches of golden blonde locks fell to the floor, I felt like a snake shedding old skin. I looked into the mirror and saw my appearance shift—I looked younger, lighter. The weight of the last year seemed to disappear from my face.

I half-jokingly wondered if it was possible that I was storing the trauma of my relationship with Marcus in those strands of hair, and now that so much had been cut off, I could finally move on and fully heal. Or maybe I was just happy that I'd listened to myself—a new trend—versus doing what other people wanted me to do. Either way, I didn't miss having long hair one bit.

Besides the outward actions of deleting old photos and cutting my hair, one major internal shift needed to occur before I could truly heal and move on. The best term I can find for this shift is radical responsibility. As long as I saw myself as a victim, I stayed in a victim mind-set, unable to transform into the fully empowered version of myself.

But it was tricky because part of me was certain I was a victim, and I had all sorts of evidence to prove it: I didn't know what I was getting into when I decided to trust the sparkly-eyed guy sitting across from me at the Sanctuary; I didn't know Marcus had anything less than my best interests at heart when I gave up my life in Hawaii to move to Texas; and I never could have fathomed that my life would be turned upside down and ripped apart because I continued to follow my heart—or did I?

As much as I felt like a victim of my circumstances, I had to take responsibility for the fact that there were plenty of warning signs along the way and that, although Marcus had me fooled, I played a part, too. I hadn't been completely blindsided. But lifting myself out of victimhood wasn't easy. No one wants to take responsibility for the questionable choices that led them to the place they now find themselves. But going around blaming others isn't the answer either.

Something magical happens when you take radical responsibility for the choices and decisions that led you to where you are—anything becomes possible. What happened, happened. The damage has already been done. It's over. And now it's up to you. Do you operate from a place of strength and power, or do you walk around at the mercy of other people's myriad dramas and traumas? Once you can take radical responsibility for playing a part in your own story, healing is possible.

The only problem is that you can't control how long it might take to heal. There's no tried and true formula for exactly how many days, weeks, or months must pass before you feel like yourself again—if you can even remember what yourself feels like. This was the hardest part to swallow because I assumed that after about two months of separation from Marcus, I'd be back on track as if nothing had happened. Two months was the time I'd allotted myself before I would be bouncing back into life as I knew it before everything fell apart.

But I couldn't control how long it would take to heal because healing isn't linear. There are ups and downs, twists and turns, and unexpected leaps forward and setbacks. And there's no way to avoid it.

When I found myself still having adverse physical reactions to anything having to do with Marcus a whole year later, I had to surrender my timeline and allow healing to take place naturally without the added pressure. It was time to simply be at peace with where I was and know that one day that painful crack in my heart would be the source of my own enlightenment.

As Rumi said, "The wound is the place where the light enters you."

Twenty-four Finding Freedom

The smell of microwaved stuffing wafted through my sister's house. Our family had finally gathered together on the Friday after Thanksgiving, having postponed the holiday due to my father's weakening health. We didn't know what was happening to his body, but he described severe pain in his lower abdomen, waving it off as the same old hernia pain he'd suffered on and off for the last eleven years.

My dad adamantly refused to see a doctor and for good reason, I suppose. He had just spent eight weeks in the hospital after undergoing open-heart surgery in September. Since the surgery, his whole life seemed devoted to doctor's appointments, blood draws, and various rehab therapies—none of which he wanted to do at all. No amount of hernia pain was going to send him back to yet another doctor. But that evening, as he sat hunched over with little Ocean nestled in his lap, he was clearly not well.

The surgery had taken a lot out of him. I didn't know what open-heart surgery entailed until my father faced an emergency quadruple bypass. I didn't realize his collarbone would be snapped in half so that doctors could maneuver his chest muscles to access his heart. He was hooked up to a machine that pumped blood through his body while his heart was stopped and operated on. Just thinking about his procedure was enough to make me queasy—I couldn't imagine being the one going through it. Still, as a nurse rolled my dad into the surgery prep room, he was laughing and cracking jokes like he'd done his whole life.

Dad was different after the surgery. His humor was harder to come by, and his once tall, strong stance was now permanently hunched over with a newfound frailty, like a sunflower wilting with the waning sun. It was hard for me to see him like this. It was hard for all of us to see him like this, but we held on to his doctor's words, that this surgery had been necessary and would significantly prolong his life. Without it, the doctor said, my dad could be walking down the street and drop dead from a heart attack. If he survived the surgery, he'd have a new lease on life.

But ten weeks after the operation, my dad was in so much pain he could barely walk across the room. How was this his new lease on life? Our gathering, however, wasn't the time to question. We tried to make the most of our time together—at the piano, my mom's fingers ran up and down the keys as she played her signature compositions, melodies I'd heard since I was a child. My parents' five small grandchildren—my sister's three kids and my two babies—took turns sitting in Grandpa's lap, while the others ran about, chasing each other from room to room. My brother-in-law took charge in the kitchen, attempting to put the meal together as quickly as possible as he passed dishes in and out of the microwave. I walked around with my iPhone videoing the strange scene, an equal mix of somber and celebratory.

Once we were finally all seated, a feat in and of itself, my sister spoke in the most upbeat voice I'd heard all evening. "Why don't we go around and say what we're thankful for? Dad, you start!" Her enthusiasm was over the top in an attempt to lift his somber expression.

We all looked at Dad, who closed his eyes for several seconds, trying to gather his thoughts amid the chaos of squealing toddlers and squirming infants. When he opened his eyes again, they were full of tears. "I'm grateful to be alive," he said slowly and contemplatively, "and surrounded by the people I love."

His words cut straight into my heart. A single thought struck me. *This is our last Thanksgiving together.*

While I had a strong knowing that my dad's life wouldn't last another Thanksgiving, what I didn't know was just how soon he would pass away.

Three days later, when the hernia pain still hadn't gone away, my sister drove Dad against his will to the doctor, where a supposedly low-risk operation was scheduled for the next day. Since he'd already survived open-heart surgery, we weren't overly concerned about a simple hernia operation. After seeing him off into the operation room, we returned to our daily lives, planning to see him again the next morning in recovery.

During this "simple procedure," however, my dad unexpectedly went into cardiac arrest and passed away—peacefully, we were told—with a nurse reciting the Lord's Prayer by his side. His passing was so quick that we didn't even get a phone call until it was too late. None of us—not my mom, my sister, or me—were there for his last moments.

What I had feared since childhood had finally come about—my dad was gone. As my dad's health slowly declined over the last several years, sometimes I thought about whether I'd be able to handle his death. A consistent thought that ran through my head as I looked toward the future: *I need to make sure I'm married when Dad passes away so that I'll have a husband to support me and be there for me.*

But now, here I was, not only still unmarried but also a single mom to a four-month-old and a seventeen-month-old, and no man in sight. With my mom and sister struck with severe shock and grief after Dad's passing, it was my turn to be the strong one. I was amazed at how that strength naturally drew out of me, like a warrior-in-training given her first full-fledged assignment. I was ready and prepared for this role—everything had been leading up to it. And even more amazingly, I felt a deep inner peace around my dad's passing.

The death of my beloved father instigated a deep revelation of everything I'd been through in the past year since I landed in California, forcing me to grapple with the symbolism of it all.

When I showed up at my parents' apartment—injured, newly pregnant, and heartbroken—I had no idea that my dad had only twelve months to live. If my relationship with Marcus hadn't fallen apart when it did, and if Paul hadn't sent me off to California so he could cover up the car incident on the Church campus, then my last year with my dad would never have happened. He would have passed away, and I would never have had that time with him. One of the greatest joys of my dad's final year was the time he spent with Skye. She brought such life back into him after his open-heart surgery, and the joyous admiration he held for her was clearly mutual—Skye adored her grandpa "Baba," and to this day, she remembers him fondly even though she was just a toddler when he passed away.

Buddhism teaches that one can forge a path to a fulfilling and enjoyable life if one has the depth of faith to regard everything as a source for creating happiness and value. Yet conversely, if one sees everything in a negative or pessimistic light, their life will gradually but inevitably be plunged into darkness. The choice was mine to make. But how could I take the painful, even tormenting, experiences I'd been through with Marcus and turn them into a source of happiness? The only way was to come to terms with the fact that I'd had an appointment with destiny, that everything I went through was a prerequisite, so to speak, for the future growth and expansion of my soul. The healing and learning that such an experience forced upon me couldn't be grasped any other way than living through it.

Buddhism also teaches that before we are born—from the perspective of our fully enlightened selves—we pick our parents, our birthplace, and the soul lessons we want to experience. I've subscribed to this belief not simply because my parents passed it down to me but because it's how I've made sense of this chaotic, often-confusing world. As the French philosopher Pierre Teilhard de Chardin said, "We are not human beings having a spiritual experience. We are spiritual beings having a human experience." From this stance, I can see that fundamentally transforming from victimhood into embodied empowerment is an assignment I chose for this lifetime. So, even if I had made wiser choices about Marcus, my story would have found another way to manifest, perhaps at a different time, perhaps with someone else, yet the lessons would still have to be learned.

Karma. Fate. Destiny. These words are thrown around, but what do they mean in our day-to-day lives? If you're at the mercy of fate, then where is your power? If destiny controls your choices, where does free will come in? Looking at my own experiences with the gift of hindsight, it all starts to make sense. What I went through with Marcus is bigger than the story I've detailed throughout this book.

After Dad died, I came across a handful of cards that I'd written to Marcus during our relationship, and in each one I elude to the same powerful word—destiny. In the cards, I wrote about how "glorious and divinely ordained" our meeting was and how I was so glad our paths had crossed. At first, the cards made me sick to my stomach. How could I have been so fooled, so deluded? Or maybe, just maybe, there truly was some unstoppable force pulling us together because while I had choices along the way, I also had a destiny to fulfill—one that included breaking a karmic pattern held for many lifetimes, a pattern of disempowerment.

My time with Marcus wasn't a random experience nor was it punishment for making mistakes and trusting someone who never should have been trusted. It was the ultimate way to shift something so deeply that the reverberation of my empowerment would affect not only me and my children but also generations to come. A pattern has been interrupted, and now there's no going back.

On October 31, the morning after Marcus hit me with the car and while Paul was ordering me to "go, go, go," I ran into the familiar blue bathroom to make a phone call before Paul could catch up with me. I called my elderly Buddhist leader, Eve. I was worried that if I told her what was going on, it might be a little too much for her to handle.

After I spoke, however, she calmly repeated with utter assurance, "This is all happening for your protection. This is all happening for your protection."

I had no idea what she was talking about. Before she could explain, Paul barged in and asked to whom I was talking. When I told him that I was talking to my Buddhist leader, his face seemed to soften. Perhaps he had worried I was speaking to lawyers, which is what I should have been doing. Or was it?

Speaking to lawyers, staying in Dallas to pack up, and reconciling with Marcus—everything I strongly felt I should have done—would have created an entirely different outcome, and one in which this story of growth, change, and freedom would not exist. Eventually, I had to embrace the fact that the traumatic way I was forced to leave my beautiful home and dysfunctional relationship was indeed protection. Truth be told, being hit by the car and subsequently kicked out of our home was the only way I could have left at all. Those painful, traumatic events truly were a protection from staying in that relationship for another five, ten, or twenty years.

The undesirable ending allowed for another kind of profound protection. If I had been given the time to properly pack my belongings in Dallas and stay an extra week as I desperately wanted to, my son, Ocean, wouldn't have had a chance to be born. A new life, an entire person with a heart full of pure gold, would not exist. Instead, on top of everything else, I would have had to face the emotional consequences of having an abortion.

The idea of changing "poison into medicine"—taking the most difficult obstacles in your life and turning them into a source of growth and happiness—is a key Buddhist concept and one I've understood since I was young. When it came to the way my relationship with Marcus ended, however, I just couldn't see any good in that situation—all I could see was the poison. I spent night after night crying on my parents' couch, repeating, "If only I had done things differently... if only it could have ended differently." Yet, now I can see clearly that it is precisely because of how things ended that I have a beautiful baby boy, a soul with a huge mission on this planet who chose the exact circumstance of his birth.

Some say that forgiveness is the only path to healing, and yet forgiveness cannot be forced or inauthentic. I've come to learn that while forgiveness of a person, on a deep soul level, is healing, forgiveness of someone's wrongful actions is never necessary or even helpful. You can forgive the person without forgiving their actions. For me, the hardest and most important work was forgiving myself. I held so much deep anger toward myself for being too naive, too trusting. For ignoring the red flags, for making excuses as to why everything was okay or was somehow going to be okay. For becoming a single mother, for abandoning a life I loved in Hawaii, and most importantly, for putting someone else's life above my own. Forgiveness, of both yourself and others, gives you the brilliant opportunity to step into the present rather than being consumed by the past. As Oprah succinctly puts it, "Forgiveness is giving up the hope that the past could be any different."

I'm not one to quote Bible verses, but there's a proverb that often floats into my mind: "A man reaps what he sows." The Buddhist concept of karma goes right along with this premise, teaching that sooner or later, one's karma—an accumulation of past actions, both good and bad—will catch up to them. Cultivating a deeper understanding of the law of karma and its unwavering strictness allowed me to let go of my initial need for revenge and fairness and finally shift the focus to moving forward, as the Buddhist concept *hon'nin myo* teaches. This Japanese term is best translated as "from this moment forward," yet moving forward still takes into account the immutable law of cause and effect.

While one intense chapter of my life has come to a close, others have just begun to open. As of this writing, I'm in graduate school full time at New York University, babies and all, living in my hometown of Manhattan—a place I once thought I would never return to. Surrendering my plan to a higher plan has allowed opportunities and support systems to arise that I couldn't possibly have imagined for myself. And despite the fact that my current reality looks different from what I once imagined, I am truly grateful for it all.

As life continues to unfold, I always keep my genius—my attendant spirit—by my side. If my little "genie" has done anything for me, I'd like to think she has helped me see the whole from the parts—the big-picture lessons from the myriad singular events. This wide-angle view is what allows me to move forward toward clarity and confidence.

Eris Rising

My happiness now depends on fully owning my power as Eris courageously represents—living and acting from a state of empowerment rather than one of fear. It's from that place of true strength and authenticity, like the phoenix rising from its own ashes, that my wings have been formed once again, and I can finally be free.

Acknowledgments

First and foremost, I want to thank my mom, Adrienne. She is a living example of what a mother's unconditional love means. Thanks to her unwavering support and encouragement, not to mention countless hours of childcare for my babies, I was able to complete this book.

Thank you to my late father, David, whose grounded, stable presence in my life, as well as constant stream of humor, has stayed with me and inspired me to stress less and see the lightness of life, two important qualities when moving through difficult situations.

Thank you to my sweet, sweet children Skye and Ocean. I love you two cuties more than words can possibly express, and I so appreciate your support, given to me in the form of endless hugs, kisses, and laughter.

Thank you to my editor, Heather, for your generosity of time and knowledge, as well as utmost patience with me as I juggled full-time graduate studies, an infant and toddler, and writing this book.

Thank you to my Buddhist community: fellow members and leaders for encouraging me to "turn poison into medicine" and inspire others to do the same.

Last but not least, I give thanks to the real-life characters of this book who made this story possible and who played a key part in my journey—and vicariously, by reading this book, in yours.

About the Author

Born and raised in the heart of New York City, Courtney Ramm has followed her passion for dance since childhood, which led to a career as a professional dancer, choreographer, and teacher. She's directed dance schools, performed, and taught all over the world, from Singapore to Thailand to Manhattan.

With her Master's degree in Dance Education, Courtney has led wellness retreats in Hawaii, focusing on empowerment and transformation. Courtney is the founder and artistic director of the nonprofit dance company, RammDance. She blends her love of dance with holistic healing, and is a certified Pilates instructor, Yoga teacher, Ayurvedic consultant, Theta healer, Master Detox Chef, and Reiki practitioner.

Alongside her focused training and career in dance, writing has always been one of Courtney's passions. She knew she would write a book—although she never imagined her memoir would take such a twisted turn.

Courtney is a full-time single mama to two toddlers. *Eris Rising* is her first book.

Made in the USA
Middletown, DE
04 May 2022

65188348R00187